MARCO BELLOCCHIO:
THE CINEMATIC I IN THE POLITICAL SPHERE

Marco Bellocchio is one of Italy's most important and prolific film directors, with a career spanning five decades. In this book, Clodagh J. Brook explores the tensions between the public and the private, the political and the personal, and the collective and the individual as central motifs in Bellocchio's films. She looks at the role of autobiography, psychoanalytical approaches, and politics in Bellocchio's work, while at the same time addressing fundamental issues in film analysis, such as film production and distribution and the relationship between film tradition and contemporary culture.

Focusing on Bellocchio's uniquely political approach to film-making, the study investigates what it means to create personal or anti-institutional art in a medium dominated by a late-capitalist industrial model of production. Brook's readings of Bellocchio's often enigmatic and perplexing work suggest new ways to approach questions of subjectivity, objectivity, and political commentary in modes of film-making. In its assessment of the personal art of a director within a public medium, *Marco Bellocchio* is an important contribution to our understanding of film.

(Toronto Italian Studies)

CLODAGH J. BROOK is a senior lecturer and head of the Department of Italian Studies at the University of Birmingham.

CLODAGH J. BROOK

Marco Bellocchio

The Cinematic I in the Political Sphere

UNIVERSITY OF TORONTO PRESS
Toronto   Buffalo   London

© University of Toronto Press Incorporated 2010
  Toronto Buffalo London
  www.utppublishing.com
  Printed in Canada

  ISBN 978-0-8020-9710-1 (cloth)
  ISBN 978-0-8020-9651-7 (paper)

∞

Printed on acid-free, 100% post-consumer recycled paper with vegetable-based inks.

Toronto Italian Studies

Library and Archives Canada Cataloguing in Publication

Brook, Clodagh J.
Marco Bellocchio : the cinematic I in the political sphere / Clodagh J. Brook.

Includes bibliographical references and index.
ISBN 978-0-8020-9710-1 (bound). – ISBN 978-0-8020-9651-7 (pbk.)

1. Bellocchio, Marco, 1939– –Criticism and interpretation. I. Title.

PN1998.3.B454B76   2009   791.4302'33092   C2009-906292-5

This book has been published with the aid of a grant from the Arts and Humanities Research Council, United Kingdom.

University of Toronto Press acknowledges the financial assistance to its publishing program of the Canada Council for the Arts and the Ontario Art Council.

University of Toronto Press acknowledges the financial support for its publishing activities of the Government of Canada through the Book Publishing Industry Development Program (BPIDP).

Contents

Note on the Text

All Italian citations from film dialogues have been taken directly from Marco Bellocchio's films as released on DVD or videocassette, except where stated. To ensure accuracy I have provided my own translations, rather than quoting the English subtitles (where these exist). I have also cited from published and unpublished screenplays, as indicated. Unpublished screenplays were consulted at the Scuola Nazionale di Cinema in Rome.

Acknowledgments

I would like to express my thanks first and foremost to the Biblioteca 'Luigi Chiarini' and the Cineteca Nazionale, at the Scuola Nazionale di Cinema (SNC) in Rome. Their resources, including important unpublished material by Marco Bellocchio, were invaluable to this research. I am also grateful to the exceptionally helpful staff at the offices of the Pesaro Film Festival in Rome, who kindly granted me access to Bellocchio's short films and documentaries, and to La Sapienza University, Roma Tre University, the Biblioteca Nazionale in Rome, the Università Cattolica del Sacro Cuore in Milan (especially its department dell'Arte, della Musica e dello Spettacolo), the Cineteca di Bologna, the Istituto Gramsci (Rome), the very helpful Fondazione Basso in Rome, the librarians (particularly Zbig Gas) at the University of Birmingham, and to Marco Bellocchio for his help and clarifications.

I am grateful to the UK's Arts and Humanities Research Council (AHRC Research Leave Scheme 2007) and the University of Birmingham for awarding research leave to help me complete this book; my warmest thanks go to everyone at the Department of Italian Studies in Birmingham for their interest and support.

Finally, I would like to take this opportunity to remember all those who have been close to me while I wrote *Marco Bellocchio: The Cinematic I in the Political Sphere*. Two people – Maurizio Locusta and Bruce Comens – deserve special mention, not only for their friendship during these years but also for our conversations, which have contributed to the development of some of the ideas in this book. Cath, Patrick, my family in Ireland, the Raiconi family (in whose house the manuscript came to life), and my friends in Rome have all been wonderful – encouraging, supportive, and kind.

An earlier version of the sections 'Massimo Fagioli and Group Therapy' and 'Massimo Fagioli's Model of the Unconscious' was published as 'Beyond the Controversy: Marco Bellocchio and Fagiolian Psychoanalysis' in *Italian Quarterly* (winter 2005, pages 55–66). The section 'The Oneiric and States of Hesitation' is based in part on 'The Oneiric in the Cinema of Marco Bellocchio,' published in *Italica* (volume 84, summer – autumn 2007, pages 479–94). I would like to thank the editors of these journals for granting permission to reprint the articles in part. I would also like to thank Marco Bellocchio for granting permission to print the photograph for the cover of this book.

MARCO BELLOCCHIO:
THE CINEMATIC I IN THE POLITICAL SPHERE

1 Auteur and Autobiography

Marco Bellocchio's filmic output is built upon the complex issues surrounding the interrelationship of the public and the private, the political and the personal, the collective and the individual. During the 1960s and 1970s these issues were bitterly negotiated in Europe, when – against a backdrop of postmodern theories – the idea of committed film-making struggled against the notions of a more private and introspective cinema of the 'I,' and now, in the new millennium, they have returned to Italian cinema. *Impegno*, as Burns (2000) has argued, is now fragmented, with film-makers currently tackling issues as diverse as prostitution, the mafia, gay rights, terrorism, and Berlusconi. Bellocchio's film *Buongiorno, notte* (*Good Morning, Night*, 2003) can be read in the light of this, albeit fragmented, return.

The dichotomy of private and public, so crucial to cinema and especially to Italian cinema, touches on some of the fundamental issues of the medium. What does it mean to make personal, or anti-institutional, art in a medium that is dominated by a late-capitalist industrial model of production? Is there such a thing as the private and personal in a medium as public and political as cinema? Does subjectivity undermine and negate the political, thereby rendering political comment biased, incomplete, or invalid? Should the political be screened only through objective modes of film-making? How is a character's subjectivity portrayed in a medium that has an eye but no 'I,' no stable first-person pronoun?

The issues of public and private go to the very heart of Marco Bellocchio's cinema and create questions and debates that are perplexing and at times irresolvable. For instance, *Buongiorno, notte* may be read as a film about the unconscious rather than as a film about the Aldo Moro kidnapping and murder. Films that repeatedly document clashes with institutions may be interpreted either as an attempt to portray power mechanisms in society or as a rather obsessive working out of the relationship between self and other. Or, to turn the argument on its head, perhaps we should be reading Bellocchio's private cinema as political. Perhaps *Salto nel vuoto* (*Leap into the Void*, 1980) – often considered highly psychological and introspective – is actually a film about the climate of 1968. Perhaps *Gli occhi, la bocca* (*The Eyes, the Mouth*, 1982) is not so much a tale of love and death as it is an allegory of the *riflusso*,[1] the disillusionment of a generation of post-revolutionaries symbolized in the figure of the jaded Lou Castel, who plays the failed actor Giovanni.

Of all Italian film-makers it is the director Bellocchio who, during more than forty years of film-making, has battled most intensely with the complexities of 'self' and 'other' – and on a variety of levels. His films encompass a broad spectrum of production methods (from collective to individual film-making), production companies (from large networks such as the national broadcaster Radio Televisione Italiana (RAI) to his own company, Filmalbatros Srl), and source material (adaptations, screenplays written collectively, and screenplays written solely by him). This signals a profound experience of both personal and collective film-making. Furthermore, Bellocchio's most enduring theme – the only one, perhaps, that links the films made during those forty years – is the rebellion of the self against an 'other,' which is represented in turn by society, institutions, artistic traditions, and father figures. Like Bernardo Bertolucci, Pier Paolo Pasolini, and numerous other post-war Italian film-makers, Bellocchio has a fascination with both political ideologies and psychoanalytic theories, which signifies an enquiry into not just one side of the equation (the political and public) but also the other side (the private and subjective), and the interface between them. The public-private debate is also crucial to the films' reception. If issues of 'auteurship' are not approached, then, for example, the court case and polemics surrounding the paternity of *Diavolo in corpo* (*Devil in the Flesh*, 1986) become incomprehensible. Without an understanding of the shifting relationship between political and private it becomes difficult to navigate the debate that issued from films like *La Cina è vicina* (*China Is Near*, 1967) and, more recently, *Buongiorno, notte*, where critics typically judged the films in terms of their political content (or political content manqué) without engaging fully with the problematics of a cinema that I will argue is often not in fact *strictly* political.[2]

Constructing an Auteur

> Mi chiamo marcobellocchio, garantisco
> percentuale cento per cento film d'autore,
> è nell'interesse del produttore la mia libertà.[3]
> — Marco Bellocchio, from his poem 'ANAC,' 1969

Writing a monograph on a director conjures an underlying presumption that there exists a body of films directed by him that in some way bears, at the very least, a trace of his ideas, of his style. It also implies that the director has been able to impose himself on his films. More radically, one might suppose that such a book would present the films as repositories of encoded autobiographical material that attentive critical reflection can seek to decode – the director's life, seen as somehow wedged in between the props of this the most collaborative of all art forms. It implies, too, that the films are to be interpreted as fundamentally belonging to the director and not, for example, to the actors Lou Castel or Sergio Castellito, to the playwrights Luigi Pirandello or Anton Chekhov (from whom Bellocchio adapted theatrical pieces), nor to his producers and costume designers. Perhaps it suggests also that Bellocchio's stylistic and thematic trajectory is necessarily more compelling than his films' intricate relationship with the genres, styles, and themes of the time. Writing a book on a single director, in other words, suggests a kind of ultimate control for a figure who, to use Francesco Rosi's term, acts as a kind of chef, attentively overseeing the buying and mixing of ingredients.[4]

Director authorship has been considered highly problematic for a long time, particularly in relation to a director such as Bellocchio who has been involved in highly collaborative modes of film-making and whose films do not easily constitute a body of work with an instantly recognizable stylistic signature – as do the films, for example, of Michelangelo Antonioni, the mature Federico Fellini, or, more recently, Paolo Sorrentino. Therefore, although the choice to write on a single director belies having only a hunch that there is a body of work with some coherence behind the name, it denies neither the fragmentary and collaborative nature of Bellocchio's films nor the importance of looking at his films in other contexts. Interesting work that isolates *Buongiorno, notte* from its auteurist and production context in order to relate the film to its socio-political context – particularly that of terrorism – has been done recently by, for example, Ruth Glynn (2008), G. Lombardi

(2008), and Alan O'Leary (2008), and the interrelationships between individual films and their literary sources have been usefully undertaken by quite a number of critics (Aste 1998; De Giovanni 1989; Bini 1993; Yacowar 1989).

Collaboration and Production

With few exceptions, Bellocchio has assumed extensive control over the film-making process throughout his career. He is almost always the scriptwriter for his films, either alone or with collaborators. Even where films have been commissioned – *Sbatti il mostro in prima pagina* (*Slap the Monster on Page One*, 1972); *Buongiorno, notte*; and the adaptations of literary texts for RAI – Bellocchio's hands have not been tied. In the case of *Buongiorno, notte*, for example, RAI only wanted a film that broadly treated 'terrorism'; it did not specify which terrorism.

Bellocchio generally retains the position of principal writer in the preparation of the scripts and the position of 'chef' (to use Rosi's term) on set. He has called on a range of different collaborators over the years, selecting them both on the basis of a professional and personal understanding and, perhaps especially, for their ability to develop a perspective that will fill in the gaps in Bellocchio's experience or expertise. He specifically chose Goffredo Fofi to work on the script of *Sbatti il mostro in prima pagina* because of Fofi's knowledge of politics. Bellocchio also remarks on the importance of Daniela Caselli's collaboration on the screenplay for *La balia* (*The Nanny*, 1999) in terms of her ability to bring a female perspective to the original material, a short story by Pirandello, who Bellocchio terms 'un grande misogino' [a big misogynist] (Turco 2000, 61). Analyst Massimo Fagioli's input from 1980 to 1994 reflects Bellocchio's desire to better understand character psychology and motivation. Collaboration on the screenplay generally takes the form of an intense consultation in which the co-screenwriter brings new ideas to the structures that have already been developed by Bellocchio. In other words, with the two prominent exceptions discussed below, collaboration at the level of screenplay is seen as closer to the process of grafting after a tree has taken root rather than that of planting seeds together in the same soil. On set, Bellocchio's collaborators remark on his openness to their suggestions, and, for instance, Giuseppe Lanci appears to have significant control over lighting, Sergio Ballo over costumes, Sergio Castellito over acting style, and Carlo Crivelli over the soundtrack.[5]

Bellocchio's generally high level of control over the process of film-making is supported by models of production that facilitate a certain artistic independence, models that are particularly well developed in Italy. His first three films were overseen by independent producers who supported art-house cinema. The film that launched Bellocchio's career, *I pugni in tasca* (*Fists in the Pocket*, 1965), was produced by a small independent company – Doria Film – and financed largely by Marco's brother (Costa 2005, 62). Doria Film gave Bellocchio a very free reign (Aprà ct al 1965, 490), but the limited funds available to him for this first venture are nonetheless inscribed in the film's texture. The film lacked 'stars' or even faces familiar to the public. Bellocchio claims that he had wanted the foreign actors Susan Strasberg (for Giulia) and Maurice Ronet (for Augusto), but, owing to budget constraints, he had to make do with what he got (Costa 2005, 62), and the cast was therefore almost unknown at the time.[6] Moreover, to save money, the film was set in Bellocchio's mother's villa, using his mother's furniture, and all shooting took place in the area around Imola, his native territory. Bellocchio was fortunate: Lou Castel played wonderfully the part of the young rebellious epileptic, and the bitter, wintry environment of Emilia-Romagna, with its provincialism and sense of enclosure, lent itself to the torturous themes of incest, suffocation, madness, and death. Despite its small budget, *I pugni in tasca* became one of the most critically acclaimed films of that year, grossing a respectable 148 million lira.[7]

After the initial years of his career, when he had the backing of first Doria Film for *I pugni in tasca* and then auteur-friendly Franco Cristaldi of Vides Cinematografica for the subsequent *La Cina è vicina* and *Nel nome del padre* (*In the Name of the Father*, 1971), Bellocchio turned to European co-production, a formula that marked his films for twenty years, from *Marcia trionfale* (*Victory March*, 1976) until it was interrupted in 1997; it returned with *Il regista di matrimoni* (*The Wedding Director*) in 2006. Co-productions have long been a popular production solution for Italian cinema, whether auteurist or mainstream, and have left a tangible mark on Italian filmic products. In 1969, 27.1 per cent of Italian takings stemmed from co-productions with either other European countries or the United States (Micciché 1995, 89), and some of the most successful films in this period, including Pietro Germi's *Divorzio all'italiana* (*Divorce: Italian Style*, 1961) and Michelangelo Antonioni's *Blowup* (1966), were co-produced; not to mention the co-production of whole genres in the mid-sixties – from the spaghetti western to the peplum.

As Bellocchio's great authorial freedom in his work with the independent production company Cristaldi (formerly Vides Cinematografica) becomes evident in the filmic text, giving him the scope to make bitter head-on attacks on the Italian political and ecclesiastical systems and allowing him to begin to develop a personal style, so the marks of co-production appear in the films in different ways: there is still much freedom with regard to subject matter and style, but non-Italian actors are now incorporated. The casting of French actress Miou-Miou (*Marcia trionfale*), Anouk Aimée and Michel Piccoli (*Salto nel vuoto*), Maruschka Detmers (*Diavolo in corpo*), Béatrice Dalle (*La visione del Sabba* [*The Witches' Sabbath*, 1988]), and so on, is a direct result of the need to incorporate French, and occasionally other European, actors into the films in order to meet the legal requirements of the co-production contract,[8] and it is not entirely a result of Bellocchio's personal or professional choices. Co-productions are also signalled in the persistent use of dubbing in Bellocchio's cinema. Italy's cinema, alongside India's and Japan's cinema, has been heavily marked by dubbing until recently; in Italy, widespread use of direct sound was made only after the release of Nanni Moretti's *Ecce bombo* (*Ecce bombo*) in 1978 (De Bernardinis 1998, 33). Bellocchio's turn towards direct sound for *Il Principe di Homburg* (*The Prince of Homburg*) in 1997 is late, however, even by Italian standards. His use of direct sound coincides very closely with the production of those films made without foreign collaboration. He did experiment with it in three early films – 'Discutiamo, discutiamo' (Let's Discuss, 1969), *Il gabbiano di Anton Cechov* (The Seagull, 1977), and *Vacanze in Val Trebbia* (Holidays in Val Trebbia) in 1980 – none of which were co-productions. Dubbing, however, was to be an area where the control that had been removed from him in casting (through the co-production code) could be returned. Bellocchio assigned himself a significant role in the dubbing process, claiming that in the early years 'Le voci le scelgo io' [I choose the voices] (De Bernardinis 1998, 34).[9] Indeed, he claims that until the beginning of the 1990s he was always present at, and in charge of, dubbing:

All'inizio ero abbastanza investito, anche artisticamente, da questa fase del processo cinematografico. Era sempre presente un assistente tecnico, ma il doppiaggio in practica lo dirigevo io. Però, e questo mi fu definitivamente chiaro con *La condanna*, era diventata talmente innaturale per me, ormai, questa pratica di ricreazione acustica a posteriori del film, che iniziai a servirmi di un direttore del doppiaggio. (De Bernardinis 1998, 34)

[At the beginning I was quite involved in this phase of the film-making process, even artistically. There was always a technical assistant present, but, in practice, I was in charge of the dubbing process. However, and this became definitively clear to me with *La condanna*, the practice of recreating the sound after the film had already become so unnatural for me that I began to use a dubbing manager.]

Co-production was only one of the production solutions that Bellocchio used at this time. The second important element was television. Bellocchio's adaptation of Chekhov's *The Seagull* for RAI in 1977 marked the beginning of a relationship with television that has lasted close to thirty years; almost all of his films made after 1977 have received financial backing from television companies.

Television has been a crucial producer of Italian cinema since 1968, when Franco Rossi's *L'odissea*, an adaptation of Homer's *Odyssey* for RAI, became the first film produced by the new media. RAI quickly began to produce films for the small screen and, from the mid-seventies, also produced and co-produced films for movie theatres, such as the Taviani brothers' acclaimed *Padre Padrone* (*My Father, My Master*, 1977) and Ermanno Olmi's *L'albero degli zoccoli* (*The Tree of Wooden Clogs*, 1978). By the 1990s, RAI and Berlusconi's Fininvest were producing between 50 and 70 per cent of all films, making it almost impossible to think of producing a film without them (Corsi 2001, 141). Although television has been berated repeatedly by film critics for compelling films to adopt the grammar of its 'inferior' model, the promotion of quality forms part of RAI's cultural policy.[10] Moreover, it does not appear that Bellocchio's use of television to produce films led to an adoption of a particular style. Conversely, his comments on this relationship point repeatedly to the greater artistic freedom experienced with RAI than with other producers:

La televisione mi ha dato tranquillità. Il problema del successo di pubblico, che l'industria privata del cinema continuamente ti reclama perché nel profitto trova la sua ragion d'essere, è sempre stato per me una persecuzione, che mi angoscia e mi fa lavorar peggio. (Tassone 1980, 44)

[Television gave me peace of mind. The problem of box office success, which the private cinema industry is always demanding since profit is its raison d'être, has always been a form of persecution for me, one that causes me distress and negatively affects my work.]

In other words, somewhat paradoxically, working for RAI seems to remove the problems of market and audience response, facilitating a cinema that is not necessarily popular and successful in terms of audience share.[11]

Finally, in the later part of his career, like many other directors (including Roberto Benigni and Nanni Moretti with Melampo Cinematografica and Sacher Film, respectively), Bellocchio founded his own production company, Filmalbatros Srl. In 1994, he made his first film with its backing, *Il sogno della farfalla* (*The Butterfly's Dream*). The company has co-produced all of Bellocchio's feature films – until *Vincere* (*Vincere*) in 2009 – along with his two documentaries *Sogni infranti* (*Broken Dreams*, 1995) and ... *Addio del passato* (Farewell from the Past, 2002). Like Moretti, Bellocchio runs a film festival (the Bobbio Film Festival), which has its own prize, the Gobbo d'oro (the Gobbo bridge is the town's symbol).

Although Bellocchio's film-making is generally characterized by a high level of creative control at the level of production, there are certain films that problematize this. They include the collectively made documentaries and two feature films that Bellocchio claims do not feel his own. The first of the features, *Sbatti il mostro in prima pagina*, was a film that Bellocchio took over from director Sergio Donati when it was in its first week of shooting. Bellocchio tried, with the help of cinema maker and critic Goffredo Fofi, to turn the film from something ideated by a maker of spaghetti westerns to a left-wing political thriller. However, he admits that 'it still feels like a film which I took over' (Zalaffi 1973, 231), and despite the incorporation of his own team of collaborators, including personal friend and actress Laura Betti, the film remains a rather generic product, part of the strand that Miccichè (1995) terms *cinema civile*, which was a commercial political subgenre of the time.[12] In a later film, *Il sogno della farfalla*, Bellocchio also took over a screenplay that he had not written, working with a text prepared by someone wholly outside the world of cinema, his psychoanalyst, Massimo Fagioli. Despite making changes to the film's cultural references and taking control of the directorial aspects of the film's production, Bellocchio has never claimed the film as ultimately his, referring to his role of director as closer to that of an actor: 'Non era stata scritta da me ... sono stato come un interprete ... nell'essere regista ... l'origine era di Fagioli' [It wasn't written by me ... I was like an actor ... while I directed it ... Its origin was Fagioli's] (Turco 2000, 60).

The documentaries, especially the two made in 1969 for the extra-parliamentary political group Unione dei Comunisti Italiani (marxisti-leninisti) [Union of the Italian Marxist-Leninist Communists]) (UCI [m-l]), provide further examples of works where Bellocchio does not assume full control over the film-making process. *Paola* (*Il popolo calabrese ha rialzato la testa*) (Paola [The Calabrian People Have Raised Their Heads Again]) and *Viva il 1° maggio rosso e proletario* (Long Live the Red and Proletariat May 1), together with his documentaries made in the 1970s – *Matti da slegare* (*Fit to Be Untied*, 1975–76) and *La macchina cinema* (*The Cinema Machine*, 1978) – were all directed not by Bellocchio alone but by collectives; even during shooting, Bellocchio's voice was but one of a group. *Matti da slegare*, commissioned by the *Assessorato Provinciale alla Sanità di Parma e Emilia Romagna* to explore the diabolic state of Italy's mental institutions, was co-directed by Bellocchio with Stefano Rulli, Sandro Petraglia, and Silvano Agosti. This same team would work together two years later on *La macchina cinema*, a documentary exploring the then-current state of Italian cinema. Although these commissioned documentaries, together with *Sbatti il mostro in prima pagina* and *Il sogno della farfalla*, only amount to a fraction of the films made by Bellocchio, they problematize his opus in its entirety, allowing uncomfortable questions to rear their heads. Should these collectively made documentaries be considered alongside the feature films over which Bellocchio clearly had direct control? What is the position of the commissioned film *Sbatti il mostro in prima pagina*? What of films like *Enrico IV* (*Henry IV*, 1984) and *Buongiorno, notte*, where the subjects for the films were proposed by RAI? On another note, can Bellocchio's adaptations really be seen as *his* films? Where, in all of this, is there space for the idea of an *auteur*?

These are questions which will be addressed at various stages in the book. Bellocchio's film-making undergoes specific and identifiable influences at particular points, especially those of the Marxist-Leninists on the early documentaries, of Fofi on *Sbatti il mostro in prima pagina*, and of Fagioli on a range of films from 1980 to 1994. His film-making also inevitably reflects the on-set and post-production collaborations in the creative decision making. Moreover, it is clear that Bellocchio's cinema is deeply and necessarily marked by the cinema apparatus, whether it be that of independent cinema or of co-production. In this sense, his cinema is always a result of an intricate relationship with an industry and a mode of production; it is never absolutely personal. However, Bellocchio's position outside popular cinema nonetheless permits a surprisingly high degree of freedom. His influence at the level of screenplay and his position as 'chef' generally enable him (with certain exceptions) to create substantial space in his films for the personal, should he decide to use it.

The Zigzagging Path

Despite the complexity of the film-making process, the demands of production and collaborators, and pure chance, there is still a widely held notion that art cinema – as opposed to mainstream cinema – is in some way personal. There are genuine reasons for this. As Neale has pointed out, the idea is 'manifest both in policies to support and to fund new film-makers ... and in the prevalence of auteurism within the discourses circulating centrally across the institutions involved in Art Cinema as a whole' (Neale 1981, 36). The prevalence of the idea of the auteur enables directors to construct themselves as such; it is a choice that is not just personal but also political, because it is only with the complicity of the film industry, the cinema critics, and a government whose ideology is supportive of the notion of the auteur that such a practice is enabled (see Wood 2005, 110–135).

Bellocchio has consciously constructed himself within the tradition of auteur cinema making, despite occasional directorial sorties into more mainstream genre film-making. In an interview with Peter Brunette (1989), in which he discusses his latest film (*La visione del Sabba*), he is clearly aware of the advantages that this brings, remarking that the film is typically European because

> [it] demands a public which is sensitized to a *cinéma d'auteur*, a sophisticated public which sees a certain value in film, which is not as concerned with popular success ... In Europe, partly from tradition and partly from history, there's still a way to approach a kind of universality but which leaves popular approval out ... Italian producers no longer have any hope for an Italian market, they're trying to open things up to an international audience. They need a certain number of products that can be marketed abroad. Thus the 'auteurs' have the possibility of making films that can at least potentially be shown here, for example, at the Montreal Film Festival. They have an advantage because they are useful to the producers in making a profit.
>
> (Brunette 1989, 53, 54, and 56)

Bellocchio's construction of himself as an auteur has been relatively successful, especially in Italy but also in France and to a lesser extent in other European countries and the United States. Within Italy, Bellocchio's name commands a certain level of power: it attracts funding from the government and support from the national television producer, RAI, and others, and attains an airing at film festivals and on Italian television – although not necessarily in prime time. Internationally, many of his films have circulated in film festivals and dedicated art-house cinemas, and DVDs have been produced for the international market. *Buongiorno, notte* benefited from being co-produced by the big international company Sky. However, his name has not attained the international currency of Fellini or Moretti. It does not have the transversal power of Pasolini, which attracts audiences in the diverse fields of poetry, prose, film, and intellectual debate. Nor does it have the appeal of Pasolini to specific subgroups. Recognition as an auteur beyond Italy and France – two countries deeply interdependent in terms of their national cinemas – has in fact been somewhat hard to attain.

There are a number of reasons for this. For one thing, Bellocchio tends to collocate himself almost exclusively within Italian and European contexts. Only two films, *Il sogno della farfalla* and *Il Principe di Homburg*, were shot outside Italy (in Greece and Bulgaria, respectively). Not one film has been shot in the United States. Casts are almost exclusively either Italian or French, with occasional actors from other parts of Europe. American actors simply do not figure. Bellocchio dismissed the idea of casting Richard Gere for *Gli occhi, la bocca* as he did not want to shoot in the United States (Malanga 1998, 186). Most internationally recognized Italian auteurs, on the other hand, have been keen to attract Anglo-American casts, from Pasolini with Terence Stamp in *Teorema* (*Theorem*, 1968) to Fellini with Donald Sutherland in *Il Casanova di Federico Fellini* (*Fellini's Casanova*, 1976) to Bertolucci with Marlon Brando in *Ultimo tango a Parigi* (*Last Tango in Paris*, 1972). Even Moretti uses Jennifer Beals in a cameo role in *Caro diario* (*Dear Diary*, 1993). Moreover, the subject matter and the polemics of Bellocchio's films often tend to target a local and Italian audience, one already familiar with, for example, the political climate of the Italian left. *Buongiorno, notte*'s international success comes from the treatment of a major Italian event, the Aldo Moro kidnapping, in the context of high-profile contemporary concerns (terrorism) and is subjected to universalizing discourse, which makes it accessible beyond national borders. Until recently, too, Bellocchio's cinema has resisted another crucial selling point of Italian cinema abroad: the screening of Italy's beautiful cities and landscapes and its 'charmingly rustic' people. Successful exports typically brandish these visual aspects, which are considered so romantic abroad: Nanni Moretti's Rome and the islands near Sicily in *Caro diario*; Roberto Benigni's soft-toned Tuscany in the first half of *La vita è bella* (*Life is Beautiful*, 1997); Emanuele Crialese's bright and blue Sicily in *Respiro* (*Respiro: Grazia's Island*, 2002) and 'charmingly backward' Sicily and Sicilians in *Nuovomondo* (*The Golden Door*, 2006). Bellocchio's focus on interiors does not open his films to this kind of audience. Only since *La balia* have his images begun to dialogue with the monumental and natural beauty of Italy; *L'ora di religione* (*The Religion Hour / My Mother's Smile*, 2002) screens elements of monumental Rome, and *Il regista di matrimoni* is set in a magnificently blue Sicily.

Perhaps the deepest problem with regard to Bellocchio's emergence as an auteur is the metamorphosing of style and approach in his opus. It has enabled the director to reinvent himself repeatedly but has led to difficulties in identifying the nature of a 'Bellocchian' film. His films are not a single product, easily identifiable in terms of theme and style, as are the films of the big international names like Fellini, Antonioni, and Moretti or the big national names of Leonardo Pieraccioni, Gabriele Muccino, and Carlo Verdone. He fails to create a package that would make his films instantly recognizable to the public and give producers some kind of guarantee as to their quality. There are few elements that traverse his oeuvre and become constants. Although his name can be linked to political film-making, especially with regard to the contestation of 1968 and Italian terrorism, in only two films since 1980 – *Buongiorno, notte* and *Vincere* – is politics actually placed in or near the foreground. One might argue instead that a Bellocchian film is one which dialogues with psychoanalysis – especially the controversial brand of psychoanalysis proposed by Massimo Fagioli (see chapter 3). However, in Bellocchio's early films Fagiolian psychoanalysis is absent, and since 1994 any influence is decidedly indirect. One could turn to the geographical setting and argue that Bellocchio's name is conjoined to his native, northern province of Emilia-Romagna. However, although the province certainly created the atmosphere of some of the early films, since the mid-1980s not one of his feature films – with the exception of *Sorelle* (Sisters, 2006) – has been set there. The filmic style too shifts and changes, from touches of the nouvelle vague in *I pugni in tasca* and *La Cina è vicina* to the long, still takes of the 1980s; from the partially realist style of *I pugni in tasca* to the grotesque in *Nel nome del padre*; from the popular genre film (*Marcia trionfale*) to the oneiric, ambiguous, personal art film (most of his films made between 1980 and 1998). Very little is embedded across the range of his films, beyond Bellocchio's enduring theme – rebellion against institutions and father figures – a theme that he shares with other sons of 1968 such as Bertolucci, Marco Ferreri, and Jean-Luc Godard. In other words, one might be forgiven for wondering what the adjective *Bellocchian* might mean, a quandary that one perhaps would not have about *Viscontian* or *Fellinian*.

Rather than presenting a unified whole with a distinctive identity, Bellocchio's cinema comprises a series of overlapping phases. These phases largely coincide with the transformations in Bellocchio's way of conceiving cinema, although the impact of new collaborators – directors of photography, composers, and so on – is also instrumental in changing the atmosphere of the films. Three phases can be identified. In the first, which can be described as stretching from his debut, *I pugni in tasca* (1965), to *La macchina cinema* (1978), Bellocchio's output is fragmentary and varied. He experiments with a variety of voices, quickly discarding them. This period is marked by angry rebellion against bourgeois norms and by political activity, although they are not sufficient to lend the filmic products a clear identity, given the extreme diversity, both in genre (documentaries, detective thrillers, melodramas, and literary adaptations) and in style (the grotesque in *La Cina è vicina* and *Nel nome del padre*, the Brechtian in 'Discutiamo, discutiamo,' and *cinéma vérité* in the documentaries). Even the tone fluctuates: the ironic detachment that characterizes most of the feature films in this period is countered by the earnest political engagement of the political documentaries. One feels too the lack of any coherent team of actors and creative or technical operators around Bellocchio at this time. There is a marked tendency to work with editors, cinematographers, actors, musical directors, and even producers on an ad hoc basis. The fragmentation of this early period, with its stops and starts and searching, clearly tends to block the emergence of a distinct auteur product.

The second phase is marked by a much stronger sense of artistic identity. I suggest that it begins in 1979 with the making of *Vacanze in Val Trebbia*. Bellocchio seemed to use this otherwise insignificant film as a fertile ground for experimenting with new ideas before they suddenly leaped into existence in a more developed form in his minor masterpiece, *Salto nel vuoto*, the following year. There is suddenly a new coherence in style and theme, with the kind of predictability necessary for auteur construction. This phase is marked by a shift away from public and political terrains and towards psychoanalysis, the language of the unconscious. Female characters emerge and come to the fore, and nudity and sex scenes become part of the fabric of the films. Interest in the private world of the main characters, by delving into unconscious motivations and the unsaid, leads to the steady development of the characteristic style of this period: long, still takes, close-ups, the near abandonment of classic shot-reverse-shot cinematography, and the dominance of enclosed spaces. The films slow down and become more silent and more intellectual. Oneiric elements appear for the first time, and gradually the films become more slippery, more difficult to interpret, more inward, and more abstract. The period seems to culminate with *La condanna* (*The Conviction*, 1991), a film in which the female body is at the centre of the male discourse, and Fagiolian psychoanalysis provides the unrelenting framework for the discussion of sexual relationships.

In this second period Bellocchio begins to build a team of collaborators. Although it would be impossible to talk yet of close and unbroken collaboration like that found on the film sets of the mature Fellini or Antonioni,[13] the persistent sense of a team leads to a more coherent and consistent product. Giuseppe Lanci, who had worked as a cameraman with Bellocchio from time to time since the very beginning of Bellocchio's career, took over the role of cinematographer in 1980 for *Salto nel vuoto* and worked with him in this capacity for every feature film – with the exception of *Il sogno della farfalla* – until he left Bellocchio's team in 2001, choosing not to be involved in *L'ora di religione* for religious reasons (Iadanza 2001, 52). The composer Nicola Piovani, who had worked with Bellocchio since *Nel nome del padre* in 1971, was replaced from the time of *Diavolo in corpo* (1986) by Carlo Crivelli, who then worked with Bellocchio until *L'ora di religione* and again for *Vincere* (2009). Both Crivelli and Piovani lend their particular stylistic signatures to the musical soundtrack. In this phase Bellocchio also retains editors for long periods. From 1982, with *Gli occhi, la bocca*, Mirco Garrone is involved in editing, being replaced in the mid-nineties by Francesca Calvelli, who has worked consistently with Bellocchio ever since. Finally, the significant presence of Bellocchio's psychoanalyst, Massimo Fagioli, needs to be mentioned. As will be argued in chapter 3, it is his presence in a variety of roles (scriptwriter, consultant, editor, and assistant director) that is crucial in conferring the particular tone and psychological content to the films of this stage.

The third period was already in preparation in *Il Principe di Homburg* and *La balia*, which could be read as transitional films. It develops fully, however, with *L'ora di religione*. The films in this phase undergo important changes. The rupture with Fagioli after *Il sogno della far-falla* leads to a diminishing of the intellectual discourse about the unconscious, although Fagioli's ideas can still be felt. There are also significant shifts in content, especially in relation to the treatment of fathers; the anger towards these figures begins to fade. The 'angry young man,' rebellious and iconoclastic, with which Bellocchio's name was associated after his debut in *I pugni in tasca*, seems to have defini-tively disappeared, although rebellion still remains on some levels. Another notable change is in the target audience. Since *La balia*, Belloc-chio's films appear to be drawing again a more mainstream and inter-national public. The use of the popular actor Sergio Castellito in *L'ora di religione* and *Il regista di matrimoni*, the decision to tackle key histori-cal moments – the Aldo Moro case and fascism – and the entry of a big international company like Sky into the production team are all signs of a change of gear. One might be tempted to argue that Bellocchio has finally quit rebelling and become part of the establishment.

Important changes have taken place during this period in terms of Bel-locchio's creative team. Since *La balia*, Daniela Ceselli has been working steadily with Bellocchio as assistant director or co-writer. Since *L'ora di religione*, Pasquale Mari has taken over as cinematographer (although he was replaced by Daniele Ciprì for *Vincere*), and Riccardo Giagni as musi-cal director (although Crivelli returns for *Vincere*). The style that Giagni brought to the films marks a shift from the uncomfortable and disturb-ing contemporary scores composed by Crivelli in the 1990s and plays an important part in not only the tone of the films but also their market-ability. Giagni adopts more accessible classical, pop, and world music. The music of Pink Floyd in *Buongiorno, notte*, for example, is a dramatic departure from previous scores and caters to more mainstream tastes.[14] During this period there are departures too in the use of technology, which have improved the quality of both image and soundtrack and, combined with the change in core players on the creative team, have led to a significant transformation in the atmosphere of the films. The Dolby system was first used in *Il Principe di Homburg* (a film that also marked the definitive shift to direct sound), transforming the sound world of the films and lending it a new complexity and richness. *Buongiorno, notte* was the first of Bellocchio's feature films to be shot using digital technol-ogy. The visual discourse too has gradually become more sophisticated and polished, and the image has grown in significance, pushing the explanatory and theoretical dialogue that characterized much of Belloc-chio's earlier cinema to one side, but never wholly eliminating it.

This periodization is naturally a simplification, constructed to confer order and unity on the diversity of an oeuvre that tends to resist it. Bellocchio's trajectory remains a contradictory one, for which the director himself uses the term *zigzagare* (Bernardi 1998, 6). Bellocchio comments that those whom he considers to be the greats of Italian cinema – Fellini, Antonioni, and Rosi – have an oeuvre which is '*tutt'uno*' [a whole], whereas he experiments with '*strade diverse*' [different paths] (Tassone 1980, 22). The *zigzagare* is not, however, limited to this experimentation but belies an inconsistency of quality. Bellocchio failed to repeat the success of *I pugni in tasca* in the films that followed, and many of his films of the seventies represent an attempt both to break away from the matrix that this film had imposed and to return to the success attained with his first film. Some of them, like *Marcia trionfale*, while successful at the Italian box office, were too close to the schema of genre cinema to be considered *film di qualità* [quality films] and only damaged his reputation among critics as a serious director. 'Discutiamo, discutiamo' (Bellocchio's contribution to the multi-authored film *Amore e rabbia*), while lauded by some critics as an instance of committed Brechtian cinema, to many simply seemed poorly shot and poorly acted, reducing the student revolt to a series of banal schemas and to self-exorcism (see, for example, Micciché 1995, 217, and De Bernardinis 2005, 152). From the 1980s, when Bellocchio was heavily influenced by Fagioli, such was the hostility to the analyst – widely considered to be a kind of manipulative guru – that, although the second phase helped to consolidate some sense of an identifiable auteur, the very consolidation was often negative. The 'Fagiolian' films were said to be too heavy and verbose for cinema, and in their reviews critics often vented real rage against Fagioli's peculiar brand of psychoanalysis. Bottiroli (1986, 68), for example, says that Bellocchio 'paga un tributo assai alto alle bêtises anti-psicanalitiche ... del suo mentore, Massimo Fagioli' [pays a high tribute to the anti-psychoanalytic stupidities of his mentor, Massimo Fagioli], and many other critics have made similar criticisms (see, for example, Cosulich 2000, 24).

The inconsistency in quality, theme, and cinematic style has led to Bellocchio emerging incompletely as an auteur of international repute. However, his self-conscious construction within the productive parameters of auteur cinema making in terms of working practice, productive environment, and themes means that even where his films lack the immediate recognizability of an Antonioni or a Moretti, they are inscribed with the codes of auteur film-making.

Bobbio and *My Mother's Smile*:
Autobiography in Bellocchio's Cinema

Bellocchio's construction as an auteur – with the control over the film-making process that this implies – enables him to weave personal material into his films. This material is a recurring feature of his cinema, imprinted even on the early political films. Autobiographical material is, nevertheless, almost never present in its own right but appears conjoined with other fictional genres. To speak of Bellocchio's cinema as one of self-expression makes little sense, not because the collaborative, productive environment of film-making renders this problematic (and it does), but because autobiography is clearly not the ultimate goal of his cinema. Fiction rather than self-expression dominates, and where autobiographical motifs do appear, they exist principally as raw material to be transformed by storytelling. This is true even of the two films, both minor productions, which announce themselves at least in part as autobiography: *Vacanze in Val Trebbia* and *Sorelle*.

Vacanze in Val Trebbia, just forty-seven minutes long, is to date Bellocchio's most autobiographical and private work. It narrates a family holiday in the Trebbia Valley of Marco Bellocchio's native Emilia-Romagna and features a film director called Marco (played by Bellocchio), a wife (played by Bellocchio's then-wife, Gisella Burinato), and a son (played by their son, Pier Giorgio). It records what on one level appear to be typical family holiday scenes: Marco watches a children's play, argues with his wife, talks to friends about selling the family home, and sits with his family on the banks of the river. The inscription of the home movie code is reinforced by amateur camera movements and positioning: grainy 16 mm film stock, fixed camera positions, jerky filming, harsh jumps between scenes, inaudibility, discontinuous temporality, and so on. One would, therefore, be easily tempted to interpret this as a purely autobiographical movie. However, the apparent spontaneity and reality of what we see is not as natural as it seems, and as the film proceeds, the 'real' is progressively undermined. Oneiric material repeatedly interrupts the realism of the home-movie mode. In the first scene, for instance, while watching a predictable children's production of *Pinocchio* with other parents, Marco suddenly 'sees' adolescents re-enacting the martyrdom of Saint Sebastian in the woods beyond. From this point, the film shifts uneasily between realism and hallucinatory or dream sequences.

It is not just the presence of the oneiric that points to the constructed nature of the scenes. In one episode, for example, Marco and his wife,

Gisella, are framed while they are sitting outside on the terrace of their villa. They begin to argue. Gisella says that she hates coming to Bobbio and wants Marco to sell the house. Bellocchio points out that selling the house is far more complex than she thinks as it means separating from the past. Although the alternating shot and reverse shot, typical of fictional on-screen arguments, has been suppressed in favour of a single take that shows Gisella's face and Marco's back, the camera does not remain still and creeps slowly towards the couple as they argue. This camera movement, although subtle, is significant because it implies that there is a third party – in the form of a camera operator – on the terrace. In other words, this domestic row is not something caught spontaneously by a video camera that was left running by chance but is something prepared and shot deliberately. The fact that Gisella and Marco ignore the camera during the argument, never once glancing at the operator (and so towards the screen and the spectator) as they presumably would if this were a real argument, coupled with Marco's and Gisella's clear suppression of laughter as they recite some of their lines, reinforces the impression that what we have here is a scripted scene rather than a real argument. Fiction and autobiography are conjoined.

In 2006, two-and-a-half decades later, *Sorelle* plays a similar game in its genre-crossing. The film, again a minor work, is sewn together from three shorts that were shot in conjunction with Bellocchio's Fare Cinema school in Bobbio. It uses relatively amateur modes of film-making, including a small troupe and budget. Like *Vacanze in Val Trebbia, Sorelle* casts family members in the central roles and is set in and around Bobbio, referencing not only Bellocchio's personal past but also his professional film-making past. Clips from the two films previously shot near Bobbio (*I pugni in tasca* and *Vacanze in Val Trebbia*) are intercut into the film, setting up a dialogue between *Sorelle* and its predecessors.

Sorelle is more obviously fictional than *Vacanze in Val Trebbia*. For instance, although family members and friends are cast in the central roles, the roles do not exactly mirror the extra-filmic relationships.[15] Although the little girl, Elena, is played by Bellocchio's daughter, Elena, and her great-aunts are played by her real great-aunts, her uncle is played by Pier Giorgio Bellocchio, who is actually her half-brother, and the distant mother is played by Donatella Finocchiaro, a professional actress and friend of Bellocchio. These later characters announce the fictionality of the film.

The fictionalizing of the autobiographical in *Vacanze in Val Trebbia* and *Sorelle* means that although Bellocchio imposes his private autobiographical voice, this, rather than revealing, becomes its own opaque mask. We cannot learn more about Bellocchio from these films than we already know because they do not purport to tell the truth about him. The ambiguous relationship with the real undermines a spectator's attempts to connect the content of the film with the extra-filmic; neither film is a straightforward home movie in which the director has suddenly decided to confess his inner self. Although we are aware of being presented with some autobiographical material, we are not offered the key that allows us to decipher it, and so there is no way of knowing, definitively, where truth and fiction lie from looking at this film alone. It is impossible to tell whether or not the argument between Marco and Gisella is constructed on the basis of a real argument. Did the couple argue like this? Or is the argument invented in order to give voice to Bellocchio's uneasiness at uprooting from Bobbio? The film does not provide answers to these kinds of questions.

Autobiographical material is woven throughout Bellocchio's opus, traversing the fictional universe of his films and being repeatedly reworked within the diegesis of the films. The family scenario of *I pugni in tasca*, with its absent father and dominant older brother, reflects the death of Bellocchio's own father in 1956, which left Bellocchio's older brother to run the household. The suicide of Bellocchio's twin brother in 1968 is worked through, later, in *Gli occhi, la bocca*, where the protagonist, Pippo, returns home for the funeral of his twin, who has killed himself (Aprà 2005b, 16). Bellocchio's experience of a Catholic boarding school is used as a basis for the school of *Nel nome del padre* (Cattini and Ferrero 1976, 29). The original idea behind the title and content of *L'ora di religione* comes from the choice that Bellocchio himself faced about whether or not to send his own child to a religious education class (Fusco 2001, 51).

Not only have personal themes and situations been woven into the films, but a number of characters in Bellocchio's films have been identified by Bellocchio as projections or alter egos. These are played by Lou Castel (as Ale in *I pugni in tasca*, and later as Pippo in *Gli occhi, la bocca*) (Nicastro 1992, 54) and Sergio Castellito (as Ernesto in *L'ora di religione*, and as Franco Elica in *Il regista di matrimoni*). Bellocchio has also mentioned feeling close to the character of the judge in *Salto nel vuoto* (Spila 1987, 8), and he has been linked to both Angelo and Franc in *Nel nome del padre* (Bertuzzi 1996, 94). It is common to talk of alter egos in terms of an on-screen objectivization of an auteur's self; critics, for instance, have talked somewhat unproblematically about actor Marcello Mastroianni in terms of Fellini's alter ego, or the socially inept anti-heroes of Olmi's films as his alter egos, or the suffering Monica Vitti as a female alter ego, or even anima, for Antonioni. Links between on-screen characters and their off-screen creators are at best tenuous, but the presence of some kind of relationship does suggest another place where the private and autobiographical becomes the public and fictional.

Although there are many points at which one may make parallels between the films and Bellocchio's life, two recurring instances of auto-biographical material stand out and are worth pursing. The first, which is touched upon in relation to *Vacanze in Val Trebbia*, is the attachment to or detachment from place as represented by the Bobbio-Rome geographical axis. The second is the smile, a motif that again traverses Bellocchio's film-making and is intimately connected with the body of the director.

Bellocchio was born in Emilia-Romagna, a northern Italian province that encompasses a wide sweep of land running westwards from the Adriatic Sea into the cultivated plains of the Po Valley and up into the wilder Apennine mountains. His childhood and adolescence were spent in this region, split between life in the provincial city of Piacenza and life in the Trebbia Valley, where his mother had a villa. It was only in 1959 that he left Emilia-Romagna for Milan, where he started a degree in law and a course in acting; he subsequently abandoned the latter owing to problems with his voice. In 1960, at the age of twenty-one, he finally transferred to Rome, where he studied to become a director at the renowned Centro Sperimentale. With the exception of a year spent at the Slade School of Fine Arts in London (1963-4) and, since 1995, his regular returns to Bobbio to work with his summer school, Fare Cinema, Bellocchio's adult life has centred on the capital.

The geographical axis that marks Bellocchio's life is reflected in his film-making. Bellocchio's oeuvre, taken in its entirety, records a dichotomy between city and province, and particularly between Rome and Emilia-Romagna. Moreover, it repeatedly proposes a narrative of attachment to and detachment from provincial origins. Bellocchio is not the only Italian director to represent the separation between rural beginnings and life in the metropolis. Fellini's films, for instance, narrate provincial origins in Rimini (*Amarcord* [*I Remember*], 1973) and an adult life spent in the capital (*La dolce vita* [1960], *Roma* [1972], and *Intervista* [1987]); Giuseppe Tornatore's *Nuovo Cinema Paradiso* (1988) narrates the trauma of abandoning the province (rural Sicily) for the capital. Bellocchio's attachment to place is in fact very much the stuff of Italian auteur cinema making, as any analysis of the geography of the films of Rosi, Olmi, or Pasolini confirms.

In Bellocchio's narratives, the landscape of Emilia-Romagna repeatedly figures as a marker of provincialism, insularity, stasis, and suffering. This does not reflect so much the real Emilia-Romagna as it does Bellocchio's personal views on the area. The province is presented as a dreary constant in the early feature films: *I pugni in tasca* is shot in Piacenza and at the family villa near the country town of Bobbio; *La Cina è vicina* is shot in generic Imola and Dozza, both in Emilia-Romagna; *Marcia trionfale*, although appearing to be set in an anonymous location, was nevertheless filmed at a disused barracks in Reggio-Emilia. Both *I pugni in tasca* and *La Cina è vicina* sketch an unflattering portrait of a wintry landscape in which is housed a petty, sick, provincial society, a place where social patterns repeat themselves like viruses, where rebellion is doomed to failure, and where revolutionary ideas fail to take hold.

It is only in the early eighties that there finally comes a definite, if not quite definitive, break with the province. This is worked through in two films: *Vacanze in Val Trebbia*, which presents the argument directly and codes it in terms of the director's autobiography (a director called Marco returns to Bobbio from Rome); and *Gli occhi, la bocca*, two years later, which re-presents the problem in more obviously fictional terms, narrating the story of an aging actor (Lou Castel) who returns to Emilia-Romagna from the capital for the funeral of his twin brother. In both films the emphasis is on the return to the province, with Rome present only as absence. In the first, the encounter with the provincial past brings little reconciliation or acceptance. The memories of Marco's childhood, which appear as oneiric sequences, are poorly integrated into the protagonist's life, as if the adult had failed to recognize and accept them. Moreover, the finale of the film records a child running naked towards Bobbio, which suggests that this child still clings to the town and is therefore still at war with the adult who is trying to rid himself of the place by selling his family house and rejecting Bobbio as a place in which 'si soffre' [one suffers]. The second film, *Gli occhi, la bocca*, although reiterating the break with the past, seems to offer a certain level of inner reconciliation. The break is made explicit when the father (Michel Piccoli) says to his son, Pippo (Lou Castel), 'Adesso basta, e finiscila con i pugni in tasca' [Now, that's enough; leave the fists in the pockets behind you], an admonishment that is autobiographical both for Lou Castel and for Bellocchio: the era of *I pugni in tasca*, of frustrated rebellion, and of the provinces has ended, and it is time to find a new mode of expression. These two films seem to put the ghosts of the provincial past to rest. After 1982 the world that Bellocchio left behind at the age of twenty will only re-surface again in minor works: some short films set in Bobbio, which would be used for the film *Sorelle* in 2006.

In the eighties, Rome – Bellocchio's adopted city – slowly comes to the fore as a location.[16] *Salto nel vuoto* (1980), the first film shot in the capital, is set in the comfortable middle-class district of Parioli (although the apartment itself was actually reconstructed in a studio). However, in this, Bellocchio's first Fagiolian film, the city stands very much at the margins, while the space within the apartment dominates. Only in *Diavolo in corpo*, and later in *L'ora di religione* and *Buongiorno, notte*, is there a profounder interaction with the capital and its religious and political history. The city takes a central position, both visually and thematically, in *L'ora di religione*.

Whereas Rome tends to embody public, civic, or socio-political comment, as the centre for the Italian state (embodied in the Vittoriano building in *L'ora di religione*) and the Church (the Vatican in *L'ora di religione* and *Buongiorno, notte*), Emilia-Romagna testifies to a deeper autobiographical attachment. It is specifically the Trebbia Valley (in which *I pugni in tasca* and the semi-autobiographical *Vacanze in Val Trebbia* and *Sorelle* are set) that is linked to Bellocchio's personal cinema making. Images of Piacenza in *I pugni in tasca*, and the Po River, Bologna, and Faenza in *Gli occhi, la bocca*, seem somewhat detached and generic – probably in part because they resonate with Emilia-Romagna's long cinematic history. After all, the province is home both to the Don Camillo films of the fifties and to some of the most internationally significant auteur cinema of the sixties and seventies: Pasolini's Po Valley, Antonioni's Ravenna, and Fellini's coastal Rimini. In contrast, the Val Trebbia, fresh in terms of cinema history, is rooted more deeply in the personal of Bellocchio's cinema.

Bobbio and the Val Trebbia come to signify a personal link with location, which can be seen in the very mise en scène of *I pugni in tasca*, *Vacanze in Val Trebbia*, and *Sorelle*. In these films Bellocchio's private world overlaps with film-making's public world through the use of locations, furniture, paintings, and objects that take up different positions and meanings in the private and autobiographical spheres on the one hand and in the public spheres on the other. *I pugni in tasca* was shot at Bellocchio's mother's house outside Bobbio and incorporates the furniture with which Bellocchio grew up. The camera was attentive to this, at times panning carefully across these objects, recording them. To read these objects as expressive only of the protagonist's (Ale's) bourgeois world is to miss the fact that these objects signify more to the director than they do to his character. The autobiographical presence of objects returns in *Vacanze in Val Trebbia*, where one of the beds that float down the river in an oneiric sequence is that on which Ale had slept in *I pugni in tasca*, and also that on which Bellocchio had slept as a child. In *Sorelle*, the use of personal objects in the mise en scène is repeated, and again the metacinematic element is drawn out. At one point in the film the family sits down to dinner in exactly the same dining room as that in which, forty years earlier, Ale and his brothers and sister had eaten. Flashbacks to the dining-room sequence of the earlier film, intercut with images from the present and coupled with shots that mirror the original, emphasize the extent to which deliberate parallels between the past of the house – both filmic and autobiographic – and the present of the house are drawn, stressing the *director's* memory, not that of the film's characters.

Although the use of these locations and objects is determined in part, especially at the outset of Bellocchio's career, by financial necessity and convenience, their returning presence over the years cannot be explained by such considerations alone. They clearly have a personal significance for the director, implying issues that he works out in his films. They also have a particular significance for the spectator, acting as a kind of in-joke, typical of art-house cinema. Such cinema cultivates an intellectual and knowing audience, whose pleasure is increased by getting the joke and so becoming part of a 'privileged' inner circle that holds the key to another, more hidden and private, level of the film's significance.

If Bellocchio in part works out personal emotional issues through his films, the films also reflect the concreteness of the director's material presence in the world. The corporeality of the director gets onto the screen through a gesture that weaves its way dramatically between the filmic and extra-filmic and seems to bridge the on-screen and off-screen worlds; this is the smile, or laugh, which is both talked about and screened repeatedly in Bellocchio's films. The awkward, out-of-place, or subversive laugh reoccurs with great frequency: in *Marcia trionfale* Rosanna (Miou-Miou) laughs sardonically at her husband while he tries to rape her, emasculating him; in *I pugni in tasca* the laughter of Ale (Lou Castel) is repeatedly subversive (he laughs almost uncontrollably while clearing out his mother's possessions after having murdered her); in *Nel nome del padre* Salvatore (again Lou Castel) laughs ironically at Angelo's plan to put on a play, axing Angelo's confidence; and in *Diavolo in corpo*, Giulia's (Maruschka Detmers') laugh is long and strident, characterizing her free and socially disruptive mode of being.[17]

What is interesting, however, is that this subversive laugh is characteristic of Bellocchio's own on-screen performance. In the argument staged between Marco and his wife Gisella in *Vacanze in Val Trebbia*, Bellocchio's smirking seems to undercut the words being said; in his brief on-screen appearance in *L'ora di religione* he seems again to be smirking to himself, thus undermining his harsh reproach of the film's protagonist, Ernesto; and in 'Discutiamo, discutiamo,' Bellocchio's character, a teacher, is possessed by a lack of seriousness that creates a Brechtian detachment between words (which are serious) and acting style (which is detached, mocking, and smiling). It begs the question is this detached and mocking smile ideologically motivated in a Brechtian sense, deliberately warning the spectator that what he or she is watching is fiction, or is it linked with the body of the director, with his physical modes of expression, with his life?

L'ora di religione takes the smile one step further and makes it the subject of a film. Bellocchio originally gave the film the title 'Il sorriso di mia madre' [My Mother's Smile], which is the name under which the film was released in France (*Le sourire de ma mère*) and which became the film's subtitle in Italy (*L'ora di religione: Il sorriso di mia madre*). The smile, which is the mother's smile, is also Ernesto Picciafuoco's smile, a deriding twist of the lips, indicating the character's detachment from events and his worldly wise, atheistic cynicism. It is this smile that offends Conte Bulla, who, feeling himself interrupted during his polemical discourse on the state of Italy, turns to Ernesto and accuses him of laughing at him. 'Che c'è da ridere?' [What's so funny?], he asks. Ernesto denies laughing, but this smile precipitates the duel between him and the count. The question 'Perché ridi?' [Why are you laughing?] is directed at Ernesto repeatedly and becomes one of the film's motifs.

Given the repeated occurrences of this smile or laugh in Bellocchio's opus, *L'ora di religione* becomes intertextual, referencing Bellocchio's past performances as actor along with previous occurrences of the subversive smile in his films. More radically, Ernesto's smile points to the extratextual, corporeal presence of the director; in other words, the smile for which Ernesto is criticized is actually the same distancing smile seen on the director's own face in the films in which he appears ('Discutiamo, discutiamo' and *Vacanze in Val Trebbia* especially) and in his interview performances. On one level, the body of the director seems to be the subject of *L'ora di religione*. There is certainly a link – however hard it might be to pinpoint and define – between the body of the director and the body of his films. What seems important here is Sturrock's comment (1993, 2) that the autobiographer is not an *abstraction* (as critics like De Man [1984] suggest) – being little more than a term created by the reader in order to pin down meaning in the text – but has a real face. Although postmodern theories of the author dismiss the real person, rendering him or her absent or abstract, they overestimate the fact that the author-auteur of a work has not only a set of culturally determined experiences but also a body, and that this body, along with its experiences, is reflected in the work.

It should be clear by now that Bellocchio's cinema, although tendentially focused on the fictional, harbours a relatively high level of autobiographical material, at times explicitly and deeply (as in *Vacanze in Val Trebbia*), and at other times far less obviously. Certain themes, such as the socio-political climate of the late 1960s and 1970s (to which Bellocchio frequently returns and which reflects his formative political involvement in the left-wing politics of that time), issues surrounding rebellion and conformity (central to Bellocchio's filmography and political experiences), and personal issues such as the relationship with his native territory and the suicide of his twin brother in 1969, are all insinuated into his films.

However, the question remains: Does it matter that this autobiographical material is there? After all, without knowing anything about the director, one could hazard an interpretation of *Vacanze in Val Trebbia* that would anchor its meaning to the central character, Marco, rather than to any extra-filmic Marco Bellocchio. In fact, all of Bellocchio's cinema can be read in this way, in other words, without reference to the director, since the autobiographical code is only a '*subcode* of the code of narration' (Branigan 1984, 41–2), except in *Vacanze in Val Trebbia*.

Despite the fact that the films can be read without taking their autobiographical aspects into account, the fact that autobiography exists in them does matter, and it does so for two fundamental reasons. First, the presence of private material is intimately bound up with spectator pleasure. If a spectator who has little knowledge of the director Marco Bellocchio watches *Vacanze in Val Trebbia*, he or she may feel distanced or even betrayed by the film's procedure and will certainly be aware of 'being in the dark.' Similarly, in *Sorelle* the flashbacks to Bellocchio's earlier films become illusive and alienating. However, for the typical

Italian follower of art-house cinema, who consumes not only films but also cinema journals and the cinema pages of broadsheet newspapers like *La Repubblica* (ANICA 1987, 16), this private and autobiographical material takes on a different meaning. Sharing the director's in-joke (whether it be his casting of family members, his referencing of objects he owns, or his nods to films he has made) is an important part of the pleasure of cinema-going within the auteur circuit, a pleasure associated with the cultish discovery of the unknown or little known; the sharing of this in ensuing conversations is part of the experience of art-house cinemagoers, an experience that tends *always* to go beyond the filmic text. The argument, propounded by critics like Tormey, for instance, that we should concentrate only on the filmic text as a 'self-expressive object'[18] does not take into account this whole socio-cultural ambient around art-house cinema that makes the film more than an individual text and encourages links between films and between those films and their directors.

The second point is that although the films may be interpreted without recourse to an autobiographical reading, the discovery of autobiographical elements amounts to the discovery of the director's signature in the films, a signature that defies the commercial and public nature of the film-making medium and that, in revealing a link between the director as chef and the film as product, draws attention to the power of the director. Autobiography is therefore per se a political tactic, inscribing the director into the text and thus showing how the private and individual still inheres in an apparently rigidly impersonal, public, and collective medium. In this sense, autobiography is power.

Conclusion

The existence of a category of film-making termed art house, with its own industrial productive methods and distributive circuits, enables directors like Bellocchio to construct themselves and be constructed within an alternative space that has profound implications for the ensuing films, both in terms of their production (that is, what goes into them) and their consumption (what is considered relevant to take from them). In the whole arc of the production and consumption of such films, the personal, as autobiography and as stylistic signature, is given a far more significant place than it is in commercial cinema. Personal cinema becomes an important, often hidden, code within the public institution of cinema.

2   Bellocchio's Political Cinema in the Sixties and Seventies

Bellocchio is commonly categorized as a political film-maker. Michalczyk (1986) unproblematically classifies him as such alongside Pasolini, Rosi, and others in *Italian Political Filmmakers*. However, I am not convinced that Bellocchio is so easily characterized, either in terms of classifying his cinema in its entirety as the work of a political film-maker or even in terms of interpreting particular films, like *Buongiorno, notte*, as such despite their avowed political content. This chapter will explore whether, and to what extent, Bellocchio's earlier films are political, what is meant by *political* in this regard, and how politically engaged they may be considered to be.

As soon as we discuss politics in relation to Bellocchio's cinema, a terminological problem arises that needs to be settled at the outset. The word *political* is subject to a number of different interpretations. As far as this book is concerned, two principal meanings need to be distinguished. In the first, *political* signifies an explicit relation with institutional politics and implies a relation to governance by the state. Not all Bellocchio's cinema is political in this sense, although some films clearly do treat institutional politics: 'Discutiamo, discutiamo' and the two militant documentaries for the extra-parliamentary UCI (m-l), all shot in 1969, are clearly political in this sense. Other films make explicit mention of institutional politics: Bellocchio's early short, *Ginepro fatto uomo* (Juniper Made Man, 1962); his second feature, *La Cina è vicina*; and the political thriller, *Sbatti il mostro in prima pagina*. After the shift to Fagiolian psychoanalysis, *Diavolo in corpo, La balia, Buongiorno, notte, Vincere* and two significant documentaries contained explicitly political material. A number of further films, like *Gli occhi, la bocca*, also strongly imply a particular political stance.

There is a second and broader meaning of *political* that is highly relevant for Bellocchio's film-making, whereby the word implies power relations. In this second sense, not one of Bellocchio's films is divorced from the political. For a start, each one necessarily interacts with the power structures of the film industry. More specifically, however, each of his films positions power relations centrally, and the struggles between self and society, individual and institution, and powerless and powerful are fundamental to his cinema making. It can be argued that while Bellocchio's films are less political in the first sense than has commonly been suggested, they are deeply political in this second sense: there is no more Bellocchian motif than the struggle against society's power bases.

The Problems of *Impegno* in the Era of Postmodernism

In the mid-sixties, when Bellocchio was first making feature films, postmodernist theories were beginning to have an impact in Italy, throwing the idea of representation into crisis and, with it, the notion of *impegno*.[1] Whereas Italian neo-realist film-makers, working before the advent of postmodernism, could still perceive a coincidence between the sign and its referent and believe that they could represent reality through cinema and perhaps effect change through their representations, filmmakers of the sixties were far more problematically situated. Postmodernist thought buried the optimistic belief in the camera's powers to faithfully record and to change reality.

In Italian neo-realist cinema of the late forties and early fifties *impegno* had a central role. However, neo-realism's conception of *impegno* was narrow and limited, both stylistically and ideologically. It reflected a left-wing vision of the world, current at the time, that was attentive to the rights of workers and peasants – that is, primarily to class – rather than to a wider range of political issues (gender, race, nation, and sexuality) which have since emerged, albeit fragmentarily, in contemporary Italian cinema. Neo-realism took an optimistic view of the role of cinema in political change. Cesare Zavattini, Roberto Rossellini, Vittorio De Sica, and other proponents of Italian neo-realism held that life could be analysed, understood, and – to some extent – transformed through film. Such faith in representability was simply erased by postmodernist thought.[2]

Under postmodernism, 'when the closed system ... is punctured and replaced by openendedness, the mimetic component of representation declines and the performative one comes to the fore,' and the process then 'no longer entails reaching behind appearances in order to grasp an intelligible world' (Iser 1987, 326–7). In other words, the idea of the play of signifiers becomes central, and the notion that one can simply represent a pre-existent reality becomes a naive illusion. It is no longer possible to wheel a camera out into the streets and record what is there, as Zavattini had proposed. The very action of setting up a camera in front of, say, a grocery store transforms that store; it is impossible not to frame it in a particular way and at a particular time, and, unless it is an extreme avant-garde cinema like some of Andy Warhol's, editing will entail the selection of some shots over others in post-production.

Jean Baudrillard's claims with respect to representation are bold. He categorizes postmodernism as an era of simulation[3] that was inaugurated by 'a liquidation of all referentials' (Baudrillard 1994, 2), and outlines the successive phases of the demise of referentiality as follows: the image reflects a profound reality; the image masks and denatures a profound reality; the image masks the *absence* of a profound reality; and finally the image has no relation to any profound reality. For Baudrillard, in high postmodernism we have reached stage four, where the image no longer simply betrays reality but is radically unrelated to it.

The detachment of sign from the world creates serious problems for any notion of *impegno*. Baudrillard is aware of this when he states, for instance, that 'simulation threatens the difference between the "true" and the "false," the "real" and the "imaginary"' (1994, 3). If writing and the production of images are no longer able to represent the world as it is, how can a writer or film-maker reveal things as they are to others in order to convince his or her spectators to get up from their seats and go out and change them?

In addition to the crisis of representation, postmodernism points to a further, and perhaps even graver, problem: the loss of faith in all grand, totalizing metanarratives, those abstract ideas – such as a belief in rational thought, progress, or truth – which have guided humankind in its attempts to make sense of the world and have inspired people to bring about transformations in the society in which they live. The loss of metanarratives has profound consequences for involvement in politics. If there is no truth, it becomes hard to say that it is 'right' to support workers and contest the bourgeoisie. If, in the context of postmodernism, ideas are myths or metanarratives that are historically circumscribed and contingent, it becomes difficult to defend the idea of giving power to the workers – another myth in a world constructed of many such myths. It is difficult too to put into practice an ideal if we know that this ideal is not an absolute but is only a relative thing, which has no final, objective status as truth. These kinds of problems tend to create paralysis rather than *impegno*.

Unsurprisingly, the era of postmodernism in the West has been marked by a withdrawal from 'objective,' realistic portrayals of a socio-political world. Attempts to describe a world in its entirety have waned. It is generally agreed that Italian cinema became inward-looking and introverted in the sixties as directors turned to filtering reality through the personal[4] – a direct result of postmodernism's undermining of any sense of a concrete and objective reality 'out there.' With the exception of the five or six years subsequent to the social upheaval of 1968–1969, when Italian cinema struck out into the political world again, making militant documentaries and contentious political films, like Elio Petri's *La classe operaia va in paradiso* (*The Working Class Goes to Heaven / Lulu the Tool*, 1971), Pasolini's documentary for the militant group Lotta Continua (*12 dicembre* / 12 December, 1972), and Gian Vittorio Baldi's *Fuoco!* (*Fire!*, 1969), it has never returned to the levels, or modes, of *impegno* that were witnessed during neo-realism. In fact, the disillusionment felt after the country became embroiled in terrorism in the mid-seventies – a clear sign that the activities of 1968 had failed in their aims to bring about a better society – led to a further detachment from political engagement, known as the *riflusso*, which deepened the trend that had begun in the early sixties. Italian cinema in the eighties, dominated by mediocre comedies and dramas, seems a world apart from the committed cinema with which Italy is historically identified.

The theoretical problems surrounding representation and grand narra-tives suggest that a politically committed cinema is anachronistic, illogical, and even absurd. Nevertheless, *impegno* continues – paradoxically – to exist, albeit without the strong ideological framework that sustained it during the years of neo-realism. Slavoj Žižek (1989, 33) has described this as a kind of pathology whereby 'they know that, in their activity, they are following an illusion, but still, they are doing it.' Burns argues in *Fragments of Impegno* (2001) that despite its decline in the later decades of the twentieth century, *impegno* did not simply cease to exist; instead, it changed, becoming more fragmentary and encompassing a far wider range of socio-political problems.

During the *riflusso*, and in contemporary Italian cinema, directors no longer focused primarily on issues of class, as the neo-realist cinema and post-1968 *cinema civile* and *militante* had, but they began to deal with a wide range of socio-political topics. Contemporary sexual relations have been explored in a great number of recent films, including Giovanni Veronesi's two *Love Manuel* films (*Manuale d'amore 1* [2005] and *Manuele d'amore 2* [2007]) and Gabriele Muccino's cinema. Gender and gay issues have come to the fore in films like Monica Stambrini's *Benzina* (*Gasoline*, 2001) and in the work of Ferzan Ozpetek. Issues surrounding immigration and immigrants have repeatedly been screened in films like Moretti's *Aprile* (*April*, 1998), Carlo Mazzacurati's *Vesna va veloce* (*Vesna Goes Fast*, 1996), and Giuseppe Tornatore's *La sconosciuta* (*The Other Woman*, 2006). The Mafia and Camorra have resurfaced in a substantial number of recent films, including those by Mario Tullio Giordana (*I cento passi / The Hundred Steps*, 2002), by Gabriele Salvatores (*Io non ho paura / I'm not Scared*, 2003), and by Matteo Garrone (*Gomorra / Gomorrah*, 2008).

Bellocchio's films, although not easily classifiable as postmodernist (for reasons that will become clear), show a keen awareness of the slipperiness of representation, the problematic relationship between representation and reality, and the splitting of signifier and signified that are typical of postmodernism. The problem of representation becomes the subject of one of Bellocchio's early films, *Sbatti il mostro in prima pagina* (1972), a 'committed' film dealing with the deceptive nature of the mass media's representation of the world. The film follows the fictional case of the brutal rape and murder of a young girl, set against anti-establishment protests during the years of terrorism. The film's plot delineates an attempt, on the part of a Milanese newspaper (a clear allusion to Milan's *Il Corriere della Sera*), to swing the forthcoming elections towards a vote for the right by framing a young male anarchist as the girl's murderer. When, however, the newspaper discovers that the anarchist is in fact innocent, its chief editor connives with the paper's unscrupulous owner to hide the truth until the elections have passed. The paper continues to frame the innocent anarchist, ignoring the discovery of the real perpetrator who is an emotionally disturbed, middle-aged porter at the girl's school. The film ends with a shot of a filthy river brimming with scum and rubbish, a clear metaphor for a corrupt world.

Sbatti il mostro in prima pagina clearly points to the gulf between reality and its representation in the media and through other official channels. This theme was topical in the early seventies, having received treatment in numerous plays and films. Dario Fo's play *Morte accidentale di un anarchico* (*Accidental Death of an Anarchist* [1970]) accuses the police of a cover-up after the anarchist Giuseppe Pinelli, wrongly suspected of orchestrating the Piazza Fontana bombing in 1969, fell to his death from a high window in a police station. Giuliano Montaldo's *Sacco e Vanzetti* (*Sacco and Vanzetti*, 1971), based on the true story of two Italo-American anarchists who received the death penalty for a murder that they had not committed, also focuses on the manipulation of facts by police and the media. In the early seventies, media representation was treated with profound distrust, especially by members of the left. A series of scandals, such as the SIFAR (Italian secret service) affair – in which General Giovanni De Lorenzo, head of SIFAR, abused his powers in order to collect detailed information on over 150,000 MPs, union leaders, and other public figures (See Meade 1990, 34–5) – and the cover-up surrounding the Piazza Fontana bombing, created a climate of distrust in which the government and the police were seen to be implicated (Meade 1990, 35–8 and 56–7). The uneasiness about representation was spawned not only by postmodernism's cynicism towards representation but also by these revelations.

Sbatti il mostro in prima pagina focuses explicitly and at length on the theme of media distortion. Near the beginning of the film there is a sequence in which the chief editor of the newspaper, Giancarlo Bizanti (Gian Maria Volonté), reprimands his younger colleague, Roveda (Fabio Garriba), for the wording of the headline he has written: 'Disperato Gesto di un Disoccupato: Si Brucia Vivo Padre di Cinque Figli' [Unemployed Man's Desperate Gesture: Father of Five Burns Alive]. Standing authoritatively above the younger man, Bizanti says, 'Ora, io non sono Umberto Eco e non voglio farti una lezione di semantica applicata all'informazione, ma mi pare che la parola *disperato* sia gonfia di valori polemici' [Now, I'm not Umberto Eco and I don't want to give you a lesson on semantics applied to the media, but it seems to me that the word *desperate* is brimming with polemical significance]. The reference to Eco and his theories of language in itself warns the spectator of the manipulation inherent in the nature of language. We then watch as Bizanti goes on to transform the journalist's title from one that might 'upset' the newspaper's reader to one that will not. The final title is 'Drammatico Suicidio di un Immigrato' [Dramatic Suicide of an Immigrant], and, once a few minor changes have been worked within the body of the article (*licenziato* [sacked], for example, becomes *rimasto senza lavoro* [unemployed]), the article becomes coherent with the paper's message and fit to be published. In this short sequence, Bellocchio's film reveals how the ideology of the paper infiltrates its every article, robbing journalists of their freedom of speech and rendering impossible any reporting of truth.

Crucially, however, Bellocchio's film does not put its *own* portrayal of reality into question; it reveals the deceptive nature of the centre-right's version of reality without unpicking its own. This means that whereas, with its citation of Eco and its suspicion of representation, the film might appear postmodern, it is in fact far from any postmodern play of signifiers. Instead, it defends an idea of truth hidden behind the distortions of the media. The plot follows the classic quest-for-truth structure of the detective genre: a protagonist (Roveda) courageously solves a mystery and finds the real rapist, contemporaneously revealing the wickedness of the other monsters – the editor and the owner of the press. In other words, the idea of truth is inscribed in the very nature of the genre to which the film subscribes. 'Truth' is also embedded in the film through the presence of real documentary inserts that appear under the opening titles. These record a right-wing demonstration, street battles between police and left-wing protestors, and the important funeral of Giangiacomo Fetrinelli, a prominent editor who had been found dead under a high-tension pylon near Milan; he had blown himself up while trying to bring down pylons to further the cause of the left. The opening sequence of the film is the result of a splicing together of scenes shot in black and white and in colour, each rigorously shot by a hand-held camera, grainy, imperfect, and therefore apparently the very embodiment of the raw 'real' (the footage from the Fetrinelli funeral was shot by Bellocchio's troupe with hidden hand-held cameras). The use of documentary contextualizes the film within the 'real' Milan of the early 1970s, suggesting that this context is somehow unmediated by filmic and media distortion and therefore true. It also implicitly gives credence to the film that follows, which, while clearly appertaining to the mass genre of the *giallo* [thriller], is doing the same work as the documentaries in revealing the corruption of the media and the right-wing interests it protects.

What emerges from Bellocchio's opus is that, despite the awareness of the unreliability of the nature of language and representation clearly shown in this and other films of the time, it is only from 1980 that the nature of the objectivity and truth of filmic reality is seriously put into question. Prior to 1980, the films turn a blind eye to their own part in (mis)representation and tend to put themselves forward as champions of the truth, while portraying the other side – the right, social democracy, and so on – as the bearers of falsehood. It is only when, in *Vacanze in Val Trebbia*, Bellocchio muddies the waters between dream and reality, creating an *opera aperta* [open-ended work],[5] and so preventing the spectator from extracting answers, that a real questioning of the nature of representational truth takes place. In the cinema of his second period, each time that Bellocchio only retrospectively marks a sequence as dream, he is showing us how easily we have been tricked by the deceptively realistic nature of film. During this phase, Bellocchio's film-making shifts – at least in part – from Baudrillard's stage two (when the image masks and denatures a profound reality) to stage four (when the image has no relation to any reality; it is its own pure simulacrum). It is no surprise that the blurring of reality and dream and the erasure of any firm notion of truth coincide with the near disappearance of *impegno* in his cinema. *Impegno* and postmodern scepticism regarding the image do not mix. Indeed, Umberto Eco links ambiguity with evasion and non-engagement (Eco 2000). The period of Bellocchio's most engaged cinema corresponds with the period in which he does not question fundamentally the existence of some kind of truth available through representation (for example, through cinema), even if he puts certain *forms* of representation into question. His cinema of this earlier period, though far from employing neo-realist codes, still lies within the realist project in its broadest sense, which, according to Hamon (as quoted by Brooke-Rose [1988, 86]) is 'identified with a pedagogic desire to transmit information' and with the consequent need to safeguard readability.

The Nature of Bellocchio's *Impegno*

Bellocchio's political film-making (in the first, narrower, sense of the term) is remarkably circumscribed in geographical, temporal, and thematic terms. It treats only one country – Italy. With the exception of two films to date, *La balia* and *Vincere*, it treats only one time period – the late sixties and seventies. Moreover, it focuses on thematic material centred only on the Italian left and extreme left. A broader, more international vision is simply not entertained, except perhaps at times by extension. However, within these strictures, as argued in chapter 1, the genres and approaches that Bellocchio's cinema employs are highly diverse: he experiments with both *cinema civile* and *cinema militante* and moves among fiction and documentary, traditional styles of shooting, and the avant-garde. In addition, his attitudes towards the political material slowly change over the forty years in which he treats it.

A distinct pattern of engagement arises from Bellocchio's biography. In the first phase, from the early sixties to 1970, he becomes progressively more politically engaged. In the second, from 1970 through the *riflusso*, his relation to politics reverses and rapidly becomes more detached. In the third phase (to which I will return in chapter 4), politics returns to Bellocchio's films, but owing to transformations in both his thinking and in society during the intervening years, the *impegno* found here is distinct from that found in the early films.

During the early to mid-sixties Bellocchio started to become seriously involved in politics. While enrolled at the Centro Sperimentale film school in Rome, he attended the meetings of left-wing extra-parliamentary groups who pitted themselves against party politics and contested both the social-democratizing tendencies of the socialist party (the Partito Socialista Italiano, or PSI) and the reformism of the communist party (the Partito Comunista Italiano, or PCI).[6] He also had slight, but significant, involvement with *Quaderni piacentini*, an extra-parliamentary political review directed by his older brother, Pier Giorgio Bellocchio. Bernardi claims that this journal was formative, citing particularly its moralism and the approach of one of its key contributors, Goffredo Fofi, who would later work with Bellocchio on *Sbatti il mostro in prima pagina* (Bernardi 1998, 23). Bellocchio's contribution is, however, limited to writing a number of poems for the journal and two articles, one on Bertolucci ('Bertolucci: Ben ti sta') and one on Nanni Loys' *Le quattro giornate di Napoli* (*The Four Days of Naples*, 1962). Both articles were published in the journal in 1963.

The articles that Bellocchio wrote in this period, which include those written for *Quaderni piacentini* and two written in 1966 for *Cahiers du cinéma* ('La revolution au cinéma' and 'La stérilité de la provocation,' published in the journal's March and April issues, respectively), provide insight into Bellocchio's public political views before he made his first political films. He professes the need to bring about change through film-making but sees little possibility of doing so in a country already institutionalized in its film industry, social democratized in its politics, and complacent in terms of its spectators. He claims that cinema *must* be political (Bellocchio 1966a, 43), defining it in the following terms:

> Un cinéma politique est un cinéma qui interprète une réalité de classe avec une objectivité absolue, afin de la provoquer, et cela, en écartant de cette réalité tous les aspects qui ne se réfèrent pas à une condition sociale, mais restent irrémédiablement particuliers, dans un style qui favorise une compréhension universelle et qui, en même temps, sauve cette interprétation du simple didactisme.

[Political cinema is a cinema that interprets the reality of class with absolute objectivity, with the aim of provoking it. It achieves this by casting off from this reality all aspects that do not refer to a social condition but are instead irredeemably private. It uses a style that makes it universally comprehensible and that, at the same time, saves the interpretation from mere didacticism.]

However, Bellocchio also seriously problematizes the cinema making of revolutionary politics, especially with regard to its ability to reach an audience. Although in the first article in *Cahiers du cinéma* he suggests that provocation is a key to making political cinema, in the second he denies the possibility of genuinely provoking a spectator. Provocation, Bellocchio argues, simply does not work: if the film does not make compromises for its spectators, average members of the public will not go to see it in the first place, so the film fails, preaching only to the converted (Bellocchio 1966b, 63). However, if a film compromises its critique in order to draw in spectators, the average spectators will still not link the provocation to their private situations, or if they do, they will only do so in a way that does not compromise them (63). Over the following years Bellocchio will try both approaches in his films, blending melodrama and politics into palatable political films (*Ginepro fatto uomo* and *La Cina è vicina*) and, later, making militant documentaries for the already converted. There are indications, however, that neither of these approaches really satisfied him.

During the student revolts of 1967–8, Bellocchio's political response suddenly shifted up a gear. He was nearly thirty at the time and would therefore have been seen as getting too old to be involved in these protests. Nonetheless, in November 1967, he was present at the occupation of the arts faculty of the University of Turin, a university whose students were some of the most militant activists of the revolts. He describes how he took part, 'stupefatto ed entusiasta' [amazed and enthusiastic] (quoted in Malanga 1998, 149), in the first episodes of the protests. He also describes an incident in which the teacher demanded to be allowed to teach, defending his moral position by stating in a superior tone that he had been interned in the concentration camp at Dachau (Malanga 1998, 149). On Bellocchio's return to Rome he was involved in the occupation of La Sapienza University:

Dopo Torino tornai a Roma. Anche lì mi infilai nella facoltà di lettere, che occupò lo stesso giorno che entrai. Mi ricordo le assemblee, coi giornalisti dei giornali borghesi che dovevano pagare l'ingresso, gli esami assediati e il diciotto per tutti, le notti in facoltà e i genitori che venivano a cercare le figlie, le telefonate a Cuba dal centrolino della segreteria occupata: 'Pronto? ... Vorremmo parlare con Fidel Castro ... è in casa?', le albe coi cornetti caldi aspettando i poliziotti ... Le cariche della polizia, precedute da tre squilli di tromba, e certi ragazzi, anonimi fino a un momento prima, che si scoprivano, meravigliandosi loro stessi, grandi combattenti di strada ... grandi parlatori, senza aver mai parlato prima ... Ecco, nel movimento collettivo, caotico e vitalissimo, ciascuno scopriva di essere un altro, e neanche quello che in solitudine aveva sempre sognato di diventare, un altro ancora, molto più originale.

(Bellocchio, quoted in Malanga 1998, 231).

[After Turin I returned to Rome. There too I infiltrated the arts faculty, which was occupied that very day. I remember the assemblies, with the journalists from middle-class newspapers who had to pay an entry fee, the exams under siege, and third-class marks for everyone, the nights in the faculty and the parents who came to look for their children, the telephone calls to Cuba from the main line of the occupied Secretary's Office – 'Hello? ... We'd like to speak to Fidel Castro ... Is he home?' – the dawns with hot croissants while we waited for the police ... the charge of the police, preceded by three trumpet calls, and certain kids, who had been anonymous up to a moment before, who, to their own surprise, discovered themselves to be great street fighters ... great orators, without ever having spoken before ... There you have it, in the chaotic and very vital collective movement, everyone discovered that they were another, and someone whom they would never have dreamt of becoming, a different person, someone who was much more original.]

The experiences gleaned from these two events were used in 'Discutiamo, discutiamo' in 1969, a short made together with the students of that very faculty at La Sapienza. Like the comments above, this short reveals that, although Bellocchio expresses enthusiasm for the movement, he is an observer more than a participator, and his commitment-lies fundamentally elsewhere.

Bellocchio was also briefly involved with the Marxist-Leninists (the UCI [m-l]), although his active political involvement stretched only from the spring of 1968 to the end of 1969.[7] His adhesion to the UCI (m-l) was, however, sincerer and more active than his adhesion to the student movement. The UCI (m-l) was one of the many small extra-parliamentary groups that sprang up in the years 1968–1969. Founded in Rome, it developed its own newspaper and in 1972 became an official political party, the Partito Comunista Italiano marxista-leninista (PCI [m-l]). Along with other Marxist-Leninist groups, it proposed disciplined organization and theoretical frameworks in place of the spontaneity and often-theoretical confusion of the student groups (Giachetti 1998, 106).

If one takes into account Bellocchio's retrospective comments on this period and his articles in *Quaderni piacentini* and *Cahiers du cinéma*, his reasons for joining the UCI (m-l) seem to stem from his belief that Italy needed fundamental and revolutionary change. Although he was also drawn to the idea of being directly involved with the people, especially the marginalized and exploited (Moscati 1998, 50), it seems to have been this revolutionary aspect that was particularly appealing.

At this time, despite his professed interest in revolution and despite the public and political nature of his film-making, what is striking in Bellocchio's comments is his emphasis not on the political policies and theories held by these groups but on the personal; this view is at loggerheads with his condemnation of the private in his *Cahiers du cinéma* article (1966a, 43). He stresses the potential for personal development that revolution offers. In an interview in the late seventies he outlines this aspect of the movement that 'si proponeva in maniera scientifica di rivoluzionare il mondo ma anche uomini che volevano rivoluzionare se stessi: il politico e il personale' [proposed, in a scientific manner, to revolutionize the world, but were also men who wanted to revolutionize themselves – the political and the personal]. He adds too that, in some ways, 'mi affascinava più il personale del politico' [the personal fascinated me more than the political] (quoted in Bernardi 1978, 3). In another interview he reiterates and amplifies this view, claiming that 'il rapporto con la politica era assolutamente non scientifico, ma morale, sentimentale, un discorso sull'integrità interna, sul non subire il compromesso' [the relationship with politics was absolutely non-scientific, but moral and sentimental, a discourse on personal integrity, on not undergoing compromises] (Menarini 1997, 38). It appears therefore that, even in the most politically committed periods of Bellocchio's career, the personal underlies the political.

During 1968–1969, in direct response to the upheaval of 1968, he made his most committed films. Within less than a year and a half he had made his first two militant documentaries (*Paola* and *Viva il 1° maggio rosso e proletario*) and the Brechtian 'Discutiamo, discutiamo.' However,

Bellocchio then steps back from what had become an unquestioning use of politics in film. Although his films continue to treat explicitly political material, the tone has changed. From 1970, after his experience in the student and extra-parliamentary left, Bellocchio's films – *Nel nome del padre*, *Sbatti il mostro in prima pagina*, and *Marcia trionfale* – will no longer unquestioningly support the left's positions. By 1977, explicit political content has almost disappeared from his cinema, although some of the associated themes remain. There is no return to the militant film-making seen in 1968–1969.

La Cina è vicina, *'Discutiamo, discutiamo,'* and Pre-contestation Impegno

When *La Cina è vicina* – Bellocchio's second film and his first political feature film – was released in 1967, there was little consensus as to whether or not it could be classified as *impegnato*, despite its open discussion of politics. The film's very title signals its contemporary political content: the words *la Cina è vicina* [China is near] refer not to any geographical proximity of the two countries but to the presence of Maoist ideas in Italy in the wake of the Chinese Cultural Revolution that was begun by Mao Zedong in 1966. The film's double plot – one strand of which is melodramatic and the other political – presents both class and party politics. The political plot tackles party politics head on as Vittorio Gordini becomes town councillor for the reformist and democratic socialist party, the Partito Socialista Unificato (PSU), which was formed in 1966 from the merging of the Partito Socialista Italiano and the Partito Democratico Socialista Italiano [Italian Democratic Socialist Party]. The film follows Vittorio's campaign to win the local elections despite the obstacles. One of the greatest obstacles is the 'Chinese' element, which emerges in the guise of Vittorio's brother, the adolescent Camillo, who is a political extremist involved with the Maoist extra-parliamentary left. A firm believer in revolution, Camillo is at loggerheads with the reformist social democracy, which his older brother has embraced, and aims to sabotage Vittorio's election campaign.

The conflict between Vittorio and Camillo is at the heart of the political strand of the plot, and two speeches – one by Camillo and one by Vittorio – synthesize the two main political positions discussed in the film. Camillo's speech comes in scene 2. Sitting in the Gordini family kitchen, he reads to his two Marxist-Leninist friends a carefully prepared discourse that treats the 'problema sessuale' [the problem of sex] and takes a highly ideological position whereby everything, including sex, is seen within the rigid schema of class. His discourse, delivered with icy seriousness, argues that for the good of the Maoist cause, their little group should gain sexual experience with an underage girl who has a medical problem. Her predicament means that she falls into a stupor during sex and therefore will not notice the substitution of her partners. The speech shows how Marxism can be manipulated to further causes that may have little to do with real revolution – one's own 'problema sessuale,' for instance.[8] A clever shot of Camillo looking at himself in a mirror prefaces the speech. The mirror is a sign of Camillo's vanity, of his position as an 'esteta della rivoluzione' [aesthete of the revolution] (Bellocchio 1967b, 27). It also suggests an intellectual disposition: he is watching himself live rather than living; he is rehearsing a semblance of life rather than living the real thing. It indicates his distance from the real.

Vittorio's speech, instead, comes right at the close of the film. He delivers it at the end of his party's election campaign, and it treats, or rather glosses over, the problematic fragmentariness in the centre left. Vittorio's address is triumphalist, prophesying that the four parties of the coalition are destined to converge. This speech is clearly meant to be read ironically as spin because in 1966, the year in which the film was shot, there was no sense of the imminent political stability that Vittorio puts before the crowd. Drake (1996, 22), for example, describes the 'disunity and schisms among the Socialists' during the sixties and the Christian Democrats' 'unwillingness or inability to compromise significantly on social and economic issues with its new allies.' By 1969, Vittorio's party, the newly united PSU, would have split back into its component parts. Vittorio's whitewashing of the fragmentariness and lack of progress of the left would have been all too transparent to contemporary spectators.

The Maoist forces of the extra-parliamentary left are portrayed as irrelevant and futile. Camillo's discourses are shown to be out of touch with reality, and his gestures – although disruptive – do not bring about change. He is capable only of small-time sabotage: he writes slogans on walls, painting the words *La Cina è vicina* on the PSU building; he sets off a small bomb within the PSU premises, which, while scaring the party members, achieves nothing further; and he sets three German shepherd dogs on his brother during his election speech. He also arranges for his male comrades to have sex with the girl who enters a hypnotic state during sex – this 'political act' actually amounts to the gang rape of a minor. The portrait of Camillo is that of a cold adolescent who masks his own desires in abstract pontificating. Moreover, under his mask of radicalism, he is still a traditional and provincial teenager who needs to believe in the sexual purity of his sister and tries to prevent her having a backstreet abortion. Camillo is also shown to be subservient in relation to the church: he can set off bombs at the PSU offices, but he still obediently serves mass and plays the piano for the priests at his boarding school. His revolutionary spirit is only skin deep and is entirely ineffectual. Bellocchio's point is that China is *not* near. The stuff of which revolution is made is not to be found in Camillo. He is just a normal adolescent, channelling his temporary rebellion into a cause; one can only imagine that this is a passing phase that will see Camillo soon in the shoes of his older brother, slipping into parliamentary politics, slippers, and middle-class hypocrisy.

Social democracy fairs little better, with Vittorio as its main exponent. Although treated in the film with indulgence rather than with the hostility shown towards Camillo, Vittorio is depicted as hopelessly bourgeois in his attention to what people will think and in his fear of ridicule. Like his younger brother, he is portrayed as hypocritical. Vittorio is capable in one breath of claiming not to be Catholic and in the next of making the sign of the cross in front of an altar. He is prepared to pass off a marriage to the working-class girl Giovanna as a political gesture. He says in his election speech, 'Sposo una proletaria socialista, una di voi' [I am marrying a proletarian socialist, one of you], despite the fact that his courtship of Giovanna has followed the classic model of the seduction by the master of the house of his maid, which is a fine nineteenth-century literary motif and quite the opposite to the stuff of revolution.

The political strand of the film thus presents a denunciation of the vicissitudes of the left, from its reformist and social-democratic wing to radical and revolutionary extra-parliamentary extremism. It portrays Italian society as coming into contact with contemporary extremist currents without being transformed by them. Camillo's revolution is an adolescent phase, which has only a minority following among the young, and is ineffectual. Vittorio's social democracy allows class domination to continue as before, and his behaviour effectively disarms the working class by absorbing them into the middle class. The right – the real enemy, one might suppose, of a director engaged in politics – is not mentioned once in the film.

Although it might be argued that the film is taking an *impegnato* line in critiquing the left and that this critique was necessary at the time, it cannot be said that the film is attempting to act as a social force for changing the world. When Fofi claims that the 'compito del cinema al servizio della rivoluzione è cambiare il mondo' [the task of cinema that serves the revolution is to change the world], it is clear that Bellocchio's film does not achieve, or even attempt to do, this. It offers only negations; it offers no guidance on how to proceed; it offers no utopias. Moreover, the film repeatedly undercuts politics both through its cinematography and by its pull towards the melodramatic code, which progressively draws the film away from the public and political sphere and into the private. In *La Cina è vicina* attention is constantly diverted from the political theme. Repeatedly, what is political in the mise en scène, in the dialogues, and in the plot slips away from any position of centrality, and this is the case right from the beginning of the film.

The opening scene begins within a public and political space: a rather bare room within the local headquarters of the newly formed Partito Socialista Unificato. The mise en scène carries heavy political meaning. On one wall hangs a portrait of Giuseppe Saragat, President of Italy at the time of filming (1964–1971) and considered to be the father of social democratic doctrine in the country. On another wall hangs a barely legible political poster for the PSU. However, the low camera angle that opens the film immediately undercuts the political significance of the setting by focusing not on Saragat or on the PSU poster but on a young couple (Giovanna and Carlo) who have made two PSU benches their bed. The camera is positioned only a couple of feet off the ground so that it stands level with the bench and the couple and not level with the political signifiers. This subtle positioning is crucial because through it Giovanna and Carlo, and *not* their political context, are placed at the centre of the frame.

The following scene plays the low-angle card again, and to great effect. We cut to the Giordini-Malvezzi family house, where Camillo is giving his long abstract political discourse on the 'problema sessuale' to his companions. He is sitting at the head of a large kitchen table; behind him a poster of Lenin has been tacked to the door. As Camillo talks, the camera unexpectedly takes up a position almost at floor level. From this position, he is suddenly far away in the background of the shot, and in the foreground we see the stone floor and a football. During this scene the camera alternates between above-table shots – particularly medium close-ups of a severe Camillo delivering his speech – and low angles that reveal the under-table activities of Camillo's meagre audience: two bored adolescent boys kicking a football for a small yapping dog.[9] The low-angle shot is literally *sub*versive (as it was in the first scene), revealing the political language as abstract, falsifying, and irrelevant. Rospo's kicking of the ball is in direct contrast to a heavy, humourless political discourse that is full of unnecessary intellectualisms and Latinisms, a discourse that is formal, lifeless, and absolutely without passion: 'Intendo per rapporto sessuale completo un rapporto *coitale non interruptus*, in posizione orizzontale, nella totale distensione del corpo secondo la sua lunghezza, con la partecipazione attiva e consapevole di ambedue i contraenti' [I mean by a sexual relationship a relationship of *coitus non interruptus*, in a horizontal position, in the total distension of the body along its length, with the active and consensual participation of both contractors]. The humor excluded from the speech slips into the subversive area of the 'under-table,' which in contrast seems to present the amused and amusing behaviour of teenage boys. The low angle encourages us to identify with the subversion and ridicule of Camillo; his discourse is clearly meant to parody the highly ideological speech that the extreme left was partial to at the time. Crucially, these shots, in shifting attention away from the discourse, also shift it away from the political meaning of the speech.

If the de-centring of attention is present on the micro-level of shot, it is also there on the macro-level of plot. The presence of melodrama in the film creates a rift in the political material, preventing it from ever firmly establishing itself. Giovanna's very first words – and the first words of the film – refer to the domestic sphere: she is concerned that her family will already be sitting down to lunch. In this first scene the political space of the PSU headquarters is transformed into a private and sexual space. In the second scene the private space (the family kitchen) is used as a political space by Camillo, but, because the posters look temporarily tacked on and the family dog runs and yaps insistently, the space never succeeds in establishing itself as political; it remains domestic. The non-establishment, or capsizing, of the political space happens repeatedly in the film. This is due to the fragile nature of the political, which is under constant threat, especially from the film's second, and melodramatic, plot.

The whole film is in tension between the political plot (Vittorio's rise through the provincial rungs of the PSU) and the melodramatic plot (the seduction of a couple of upper-middle-class siblings [Vittorio and Elena] by the proletarian couple [Giovanna and Carlo]). The first scene, in which Giovanna and Carlo wake up on the benches in the PSU headquarters, sets both plots in motion. Carlo's sexual relationship with Giovanna – which will be a trigger for the melodramatic plot – is briefly sketched; concurrently, the second (political) plot is set in motion through their comments about Carlo becoming the new socialist councillor (although in fact, we soon discover, his place has been taken by Vittorio).

Until the middle of the film the two strands are developed relatively evenly, parallel montage keeping them both moving forward. However, the seduction of a mature Elena by Carlo, occurring just before the midpoint of the film, upsets the balance. Carlo, having failed to be nominated PSU councillor, finds himself in the humbler role of Vittorio's campaign secretary and in this capacity is invited into the Gordini household. There, Vittorio leaves his sister alone with Carlo and unwittingly sets the scene for the seduction. Within minutes, Carlo is lying atop Elena on the sofa. Vittorio glimpses them and, disconcerted, bursts into the study where Giovanna, who is employed as the family secretary, is working at the typewriter. Vittorio, who has clearly been harassing the young Giovanna for some time, blurts out that if Carlo and Elena can kiss, why can't they? Giovanna, sickened by the news of her boyfriend's betrayal, initially rejects Vittorio's advances, but once she has seen the scene with her own eyes, changes her mind, runs upstairs, and hammers on the bathroom door (behind which Vittorio is now taking a bath); when she gets in and recovers from the comedy of his inadequate towel, she lets him embrace her. This scene – the first in which the four central characters appear together – puts the melodramatic strand centre stage.

Carlo's seduction of Elena generates complexities in the melodramatic plot that outweigh those of the political one. The second half of the film is drawn towards the vicissitudes of the double couple rather than to the election campaign. Elena gets pregnant and, desperate, tries to abort. However, the canny Carlo gets his ex-girlfriend, Giovanna, to monitor Elena's every move in the Gordini house, and so he is able to intervene to stop the abortion. In return, Giovanna wants Carlo to make her pregnant too, and she will pass off this child as Vittorio's. In the end, both she and Carlo – through the control of the female body – will enter the Gordini family. The final sequences of the film are crucial. The penultimate and final scenes wrap up the two plot strands. In the penultimate scene we see Vittorio giving his speech on the eve of the local elections (the pomposity of which is cut short abruptly by Camillo's organizing a cat-and-dog scrap on stage). This scene suggests that his campaign will be successful despite the antagonism of his Maoist brother, and is a vehicle for the film to conclude its discourse on the parliamentary and extra-parliamentary left. By contrast, the final scene ends within a female and private space, which is at polar opposites from the public space of the PSU headquarters in which the film began. In this final scene, direct political references have disappeared, replaced by the domestic space of the Gordini gymnasium in which Elena and Giovanna do prenatal exercises. Wearing identical white shifts, the two women, divided during the film by class and age, are now brought together by maternity (although their outlooks still differ – Elena is resigned and Giovanna is very pleased with herself). They are watched over not by any political figurehead of social democracy but by an almost life-size painting of a Madonna and child, a Madonna who also features on the cover of the book, *Sarò madre* [I Will Be a Mother], that lies on the floor beside them.

The movement of the film seems to shift uneasily from public-political space to private space, from male space to female space, finally ending up far from where it seemed to begin. The uneasiness comes from the 'interference' of a melodramatic genre. The double pregnancy and ensuing marriages see the proletariat failing to become a political force and being quietly absorbed into the middle class, being disarmed and disappearing invisibly, with any revolutionary or even reformist urge lost. The film's message is pessimistic. It sees the proletariat as a weak political force, easily corrupted by its desire to have what the richer bourgeoisie has. It does not inspire revolution but, rather, a resigned apathy, like that shown by Elena in the final scene. If we did not know that Bellocchio was a left-wing sympathizer, this film could easily be read as a piece of *anti*-left propaganda – showing the left as fragmented, ineffectual, and morally hypocritical.

La Cina è vicina is not the only film to set up an ambiguous relationship with its professed *impegno*. 'Discutiamo, discutiamo,' made two years later, similarly undermines the very *impegno* it appears to purport. 'Discutiamo, discutiamo' is an episode about the student contestation that was made for Carlo Lizzani's *Amore e rabbia* (*Love and Anger*, 1969); the latter film was conceived by Puccio Pucci and Piero Badalassi, two Catholic journalists who wanted the film to portray Christian parables in a contemporary political context (De Bernardinis 2005, 151).[10] The film's first four episodes (directed by Godard, Lizzani, Bertolucci, and Pasolini, respectively) do indeed centre on four New Testament parables. However, Bellocchio's offering, made at the last minute to fill an empty slot when the fifth director, Valerio Zurlini, pulled out, does not make recourse to parables and caused the film (originally called *Vangelo '70*) to be renamed *Amore e rabbia*, a title that reflected its political ambitions rather than its religious ones.

Shot during the summer of 1968, 'Discutiamo, discutiamo' was the next film to be released (1969) after *La Cina è vicina*. In the two years that separate the two films, a sea change had taken place. Italy's tense political climate had finally exploded in the student uprisings of 1968, and film-makers across the country were on the brink of involvement in a small flurry of militant film-making. The uprisings, which had started with the occupation of the universities of Trent, Genoa, and Turin, were now nationwide, as students contested not just the education system but the whole structure of a society dominated by the middle class (see Lumley 1990). 'Discutiamo, discutiamo' marks the beginning of Bellocchio's short-lived militant film-making and would be swiftly followed by his two propaganda documentaries for the UCI (m-l) later in the same year.

Unlike *La Cina è vicina*, 'Discutiamo, discutiamo' tackles politics head-on and without wavering. For the first time in one of his fiction films, Bellocchio does not allow the melodramatic genre to draw the episode away from its political content. For the first time too, the filmic space is entirely public (the whole episode is shot in a lecture theatre), while the domestic space of the family, couple, or individual is absent. This transformation is a reflection of a shift in focus from the individual, which is the key to the two previous feature films, *I pugni in tasca* and *La Cina è vicina*, to the collective. Representative groups (conservative students, radical students, the police, university authority figures) replace single characters, and 'chorality' replaces the monologues and dialogues of the earlier films.

In twenty-four minutes 'Discutiamo, discutiamo' narrates an iconic exemplum of student contestation. The film opens on a classroom full of university students staring blankly – their mouths exaggeratedly open, their eyes grotesquely wide and unblinking – at their teacher as he lectures them on the importance of poetry as propounded by Italian philosopher Benedetto Croce. The lesson is suddenly interrupted by a group of militant students who enter the lecture theatre and proceed to try to rouse the attentive students from their political apathy. A debate ensues in which many of the commonplaces of the contestation are trotted out: at university one learns only to obey and to command; in the universities the proletariat is radically absent; the universities are breeding a new bourgeois ruling class; culture, as inherently bourgeois, is to be despised; and the universities' token reformism is to be rejected in place of revolution. The student protest brings in the university's chancellor and finally the police. The episode ends with a medium-long shot, taken from the back of the lecture theatre, of the police mechanically hitting a row of militant students with plastic truncheons. The image fades to militant, communist red, as the rhythmic sound of the truncheons continues over the end titles in place of a traditional musical soundtrack.

The film is commonly referred to as Brechtian (Bernardi 1978, 58; Nicastro 1992, 133), and it is certain that it was meant to be seen as such, although a limited budget and lack of time certainly contributed to the Brechtian-style approach.[11] The opening sequence cuts between shots of the teacher (played by Bellocchio, who sports a conspicuously fake beard held to his face by elastic) and shots of the still, mask-like faces of students caught in a kind of rapt stupor; they stare towards the blackboard where their teacher is writing out a citation by Croce. The blankness written on the faces of the students could have been lifted straight from Brecht's description of audience reaction during performances of traditional bourgeois music. In the concert hall, Brecht (1995, 89) says: 'We see entire rows of human beings transported into a peculiar doped state, wholly passive, sunk without trace, seemingly in the grip of a severe poisoning attack ... Such music has nothing but purely culinary ambitions left. It seduces the listener into an enervating, because unproductive, act of enjoyment.' The film's opening therefore represents a critique of bourgeois culture, revealing its failure to challenge and to encourage criticism and intellectual participation; it only pacifies and renders passive those who absorb it.

Brechtian too is the film's detachment from its subject matter through the creation of an alienation effect. Any attempts to write 'for the scum who want to have the cockles of their heart warmed,' to establish the sense of the atmosphere of a particular place, have been banished (Brecht 1995, 14 and 136). With the exception of Bellocchio, the cast consists only of students from La Sapienza University. Whether they play the parts of the lecturers, the university chancellor, or the police, their beards, wigs, and truncheons are overtly just props; there is no attempt to provide realistic re-enactment. The intention instead seems to be a 'rejection of empathy' (Brecht 1995, 145), a deliberate eschewing of identification, forcing the spectator to assume an intellectual, rather than emotional, position in relation to the film. The 'total transformation in the acting' is absent (Brecht 1995, 138): some students are unashamedly reading their lines from sheets of paper in front of them. Bellocchio plays the teacher without any attempt at conviction: while he is shouting at the students not to disturb his lesson, he fails to repress a smile, showing both students and spectators that he is only play-acting, light-heartedly reciting a part with which he himself does not identify or want to be identified. The performance is being proposed as performance, and the play as self-conscious play.

Bellocchio's film follows Brechtian techniques of alienation almost slavishly. However, crucially, Brecht was using all these techniques with a particular political aim in mind rather than for their own sake. His view was that 'the new alienations are only designed to free socially-conditioned phenomena from that stamp of familiarity which protects them against our grasp today' (192). Spectators would be forced to take decisions, and their capacity for action would be aroused (39). Although Brechtian alienation is everywhere to be seen in 'Discutiamo, discutiamo,' the political outcome seems far from that envisaged by Brecht. Instead of persuading the audience to support and even join student activity, the film's Brechtianism not only fails to persuade, but it actually works to undermine the film's *impegno*.

With the very title of the episode, Bellocchio distances himself from the student contestation: the words *Discutiamo, discutiamo* are in fact ambiguous. On the face of it, the title means 'Let's discuss things,' a phrase that, in its implied demand for dialogue, pits itself against an educational system that was not promoting discussion. However, the repetition of the word *discutiamo* suggests a subtext: 'we discuss and we discuss, but we do not move beyond discussion.' The title focuses on the political talk itself and not on the outcome of political talk – action leading to change. It therefore hints at Bellocchio's lack of faith in the results of all the talk and at its repetitiousness, its folding in on itself, and its self-referentiality. The setting for the episode supports this reading, as the entire episode takes place within a windowless lecture theatre. The single door, which functions like a stage door, allows people to enter the space, but no one leaves, because the space beyond the door does not seem to exist – as if there were no 'beyond.' The space, like the discussions that take place within it, is highly circumscribed, enclosed, and self-referential. The posters on the wall depicting communism in China and Russia, the presence of the *Little Red Book* containing Mao's quotations (which some students carry and read from), and the cries of 'Ho Chi Minh' are not enough to break through the sense of enclosure.

The students' 'Brechtian' lack of serious acting, the reciting of lines, the ironic detachment from what is said, the theatrical and insular space, rather than forwarding their case, fail to persuade. The sense of righteous anger, which Brecht supported, is not present or is only present within distancing quotation marks. Despite all the anger that could be behind an argument which shows the university to be a class-oriented system that only one per cent of the proletariat have entered,[12] it is lost through the distancing techniques and through the film's spatial subtext that shows the students to be out of touch with the world beyond theirs. The argument lacks passion and conviction; it lacks its author's commitment.

One of the reasons that the episode fails to convince is the way in which Bellocchio, the actor-director, behaves within the diegesis of the film. What we see is this film's own director *laughing* at it on screen. It is hard for us not to take up this subversive position towards the film's arguments. In a sequence where some militant students seem to have become genuinely heated in their arguments, the camera, capturing this moment in a medium shot, also catches Bellocchio in the background. He is smiling. What we are witnessing is his enjoyment of the students' acting. If it were the politics that interested him in this scene, he would be as intense and angry as are the handful of more serious students.

In 'Discutiamo, discutiamo' it is no longer melodrama that interferes with the development of a serious political message but rather metacinema. On one level this film can be read, not as a rather passive transcription of a 'drammaturgia tutta a carico degli studenti romani' [dramaturgy carried completely by the Roman students] that is marred by 'un'eccessiva sottomissione nei riguardi dei ragazzi coinvolti nel corto' [an excessive submission towards the kids involved in the short] as De Bernardinis [2005, 152] suggests, but as an autobiographical comment on the pleasures of collective cinema making, of stepping outside the narrow individualism that Bellocchio had felt plagued by. His role in the diegesis is not so much as teacher (the false beard and his detached ironic attitude to the role undermines this reading) but as *director* – standing back and enjoying the fruits of his work with these non-actors as they are transformed into actors for the duration of the film. This film in fact persuades us that militant film-making in collectives can be a lot of fun; it does not persuade us that the student movement has the profundity and clout to make changes. Rather than being simply a political film, 'Discutiamo, discutiamo' is a film about the director's ambiguous view of the collectivity, about the relation between the individual (the director/teacher) and the collective, and the excitement of making cinema from the very simplest and poorest of ingredients.

The Militant Documentaries, *Nel Nome Del Padre*, and *Marcia Trionfale*: Contestation, *Impegno*, and Collectivity

Bellocchio claimed that the desire for collectivity was precisely what motivated his experience of militant political film-making over the following year (1969), when he set to work making documentaries for the extra-parliamentary group UCI (m-l). His claims with regard to participation in collectivities are well documented because he has repeatedly discussed this aspect of his work in interviews.[13] However, questions arise when one compares his claims about supporting collectivity with the position of collectives within the diegesis of his films at this time. It appears that the films tell a different and less positive story. If they do, this clearly has implications in relation to *impegno*.

Collectivity became a central ideal of the students' and workers' uprisings of 1968–9 and of the Marxist-Leninist groups that appeared during the same period; it signalled a new form of communism that was inspired by the Chinese Cultural Revolution, which had begun in 1966. Ginsborg (1990a, 302) notes, 'In contrast to the hierarchical and centralized Russian version of socialism, which had its heyday in Italy in the 1940s, the Cultural Revolution was very widely interpreted in Italy as being a spontaneous and anti-authoritarian *mass*-protest movement [italics mine].' Student groups in this period, for example, followed a model of direct democracy, with decisions taken by mass assemblies rather than small groups, and with students participating in decision making rather than having their representatives speak on their behalf (Ginsborg 1990, 305). Hierarchical forms of authority were seen as belonging to an older model of communism, and individualism was attacked as the corrupt ideological baggage of a decadent bourgeoisie. Collective action was the way forward. These ideas also affected the perception of the auteur in cinema. The individualistic, middle-class auteur became deeply unfashionable in left-wing circles. Harvey (1978, 30), for example, recounts how in France during the contestation of May 1968 one leaflet compared the cinema of directors to 'a cinema defending the interests of private property,' adding that 'the concept of authorship was linked with the concept of ownership.'

Bellocchio's two political documentaries, commissioned for the UCI (m-l) and made collectively, are without doubt his most committed works. The first, *Il popolo calabrese ha rialzato la testa* (otherwise known as *Paola* after the name of the town it investigates), explores the development of radical political consciousness among the inhabitants of an impoverished southern Italian town.[14] The investigation is a signal of the political concern at that time with the 'Southern Question.' The second documentary, *Viva il 1° maggio rosso e proletario*, shot only a few months later, is a short 16 mm film of only twenty-seven minutes. It documents the International Workers' Day marches held in Milan and Rome on 1 May 1969, focusing on the part played by the UCI (m-l) in the celebrations.[15]

These two militant documentaries are the only part of Bellocchio's film-making during this period – aside from 'Discutiamo, discutiamo' – where parliamentary and extra-parliamentary politics are the centre of focus. Unlike in *La Cina è vicina* and 'Discutiamo, discutiamo,' where the film's *impegno* is ironized or undermined, in the militant documentaries the level of *impegno* cannot be disputed; it is there, 100 per cent. There are no low-angle, under-table shots to destabilize it. However, the *impegno* of these two documentaries cannot be traced solely and directly to Bellocchio, since the heavily politicized, collective means of production almost erased the figure of the director. Instead, the producer (that is, the UCI [m-l]) was positioned as chef. In both documentaries Bellocchio did not have full directorial control: in *Paola* he was co-director alongside Paola Cosenza, and in *Viva il 1° maggio rosso e proletario* he was only one of a militant collective that included Virginia Onorato and Roberto Cacciaguerra. In *Viva il 1° maggio rosso e proletario* he was also excluded from the crucial phase of editing. He expresses his lack of control over these films in the following terms:

[*Viva il primo maggio rosso e proletario* e *Paola*] erano dei film collettivi di propaganda, del partito e quindi in qualche modo non seguivano un'ispirazione libera, personale. *Viva il primo maggio rosso e proletario* è stato un film 'collettivo' in cui io ho guidato una delle troupe e non ho nemmeno seguito il montaggio. Per il documentario *Paola* ho partecipato anche al montaggio. *Paola* doveva rispettare la linea del partito. (Minella 2004, 221)

[(*Viva il primo maggio rosso e proletario* and *Paola*) were collectively made party propaganda films, and therefore in some way they were not of a free and personal inspiration. *Viva il primo maggio rosso e proletario* was a 'collective' film in which I led one of the troupes and wasn't even involved in the editing. For the documentary *Paola*, I participated in the editing too. *Paola* had to respect the party line.]

There seems, indeed, to be little of Bellocchio in these documentaries. Unlike contemporary documentary makers such as Michael Moore, Bellocchio does not step inside the frame to guide the spectator through the material, which would enable us to reconstruct his viewpoint.[16] Instead, an impersonal voiceover, scripted by the UCI (m-l) and often contradicting the findings of Bellocchio's team (see Fofi 1980, 11–12), provides the narrative. Moreover, the focus on the individual, so central to Bellocchio's film-making, is absent. In *Viva il 1° maggio rosso e proletario*, locations are communal and outdoor (the factory and the university gates; the streets and public squares where the rallies take place) in direct contrast to those in the rest of Bellocchio's film-making. In *Paola*, interviews are held with small groups of people rather than with individuals. Gone too is the ironizing and destabilizing laugh, one of the most profound characteristics of Bellocchio's cinema. With it disappears Bellocchio's ability to undermine and ridicule his own arguments and to save his films from excessive didacticism. The suppression of the laugh is the suppression of what is most Bellocchian in Bellocchio's films: a rebellion against authority, which is not just the authority of bourgeois institutions but also the authority of the left. Therefore, although these two documentaries express deep political commitment, they do not necessarily tell us a great deal about Bellocchio's *impegno* beyond his wish to have direct involvement in such political projects at this time.

The two films that follow – *Nel nome del padre* (1971) and *Marcia trionfale* (1976) – seem to present an interpretation of the collective that is decidedly pessimistic, focusing on the frustrations and difficulties of collective action. It is tempting (though dangerous) to read these films' analyses of the collective with reference to Bellocchio's political involvement during 1968 and 1969 – both his direct involvement (as a member of a collective) and his indirect involvement (witnessing the actions of political collectives, such as those at Paola). Whatever the reasons, the view of the collective that emerges from these films cannot be easily aligned with that proposed by the left.

Nel nome del padre was Bellocchio's first feature film after his experience with militant and collective film-making. Only two years had passed since the releases of 'Discutiamo, discutiamo,' *Paola*, and *Viva il 1° maggio rosso e proletario*. Set in the pre-contestation world of 1958–9, but also allegorizing the protests of 1968, the film describes an insubordination in a Catholic boys' boarding school. The protagonist, Angelo Transeunti (Yves Beneyton), a boy from a nice middle-class family, joins the school in his final year. He resents attending the badly run, irrational, and authoritarian school and refuses to adapt. He makes no compromises to those of his own social class (the students), to the priests, or to the working-class servants. He befriends another rebel, Franc (Aldo Sassi), a boy who mirrors him but also dialectically opposes him. Franc represents left-wing ideals of collectivity in contrast to Angelo's more individualist, capitalist ideals, which imply a quest for leadership, individuality, and power. They are both, however, united in willing change. The boys' rebelliousness culminates in their staging a grotesque and angry play at the school, which is loosely based on the story of Faust and represents a bitter attack on the religious institution. Soon after the play, a revolt breaks out among the ranks of the servants, who demand better working conditions. Under Angelo and Franc's instigation the pupils follow suit. However, the two groups fail to unite, and the rebellion is quashed before it has a chance to make a real mark on the school. The ringleader among the servants (Salvatore, played by Lou Castel) is fired, and Angelo leaves the college. In the final sequences Angelo and a deranged servant, Tino (who speaks the incomprehensible language of *Flash Gordon*'s planet, Mongo), go out and cut down a 'miraculous' pear tree, where there had allegedly been a sighting of the Madonna. With this demystifying act, they impose Angelo's capitalistic rationality and rationalization on their world. They then drive away from the boarding school along a long highway lined interminably with billboards, a sign of the late capitalist consumerist culture that was just rearing up in 1958, the year that marks the beginning of Italy's economic boom (1958–63).

Nel nome del padre, though decidedly more complex and allegorical than 'Discutiamo, discutiamo' (which in comparison seems little more than a sketch), shares with it much common ground. It picks up and develops motifs such as the rebellion against teachers, the disorganized nature of that rebellion, and its failure ultimately to make enough impact. Both films represent those in power – especially the school and university hierarchy – and those trying to gain power – the middle-class students. *Nel nome del padre* broadens the discourse, however, by its portrayal of the working-class servants. This class is absent from 'Discutiamo, discutiamo.' *Nel nome del padre*, the first feature film to be made after the uprisings, is distinguished from the two earlier features

(*I pugni in tasca* and *La Cina è vicina*), in which individuals and a bourgeois family setting anchor the narrative.

Nel nome del padre is Bellocchio's first feature-length film in which there is a collective insurrection as opposed to an individual one, and the opening scenes already betray a deeply rooted pessimism. As the titles roll, a camera travels through the empty and desolate space of an abandoned school. On the soundtrack a choir sings to the insistent waltzing rhythms of Piovani's music, the rich sound of the young voices juxtaposed with, and therefore compounding, the awful emptiness of the building. It is as if the choir were a ghost from the school's past. For more than two minutes the camera acts as an anonymous eye, exploring the abandoned space through pans and stills and sweeping the high roofs in slow circles. This preface, set in the then present (1971), tells us that all we are about to see is already over. As Di Marino (2005, 147) suggests, for the viewer 'la storia di Angelo Transeunti e dei suoi compagni appartiene inevitabilmente al passato … perché gli studenti del film sono ormai entrati a far parte della società incarnando quei ruoli già prestabiliti dalla loro classe sociale e dalla loro educazione' [the story of Angelo Transeunti and his friends belongs inevitably to the past … because the students in the film have already taken their place in society, incarnating those roles that were pre-ordained by their class and education].[17] This preface does not portray a school made better by an insurrection of its pupils but a school abandoned and melancholy, left behind in the socio-political changes that swept Italy in the sixties.

In the body of the film, the pessimism continues. Bellocchio reveals the collectivity as by turns ineffectual and unpleasant. In the initial sequences of the film, pupil rebelliousness and adolescence are aligned. In vignettes that reflect the atmosphere of Jean Vigo's *Zéro de conduite* (1933) and prefigure those of Fellini's *Amarcord* that would be made two years later, the adolescent pupils are shown playing a variety of practical jokes on their teachers during lessons. This is little more than a phase of apolitical tomfoolery that cannot lead to real change and will do nothing to harm the pupils' insertion into society once they leave the school. It is this energy that Angelo, who disdains the pupils' mocking tricks, tries to annihilate in his search for a new ordered and disciplined system and that Franc tries to channel into political action. Both Angelo and Franc fail.

In a damning scene towards the end of the film Angelo tries to organize a rebellion among the boys to match the servants' strike. He asks them to voice the changes they want. Around the classroom the boys blurt out self-centred requests. One boy hazards, 'Mangiare meglio' [Better food]; another says, 'Basta con la messa obligatoria' [Enough of obligatory mass]. There is little common ground between the pupils, and almost no sense of a political program. Only Franc and Angelo have a sense of an overall program. Angelo, the new capitalist, wants a more efficient and disciplined system where the boys will learn better ('più efficenza ... vogliamo rendere di più' [more efficiency ... we want to produce more]). Franc, the socialist, is drawn instead towards the plight of the workers, which, in a prefiguring of the 1968 contestation, he links intimately to the students' struggle. The boys' discussions are as ineffective as those in 'Discutiamo, discutiamo,' although in *Nel nome del padre* the pessimism is far stronger and is no longer collocated only in the subtext of the film. When the idealistic Franc fetches Salvatore, the servants' ringleader, to involve him in discussions, the flaws in the rebellion become clearer. The already fragmented aims of the pupils are not only different to those of the servants but also incompatible. The abyss between the groups is marked visually: in the classroom where the meeting takes place, a mass of black school uniforms contrasts with the single white work coat of the servants' sole representative, Salvatore. In the end, the mass of pupils opposes Franc's idea of solidarity between the two groups, when one pupil identifies the core economic value that separates the classes: 'noi vogliamo pagare di meno e loro vogliono guadagnare di più!' [we want to pay less, and they want to earn more!].

The collective does not emerge well from this portrait, and the film dwells on its weaknesses: the pupils' petty power struggles, their bickering, and the lack of real solidarity. They are not portrayed as a true collective but as a series of individuals thrown together for a few years, who will peel off later and go their own ways. This is nowhere more obvious than in the scene in which Angelo – accompanied by a melancholic, romantic soundtrack – walks the length of the boys' narrow single rooms, looking through each porthole into the space where every night each boy withdraws from the communal spaces of classroom, dining hall, and schoolyard to nurture his individuality. Through the glass – on which is etched the school's emblem – Angelo observes one boy firing darts, another writing while tied to his desk, and another urinating at a mirror. In these shots each boy's life is portrayed as irremediably separate from the other, sunk into an individuality that is more deeply rooted and real than their collective experience.

The servants are portrayed with somewhat more sympathy than are, to use Pasolini's term, the *figli di papà* (Daddy's boys). They do not have individual spaces into which to retreat at night, but they sleep together in a dormitory (although each of them is shown disappearing into very different worlds through sleep). They have a greater sense of the collective than the middle-class pupils have: they are not shown bickering, as the schoolboys are, but instead they maintain a quiet solidarity. This solidarity emerges especially during the strike that follows the suicide of Beato, a fragile gay servant who kills himself after being rejected by one of the schoolboys. However, these servants are an odd mixture of subnormal, mentally deranged, and physically disabled working-class men who have been taken on to work through the 'benevolence' of the priests. The random and damaged nature of this collective renders it inefficient and too easily quashed, and it ultimately fares little better than do the schoolboys.

If *Nel nome del padre* represents in part a discourse on individuality and collectivity, the conclusions are pessimistic. Angelo is the only boy to really stand out from the (pseudo-)collective. The camera tends to isolate Angelo within the frame; his clean features, fair hair, tall and straight stature, stern composure, lack of eye contact with others, and the subtly different colour of his school uniform set him apart from his mainly short, fat, and darker companions. The casting plays a part in this: the French actor who plays Angelo (Yves Beneyton) has decidedly northern European, even Teutonic, features. If the epilogue of the film seems to paint an optimistic picture of the relationship between the classes, as Angelo (the middle-class student) and Tino (the deranged servant) drive away from the school together, this is not so. Although middle-class pupil and servant – rather improbably – are finally sharing a common space, the film's concluding dialogue undermines any solidarity. Angelo's final words clarify the meaning of the film: 'L'odio si può neutralizzare facilmente. Occorrono dei capi decisi, lucidi, senza crisi di coscienza che sappiano prevedere e controllare ogni parte del meccanismo' [Hate can be easily neutralized. We need lucid, decisive leaders who don't suffer crises of conscience and who know how to foresee and control every part of the mechanism]. Angelo is driving away to become a 'capo' now that his schooling is over. His desire for order, science, and efficiency, which created in him his desire to rebel against the system that he considered inadequate and inefficient, will make him a brutal and efficient leader who – unlike the incapable teachers in the school he has just left – will be able to keep a rebellion down. His Teutonic looks, strongly contrasting with Tino's heavy southern features, are certainly not irrelevant – there is something of the Nazi in Angelo, and something of a discourse on national identity lying implicitly within a film dealing with class identity. His rebellion against the system does not destroy the middle class but makes it stronger. Although both he and Franc tried to harness the collectivity, he was not on Franc's side; he was against him. The finale emphasizes the failure of the collective. After the collapse of the workers' strike and the failure of the students to join with the workers, the film ends with two individuals finally escaping confinement and going out to take their places in the world. One of these is a semi-Nazi, the other a madman. Any sense of a collective is far behind them.

This pessimistic reading of the collective does not disappear from Bellocchio's opus but rather resurfaces in *Marcia trionfale* four years later. *Marcia trionfale* was a commercial feature that earned almost two billion lire at the box office, less than the earnings of Pasolini's *Salò o le 120 giornate di Sodoma* (*Salò, or the 100 Days of Sodom*, 1975) but more than those of Steno's popular *Febbre da cavallo* (Horse Fever, 1976) (Pezzotta 2005, 157). The film narrates the story of a young graduate from the south of Italy, Paolo Passeri (Michele Placido), who enters a northern Italian barracks for a period of military service, which was obligatory in the country at that time.

The enclosed world of the barracks in which the film is set is dominated by a collectivity made up of diverse parts: compulsory military service ensures that different social strata and geographical types mingle. However, the collective is shown in a particularly negative light. It has no sense of a greater good or of a shared value system. It is controlled by small, unpleasant cliques and is a haven for bullying, male chauvinism, brutal fighting, and scatology. Passeri's outburst to a friend early in the film flatly denies the value of collective life: 'La vita collettiva mi esce dagli occhi: mangiare insieme, dormire insieme … sempre uno davanti, dietro, a sinistra, a destra e io in mezzo! Mai un momento per starmene solo!' [Collective life is coming out of my ears: eating together, sleeping together … always someone in front, behind, on the left, on the right, and me in the middle! Never a minute on my own!] Passeri's experience of collective life is of negation of personal space, comfort, and rights. This collectivity has nothing positive to offer him.

Nor is this collectivity represented as a force for change in society. Although a collective insurrection takes place in the film, just as it did in *Nel nome del padre*, the collective is again seen fighting not for shared political ideals but for selfish and individualistic goals (the insurrection begins largely because the steaks have run out in the canteen). The mutiny is set off inadvertently (by Passeri throwing his food in a bin), rather than deliberately, emphasizing the lack of any more far-reaching political plan.

The collective rebellion is futile because the army is strong enough to immediately contain it and stamp it out. An army officer shouts angrily at the mutinous crowd, and the ringleader, Passeri, is identified, isolated, and later beaten up. When an account of the beating gets as far as the newspapers, the army is forced to deal with the incident. However, the summoning of both the perpetrator of the beating, Capitano Asciutto, and Passeri does not lead to the prosecution of the captain, because Passeri has already been won over to the captain's side and defends him. A soldier has been broken in, and life in the barracks goes on as before.

Marcia trionfale is Bellocchio's last feature film to date in which a collectivity comes to the fore, and, though the film is primarily a polemic against the dehumanizing life in the barracks rather than an analysis of a collectivity, its pessimism towards collective action is indicative of the transformation that Bellocchio's cinema was about to undergo.

Conclusion

Bellocchio's *impegno* in the early years of his film-making is not as straightforward as it may seem at first. Although he was involved in militant film-making, this was only for a short time. Although he made collective films, the views towards the collectivity in *Nel nome del padre* and *Marcia trionfale* present a pessimistic and cynical portrayal of collective relations in the wake of the contestation. The utopia glimpsed briefly in the triumphal political collectivities of the documentaries had entirely disappeared by 1971. The level of bitterness towards the mass seen in *Nel nome del padre* and *Marcia trionfale* was new in Bellocchio's film-making. This is not to say that crowds were seen positively in Bellocchio's early films. In *I pugni in tasca* Ale attends a party in the town where the local people alienate him; in *La Cina è vicina* the crowd that turns out to hear Vittorio's political speech in the village square smashes his car and attacks him. However, neither of these portrayals, nor that of 'Discutiamo, discutiamo,' have the venom and disillusionment of the two post-contestation films. 'Discutiamo, discutiamo,' in particular, despite its ironic tone, presents a fairly positive view of the collectivity.

Whatever happened during the contestation years, in the early 1970s Bellocchio joined the ranks of film-makers who no longer believed in the collective utopia. From 1976, Bellocchio abandons his focus on the collective and returns to the individual. Already, in *Marcia trionfale*, collectivity is waning and individual characters are returning to centre stage. The character of Rosanna (Miou-Miou) – Captain Asciutto's wife and the woman with whom Passeri will have an affair – is the first real indication of what is to come. From the midpoint of the film, with her entrance, the film shifts away from the collective to focus on three individuals: Rosanna, Asciutto, and Passeri. Of these, Rosanna is the precursor for a new positive individual who, without ever entering into a political collective, may harbour a seed that can bring about profound change. This individual will emerge fully four years' later in the person of Marta, the protagonist of *Salto nel vuoto*.

3 The Dreaming 'I': Interiority and Massimo Fagioli's Model of the Unconscious

The symbolic opening to Bellocchio's *Il sogno della farfalla* (1994), the last film made with his analyst, Massimo Fagioli, screens two abstract cones of light, which, like cinema projector beams, cut through the darkness of what appears to be a theatre. These beams represent 'due occhi ... lo sguardo del ragazzo' [two eyes ... the boy's gaze] (Roberti, Suriano, and Turco 1994, 325) and, at least in part, the capacity of the media of cinema and theatre to enlighten, to throw light onto darkness. This brief prefacing shot, which cites the opening to another highly introspective film, Ingmar Bergman's *Persona* (1966), allegorically initiates a discourse about bringing the psyche into language, a 'sfida all'invisibile' [challenge to the visible] (Roberti et al 1994, 325) that endeavours to render the invisible visible.

In this chapter the core of my analysis centres on Bellocchio's 'sfida all'invisibile,' concentrating on the films released between 1980 and 1998 – the years in which Massimo Fagioli had most influence over the director. The films of these years are, in broad terms, focused on subjectivity, taking the private world of the 'I' as their primary concern. I will begin by outlining Bellocchio's long relationship with Fagioli, before examining Bellocchio's use of a Fagiolian-informed interiority and the implications this has for the both the style and the content of the films in this period and beyond.

Massimo Fagioli and Group Therapy

Bellocchio's relationship with Massimo Fagioli stretches over seventeen years, from 1977 until they went their separate ways after *Il sogno della farfalla* (1994). However, Fagioli's legacy can still be felt – albeit less

intensely – in the present. It was a relationship that caused a furore in
the Italian press in the 1980s, as many critics expressed their suspicion
that the director was falling under the sway of this man and his ideas
and that, consequentially, the quality of his films was suffering. These
concerns culminated in 1986 when a court case was heard to decide
the paternity of *Diavolo in corpo*, a film on which Bellocchio and Fagioli
had collaborated. In the hearings, Bellocchio charged his producer, Leo
Pescarolo of LP Film Ltd., with making significant and unacceptable
changes to the film. Pescarolo defended his position by attacking the
presence and influence of Bellocchio's analyst in the phases of shooting
and editing (Stefanutto-Rosa 1986, 12–13). Pescarolo's public defence of
his position in the pages of *La Repubblica* condemns Fagioli's control:

> È successo che si è piazzato in moviola il tuo ispiratore, gomito a gomito
> con te, entrando nel merito di una professione che ignora, e convincendoti,
> in nome della sua capacità di interpretare i sogni, a eliminare sequenze da
> te [i.e., Bellocchio] girate e montate, ad inserire materiale addirittura sfuo-
> cato, come spesso forse sono i sogni. (Stefanutto-Rosa 1986, 12)

> [What happened is that your muse set himself up in the editing room,
> working shoulder to shoulder with you in a profession of which he knows
> nothing, and convincing you, in the name of his capacity to interpret dreams,
> to eliminate sequences shot and edited by you [i.e., Bellocchio], and to
> insert material that was even out of focus, like dreams perhaps often are.]

In working alongside a psychoanalyst, Bellocchio was doing nothing new; he is not the only, nor the first, director to turn to an analyst for advice during filming. For instance, Paolo Spinola brought his
screenplay to the analyst Piero Bellanova for his 1964 film, *La fuga* (*The
Escape*); Nelo Risi turned to the analyst Franco Fornari for scientific
advice during the preparation of *Diario di una schizofrenica* (*Diary of a
Schizophrenic Girl*, 1968); and Pier Paolo Pasolini collaborated with the
Freudian Cesare Musatti on *Comizi d'amore* (*Love Meetings*, 1965). Nor,
of course, was Bellocchio the only director of this period to use psychoanalysis in his films; by the sixties, Sigmund Freud and Carl Gustav
Jung had crept into the heart of Italian cinematic culture through the
films of Fellini, Pasolini, Bertolucci, and others. However, Bellocchio's
post-seventies cinema testifies to an important cultural change in Italy:
the diffusion of vast numbers of new psychoanalytical models throughout the peninsula. Gone was much of the pre-war resistance to psycho-

analysis that was documented so well by Michel David;[1] gone too was the hegemony of the two giants Freud and Jung. Instead, by the seventies a huge range of new psychoanalytical models had appeared in Italy, including gestalt theory, family therapy, group therapy, sexology, and Lacan.[2] Bellocchio's experience, unlike that of Bertolucci, Pasolini, and Fellini, reflects this later wave.

Massimo Fagioli emerged in this new climate of the seventies, when analysis was gaining mass appeal in Italy. Although he had begun writing articles in 1962, he only sprang into notoriety when he established his seminars of collective analysis a decade later. During the mid-seventies at Villa Massimo in Rome and then in Trastevere, hundreds of people attended the sessions in which Fagioli proposed his reading of the psyche that he had been developing in his writings *Istinto di morte e conoscenza* (1972), *La marionetta e il burattino* (1974), and *Psicoanalisi della nascita e castrazione umana* (1975). In these seminars Fagioli distinguished his theories from those of Freud (he in fact was vociferous in his denunciation of the Viennese analyst) and put forward the central tenets of his own thought. He was a polemical speaker, attacking religion, homosexuality, masturbation, and intellectualism, and within a few years his ideas, together with the strident nature of their expression, led him to be expelled from the Società Italiana di Psicoanalisi (SPI). In 1980 he was expelled too from the Istituto di Psichiatria di Roma. The analysis of Fagioli's psychoanalysis by the president of SPI is damning:

> L'emissione verbale di Fagioli ... costruisce a mio parere un flusso enfatico, caotico e confuso, *non strutturato* ... Ritengo il libro di Fagioli [*Istinto di morte e conoscenza*] un 'conglomerato' di preconcezioni, impressioni e sensazioni ... Le 'cose' poste da Fagioli, a mio parere, sono essenzialmente 'urli.' (Armando 1997, 122–3)

> [Fagioli's verbal emission ... in my view, constitutes an emphatic flux, which is chaotic and confused, *unstructured* ... I maintain that Fagioli's book [*Istinto di morte e conoscenza*] is a 'conglomeration' of preconceptions, impressions, and sensations ... The 'things' posited by Fagioli, are, in my opinion, essentially 'shrieks.']

The press also railed against him, with articles in *Il messaggero*, *La Repubblica*, and *L'espresso* describing him as everything from a guru to a wild man and a 'creatore di massimodipendenti' [creator of Massimo

addicts].[3] The rejection of Fagioli, both on the part of Italian psychoanalytical societies and on the part of a large section of the press, helps to
clarify why the Bellocchio-Fagioli partnership caused such controversy
and rancour, whereas previous alignments of psychoanalysts with
film-makers either had been quietly tolerated or had generated positive interest.

Marco Bellocchio's interest in Fagioli can be dated to 15 April 1977,
twelve years after his debut with *I pugni in tasca* and a year after the
release of *Marcia trionfale*. This was the day of his first attendance at
Fagioli's seminars (Malanga 1998, 235). Just before joining the seminars,
he had been undergoing Freudian analysis, which he immediately
abandoned. Initially Bellocchio appears to have had certain reserva-
tions regarding Fagioli's methods, writing in 'Impossibile finirla,' for
instance:

L'analisi collettiva mi prendeva, anche se mi sforzavo di trovarle dei difetti,
di svalutarla … Per esempio avevo molti dubbi sulla teoria, sui libri, non
approvavo che Fagioli desse dell'imbecille a Freud ogni cinque minuti.
(Bellocchio, cited in Malanga 1998, 235)

[Collective analysis took hold of me, even if I forced myself to find defects
in it, to disparage it … For example, I had many doubts about the theory,
the books, and I didn't approve of the fact that Fagioli called Freud an
imbecile every five minutes.]

However, he was still strongly drawn to the Fagiolian experience, and
it made a deep impact on his cinema, being the catalyst behind his
shift from socio-political film-making to a psychoanalytical-subjective
approach.

The first films to realise the experience of collective analysis were
Vacanze in Val Trebbia and the feature-length *Salto nel vuoto*, both of
which were released in 1980. *Vacanze in Val Trebbia*, a highly autobiographical and experimental film, acts as a bridge between the political material in the earlier phase of Bellocchio's cinema making and the
more private, psychological cinema of the second phase. The timing of
the film's production allows us to gauge when Fagioli's influence first
began to take effect. The realistic home-movie scenes were shot in the
summer of 1978, while the oneiric scenes, which prefigure the kind of
cinema Bellocchio would make in the coming years, were shot a year
later. In 1979, Bellocchio was also preparing *Salto nel vuoto*, which again

contains introspective and oneiric material. These two films allow us to identify 1979 as the year in which Bellocchio's cinema takes its psycho-analytic turn, absorbing the experience of Fagioli's group psychoanalysis and leading Bellocchio to deal more directly with personal issues like early childhood trauma, identity, and the capacity for psychological transformation and healing. He stresses the importance of Fagioli to the genesis of *Salto nel vuoto* (whose published screenplay has an introduction by the analyst), pointing out in 1985 that the film 'nacque come idea, si sviluppò e divenne un film durante l'analisi collettiva e per me fu come una rinascita' [was born as an idea, was developed, and became a film during collective analysis, which for (Bellocchio) was like a rebirth] (Bellocchio, cited in Armando 1997, 301). Bellocchio therefore conceives of *Salto nel vuoto* as a new start after the impasse in his cinema making in the mid-1970s.

After a brief defection from the seminars subsequent to the release of *Salto nel vuoto*,[4] he returned to them in the autumn of 1984. The relationship between director and analyst grew closer, and Bellocchio began to ask Fagioli for on-set advice, particularly in relation to the psychological behaviour of central characters (Armando 1997, 379). He discussed the screenplay of *Diavolo in corpo* (1986) with Fagioli after the seminars and then, three weeks into shooting, asked the analyst to be present on set and later in the editing room, a decision that sparked the notorious court case (see Armando 1997, 380–93). Despite the negative response from the press, Bellocchio refused to deny his debt to Fagioli and dedicated his film to him. The two ensuing films – *La visione del Sabba*, which came out two years later (in 1988), and *La condanna* (1991) – saw the continuation of the close alliance of director and analyst. Bellocchio asked the lead actress of *La visione del Sabba*, Béatrice Dalle, to attend Fagioli's seminars so that she would experience the interpenetration of dream and reality that Bellocchio wanted her to portray in this film. (Dalle went but was singularly unimpressed.) For *La condanna* Fagioli co-wrote the screenplay and again worked side by side with Bellocchio on set. However, it was only in 1994 that the culmination of the two men's collaboration was reached, with Fagioli writing the screenplay for *Il sogno della farfalla*, a film that bears the strong imprint of the analyst's intellectual tone and ideas.

After this culmination came the break, however, and *Il sogno della farfalla* was the last film on which Bellocchio and Fagioli collaborated. According to Bellocchio, they each went their own way at this point, although he stresses that 'rimane il grande arricchimento di questa

conoscenza' [the great enrichment of that acquaintance remains] (Bellocchio in Cruciani and Cruciani 2003, 13). This 'grande arricchimento'
continues to make itself felt, especially in the two subsequent films, *Il
Principe di Homburg* and *La balia*, and still influences the films of the new
millennium. In an interview in 2003, after the success of *L'ora di religione* (2002), Bellocchio denied that the relationship with psychoanalysis and Fagioli was incidental and that with *L'ora di religione*, which won
widespread critical praise, he had rediscovered 'il rapporto diretto con
il me stesso più autentico, quello di *I pugni in tasca*' [the direct relationship with (his) most authentic self, that of *I pugni in tasca*] (Bellocchio
in Cruciani and Cruciani 2003, 8). Instead, he claims that the experience of Fagioli's analysis brought about 'una trasformazione del mio
fare cinema' [a transformation in (his) way of making cinema] (8) that
has remained with him to the present. In a talk given at Temple University in Rome on 29 March 2007, he still recognised Fagioli's enduring, if
indirect, legacy in his films.

Massimo Fagioli's Model of the Unconscious

The psychoanalytical model[5] on which the explorations of the psyche
in Bellocchio's mature cinema are based derives from Fagioli's theoriz-
ing of the unconscious, not as destructive and negative in essence, as
Freud had claimed, but as a positive force. Whereas Fagioli often envisages the unconscious as a calm sea, the so-called *inconscio mare calmo*,
for Freud the waters of the libidinous unconscious are turbulent and
destructive. Crucial to the difference in approach is that Freud's theoriz-
ing of the unconscious as instinctively sadistic and perverse means that
it – logically – *must* be repressed. Without this repression on the part
of society (which the individual then interiorizes), humans would tear
one another apart. Fagioli (2007, 81) claims that for Freud, 'gli uomini
sarebbero soltanto ed esclusivamente per la distruzione; vanno quindi
dominati, controllati' [men exist only and exclusively for destruction;
they must therefore be dominated and controlled]. Fagioli's positive
model of the unconscious, however, constructs a paradigm of society in
which individuals are cured by ridding themselves of aggression and
the death instinct and thereby return to the unconscious as *mare calmo*.
Transformation of the self is viable. Repression ceases to be necessary.

Fagioli's theory is founded on a conception of the unconscious as
one born healthy, a calm sea made up of positive interest and desire
(Armando 1997, 173). He posits a model of innocence, as well as a fall

from innocence that takes place in the first months of a baby's life. The baby, born happy and mentally healthy, experiences the initial moments of life as a calm sea and then reaches out to the world with interest and desire. However, the world that meets this child's desire disappoints it. In particular, the mother's irritation at her baby's unceasing demands transforms the child's initially positive rapport with the world into a frustrated and negative one. The child's desire to be fed and to get attention becomes delusion, hate, anger, and hankering (Fagioli 1996).[6] It is a theory that reflects the myth of the peaceful and idyllic origins that precede the fall. For Fagioli, one of the aims of therapy is to rediscover this lost *mare calmo* that still lies within the unconscious, sunk beneath the weight of all those deluding relationships with the Other that have shaped the analysand's life. A second aim of therapy is to recuperate a genuine bond between self and Other by reinstating it on a deep unconscious level through positive sexual relations. In the following two sections these two avenues for psychic recovery will be explored in detail.

The Calm Sea and Inner Child: Salto nel vuoto
and Il sogno della farfalla

The first feature-length film to be made after meeting Fagioli was *Salto nel vuoto* (*Leap into the Void*), and it literally screens Fagiolian motifs of the *inconscio mare calmo* and the psyche as child. It is one of two films to concentrate on these related aspects of the unconscious, the second being the most Fagiolian of all Bellocchio's films, *Il sogno della farfalla*.

Salto nel vuoto is a portrayal of the repressed and joyless lives of a middle-aged man, Judge Mauro Ponticelli (Michel Piccoli), and his sister, Marta (Anouk Aimée), who share a house in a well-to-do district of Rome. The judge is investigating the suicide of a girl who jumped from a fifth-floor window in another part of the city. His attempts to discover the person responsible for the girl's suicide lead him to a rebellious artist named Giovanni Sciabola (Michele Placido), a Dionysian character living in a barge on the Tiber. A relationship develops between this young man, who exudes Dionysian energy, creativity, and unfettered sexuality, and Ponticelli, the older man, who represents the repression of a narrow, judgmental bourgeois life and who lives not for creativity but for control. The men's very surnames point to their opposite, but linked, natures. *Sciabola* is a 'sabre,' an instrument with which to fight and wound; *ponticello* is a 'gun or sword guard,' a word which, though belonging to the terminology of battle, is the very thing that prevents a weapon from being used. Sciabola draws his sabre and challenges society; Ponticelli controls his passions and aggression and is part of the repressed world that Sciabola implicitly attacks. At the end of the film, when Sciabola enters Ponticelli's apartment, steals from it, wrecks it, and finally, standing on a table, takes out his penis and urinates over Ponticelli's belongings, this attack becomes explicit.[7]

The film also has a second axis: the relationship between the judge and his sister, Marta. Again, the sister's name crystallizes her role. She is Marta, the biblical woman who acts as a homemaker; she is the one who serves. The judge, her brother, depends on her servility and self-sacrifice for his existence. He expects her to iron his clothes, prepare his food, and run her life around his. His is an unremitting surveillance coupled with intense psychological pressure. Marta, however, slowly rebels against her brother and is supported by her maid and by Sciabola; ironically, the judge had introduced her to him, hoping that Sciabola would drive her too to suicide). As the film progresses, Marta slowly begins to assert her identity and freedom. She plucks up the courage to call her brother a piece of shit [stronzo], repeating the word to his face with real liberatory pleasure. She puts on lipstick, a sign of her budding sexuality, and leaves the house to meet Sciabola, to whom she finds herself attracted. Finally, at the end of the film, for the first time in an untold number of years, she stays away from the house overnight, going with her maid to the seaside at Ostia, near Rome. After she has left, the judge finds himself finally alone in the apartment. Aware of the extent to which he has lost control over his sister, and spurred on by his terrible death instinct, he jumps from his window. The film thus comes full circle from the suicide of a young girl in the first scene to the suicide of a judge in the last.[8]

Salto nel vuoto is a film that explores the Fagiolian ideas of transformation (represented by Marta's growing psychological liberty) and the regressive force of the death instinct (embodied in Judge Ponticelli) and demonstrates the importance of choosing the spontaneous and instinctive passion for life over the often equally strong instinct for death. The film carefully establishes the mood of repression in a darkened house, which has been organized as a panoptic octagonal by scenographer, Amedeo Fago, allowing everything to come under the control of the judge (Aprà 2005b, 15–16). When the judge returns home after investigating the suicide case, we immediately see him policing the body and spirit of his sister. He unlocks the phone that she is not to use when he is out, and he opens her handbag and extracts something from it, a gesture that shows the ease and carelessness with which he invades his sister's space. Their irritation with each other in the next sequence is played out in a lovely piece of parallel montage that shows the judge tapping on his typewriter in his study while Marta sits in almost total darkness in the kitchen and imitates the sound of the keys by drumming her fingers loudly on the table. Her brother beats down harder on the keys. Irritated beyond control, she takes two packets of meat from the refrigerator and slaps them repeatedly on the table. With his fist, her brother pounds the typewriter's keys. In the following scene at the dinner table they are, however, controlled and polite with each other again and courteously share a Valium tablet.

Marta's gradual liberation from this way of life, after years of repression, is the result of her rediscovery within herself of the lost *inconscio mare calmo*. This discovery comes to the fore – allegorically – in the closing scenes of the film, where she is at the seaside with her maid. We hear and see a tranquil sea lapping outside her window (which is an unreal image because the setting is meant to be Ostia, a seaside resort near Rome where residences are never positioned that close to the water). The tranquil water can be read as a metaphor for the healing that Marta has undergone and which has brought her literally closer to the *mare calmo* and the lost origins of her life, lodged deep within her. The lapping water also acts as a soundtrack when she leaves her narrow single bed and slips into the bed of the maid's small child, putting her arm around a child that she had previously wanted banned from her house. Her action is a signal, not only of opening to the Other but also of embracing the child within herself. Through this acceptance she finally attains peace. However, while Marta is renewing her spirit in a house on the edge of the sea, parallel editing shows Judge Ponticelli jumping lightly from the window to his death. The dialectic between the two possibilities – life and death – is thus concluded.

Il sogno della farfalla (*The Butterfly's Dream*), released in 1994, fourteen years after *Salto nel vuoto*, returns to the idea of the *bambino* and again takes up the discourse on life and death instincts. Written entirely by Fagioli, this highly intellectual work is perhaps one that best illustrates the analyst's model of the unconscious. Through the figure of Massimo (Thierry Blanc), it draws into visibility a hypothesis of what the invisible unconscious might look like. The film narrates the story of this young actor who, at the age of fourteen, makes a conscious decision to cease speaking in order to return to a primitive purity that has been lost by those around him. He chooses to speak only through the recitation of theatrical texts. At the film's outset he attracts the attention of a theatre director who becomes intrigued by the boy's silence and sets out to create a play from his unusual tale. The appearance of this director sets off a chain of persecutions: repeated attacks on the boy's alterity on the part of those who try to prize him open and turn his life into narrative and his silence into speech.

Il sogno della farfalla attempts to stage the unconscious itself, *mare calmo*, as the prelinguistic first year of life. It uses Massimo as an allegory for the experience of an infant before it learns to speak, and describes the fall from this state when, inevitably, the deluding relationships with the outside world shape the infant into an adult. In the screenplay, Fagioli describes Massimo as 'sogno, ovvero inconscio, ovvero irrazionale, ovvero primo anno di vita senza parole' [the dream, or rather the unconscious, or rather the irrational, or rather the first wordless year of life] (Fagioli 1992, 38). Massimo is living an eternal, pre-fall innocence made up of archetypes, a world that will be exploded with the 'fall' occurring at the end of the film. Within this highly private world Massimo exists as an uncorrupted ideal of himself; no self-contained monad, he is able to form genuine relationships with others, relationships which are built not on grappling, insatiable desire (the 'bramosia,' or hankering, about which Fagioli warns) but – as emblematized in his rapport with his girlfriend – on a calm joy that enables him to meet the Other on the deepest level. For Fagioli and Bellocchio, the unconscious, however unknowable and private, is not severed from the Other but is deeply implicated in it.

The figure of Massimo is inseparable from a discourse on vitality. He does not suffer from what Fagioli calls the 'fantasia di sparizione' [the disappearing fantasy], an expression of the death instinct whereby the newborn baby reacts against a new situation by using his power to make darkness with his eyes; light is the 'new' element in relation to the darkness and water of the womb (Fagioli 2007). Massimo does not annul reality but sees it fully and wishes to fully live. This is why, presumably, when we first see him, he is on stage as the Prince of Homburg, begging his aunt to intervene to save him from death by firing squad. The words of the prince, as spoken by Massimo, are, 'Non desidero altro che la vita' [I desire nothing but life].

The film's argument ultimately rests on the conflict between the calm, life-desiring perfection of the *mare calmo* and the adult world that threatens its existence. It allegorizes the fall from the initial state of the psyche at birth, a fall that marks the entry into adult life with all its compromises and failures. From the very beginning of the film, Massimo's enlightenment and silence – signs of his immersion in the irrational world of the *mare calmo* – are pitted against the blind adult world of the intellect, represented by his father and brother. Massimo's father is a lecturer in Classics; his brother, Carlo, is a scientist. The two men represent two adult ways of understanding – through science and through the arts – both of which are ultimately dismissed as false paths.[9] The father's intellectual attachment to the classical world is condemned by his wife as an abstraction ('tu scruti il segreto delle donne e non vai mai a donne' [you scrutinize the secret of women, but you never go and pick them up]), and in his lecture on *The Odyssey* at the beginning of the film the father, though recognizing the place of the irrational, fails to face it in himself, or indeed in Massimo:

Quello [Ulysses] che viene sempre considerato il grande eroe della conoscenza, in verità potrebbe essere soltanto l'espressione della grande angoscia dell'uomo greco di fronte all'irrazionale. Egli fugge dai mostri di quanto, ora, si chiama inconscio. Vuole tornare alla rassicurante casa e alla altrettanto rassicurante moglie. Occorre millenni prima che l'uomo ritrovi il coraggio di affrontare quanto, nell'uomo, non è ragione.

[He (Ulysses) who has always been considered the great hero of understanding, in reality, might be nothing more than the expression of the great anguish of Greek man in the face of the irrational. He flees from the monsters, which now we call the unconscious. He wants to return to his reassuring house and his equally reassuring wife. It would take millennia before man would regain the courage to face that which, in man, is not reason.]

Massimo's character, poles apart from his father's, is inseparable from an irrationality that the film establishes as the source of true understanding and vision. His visionary capacity enables him to see beyond the surface of things, casting light out over darkness – as in the film's opening shot. In a reversal of Enlightenment philosophy and Freudianism, it is the light of the unconscious irrational, not the light of reason, that brings vision. However, each of the characters with whom Massimo comes into contact tries to convert him, to bring him back over to the side of speech and the rational. The theatre director is the first to try, attempting to transform Massimo's prelinguistic world into speech through his commissioned play. Massimo's mother is next; she becomes complicit with the director and begins writing the script. A series of further temptations appear. Massimo, as a modern-day Ulysses or Macbeth, visits three women who try to distract him from his journey. As allegories of *Macbeth*'s witches, they are, according to Fagioli, emblematic of negation, standing for the 'fantasie di sparizione, invidia, bramosia' [fantasies of disappearance, envy, and hankering] (Fagioli 2007).[10] Even Massimo's faithful girlfriend betrays him, at the end of the film. She and Massimo go on holiday to Crete, a kind of Ulyssean voyage in which they revisit the landscapes and culture cultivated by Massimo's classicist father. Here, the girl who was the only one to instinctively understand Massimo's pure world throughout the film betrays him by turning what she knows into words in front of an audience of curious cripples in one of the Cretan villages. As the cripples gather around, she explains Massimo's silence to them and, by so doing, turns his silence into speech – just as his mother had done in writing the play. Fagioli (1992, 38) explains that it is the girl who throws the first stone by speaking, and the cripples in the village – literally – throw some more, driving them both out.

At the end of the film the whole family, which has gathered together on the island, is involved in an earthquake. This earthquake, while inflicting little physical harm on them, allegorically signals the profound shaking of Massimo's world and the loss of the *inconscio mare calmo*. The final scene, staged against a backdrop of the rocks and debris that have fallen during the earthquake, shows the family gathered, statuesque – in flowing, pastel clothes reminiscent of those of ancient Greece – around the body of the mother, who is curled up in fetal position. This 'fetal' mother represents the prelinguistic infant that Massimo has lost in the earthquake, or fall; it is the symbolic victim of the play.

Ultimately, like *Salto nel vuoto*, *Il sogno della farfalla* proposes the irrational unconscious as a beautiful essence that needs to be uncovered and defended. However, while *Salto nel vuoto*'s narrative structure leads from death to life, from adult to child, and from pain to the calm of an inner world, *Il sogno della farfalla* is structured around the more pessimistic narrative frame of the myth of the fall. As a more sustained exploration of the psyche through the figure of Massimo, this later film emphasizes the fragility of the *bambino* part of the psyche; to recuperate the child – which Marta does at the end of *Salto nel vuoto* – proves to be highly problematic. *Il sogno della farfalla*'s message is ultimately pessimistic: entry into the Symbolic, into language, is inevitable, and the calm world of the prelinguistic child cannot withstand it.

Sex, Women, and Irrationality: La visione del Sabba
and La condanna

Il sogno della farfalla's story of the *bambino* is only half the story of the psyche. Bellocchio's films tell another tale: the need for the male to recuperate the female part of the psyche in order to become whole. As Fagioli writes in *Bambino, donna, e trasformazione dell'uomo*, 'woman' represents a second aspect of the universal unconscious (male, by implication), to which the adult – as rationality – is opposed; nonetheless, the adult needs it for its completion. It is this 'female' element that will now be explored through two films, *La visione del Sabba* and *La condanna*. The first treats the woman as a projection of the male psyche that he must integrate in order to become whole, and the second deals more specifically with sex as a potential, but highly problematic, place of healing for the self.

   La visione del Sabba narrates the tale of Davide, a young psychoanalyst called to investigate the case of Maddalena (Béatrice Dalle), in which a young woman is accused of attacking a man who, she claims, had raped her. A team of psychoanalysts are trying to determine whether the girl's story is a delusion or a lie. Maddalena claims that she is a witch who was born in 1630 and, for the last four hundred years, has been searching for the right man to whom to surrender her virginity. As the film progresses, Davide is increasingly beset by dreams or visions of a world in which Maddalena is really a witch called Mad. He falls in love with Maddalena/Mad and begins to stand up against a psychoanalytic profession that would transform her irrationality into rationality. The film, which aligns psychoanalysis with the witch-hunts of the Inquisition in their common suppression of the irrational, ends with the burning at the stake of the witch Mad.

   Béatrice Dalle plays both Maddalena, the woman investigated by the psychoanalysts, and Mad, the witch hunted by the inquisitors. Mad, in particular, represents the unconscious sexual urges of the psyche – the psyche's 'vulcanicità' [explosiveness], as Bellocchio puts it (Nicastro 1992, 393). Unlike Maddalena, who is intelligent and sharp tongued, Mad is completely silent, a silence that positions her in the prelinguistic, the irrational, and, in the Lacanian sense, the pre-Symbolic – in other words, in the same kind of space occupied by Massimo in *Il sogno della farfalla*.[11] Whereas Maddalena's independent, articulate, and challenging character can even be seen as reflecting aspects of second-wave feminism, Mad undermines this in her denotations of the sensual and wordless libido: she is irrational, threatening, and invincible. Needless to say, the aligning of the irrational with woman, and the rational with man, is deeply problematic, no matter how positively the female aspect appears to be proposed in the film. The problems of this essentialist gender portrayal in Bellocchio's films will be examined in chapter 5.

Mad is a symbol of the unconscious as sexually voracious, irrational, and overwhelming. *La visione del Sabba* is therefore in part the tale of a man overcoming the fear of his own sexuality and the female aspects of the unconscious. At the film's outset, Davide is shown as a model doctor, rationally rejecting the sexual advances of his female patients. However, in the course of the film, bewitched by Maddalena/Mad, he slowly learns to integrate this sexuality and so transforms his unconscious, which has been blocked by his overemphasis on the rational. In this reading, the film's moral is that, however threatening the dark sensuality of the psyche might seem, it is a positive, liberatory, and life-giving force that needs to be accepted and not rejected. The ambiguous, open ending to the film works on this metaphorical level. Mad, having been found to be a witch by the inquisitors, is dragged out into the town square at night and tied to a stake; she is to be burned alive. It is Davide who takes a torch and sets fire to the witch's pyre. With this act, he represents the inquisitors (whom he had joined in the first dream sequence) and the world of psychoanalysts (his own profession). These two groupings represent the narrow world of male reason, a world that rejects the irrational, the 'woman,' perennially trying to tame her by rendering her rational. On the pyre the flames rise up and surround Mad, but when they die down, she emerges unscathed and in the final shot embraces Davide. This embrace between the two lovers signals both Davide's acceptance of the irrational libidinous element and the invisible and victorious nature of the female part of the psyche; male reason cannot vanquish it. Davide's psyche is now capable of accepting the feminine, the libido, the irrational.

Five year's later, in 1991, a second film – *La condanna* – again pits the female unconscious against the male, substantially developing the psychoanalytical discourse forwarded in *La visione del Sabba* and widening it to discuss sexual relationships – in particular the nature of the sexual act – in more detail. The film, which won a Silver Bear award at the Berlin Film Festival, caused widespread controversy at the time of its release owing to its deeply problematic presentation of rape; the discussion of rape, in the film, provides an emblematic point from which to unravel the sexual and psychical relationships between men and women.[12]

In the eighties and nineties Bellocchio's films repeatedly and dualistically grapple with Fagioli's binaries of rationality/irrationality, conscious/unconscious, and male/female.[13] Sex becomes a central discourse for working out these issues, coming to represent far more than just a physical union, implying rather a union on a fundamental psychical level, which permits a rehabilitation of the female within the male psyche to occur. (Neither Fagioli's theories nor Bellocchio's films show any interest in how the female psyche might deal with a male element.)

La condanna can be read as part of a progressive centralizing of a discourse on sexuality that owes its approach in large part to Fagioli but also needs to be seen in its socio-cultural context. The rise of an increasingly secular society and of second-wave feminism, and the relaxation of the censorship laws in 1962, all had their parts to play in creating a more liberal attitude towards sex in the Italian society of the sixties and seventies. In cinema, the soft-porn film had emerged, as had a dedicated network of cinemas, and at the same time there was a clear tendency to market European art-house cinema abroad as sexually explicit, thus encouraging directors to use sex more often and less cautiously in their films. The way had already been paved for Bellocchio as early as 1960 with Fellini's *La dolce vita*, and Italian films since the early 1970s had played on the saleability and shock value of sex and nudity: for instance, Bertolucci's *L'ultimo tango a Parigi* (*Last Tango in Paris*, 1972); Pasolini's *Salò* and his trilogy (1971, 1972, and 1974, respectively); Liliana Cavani's *Il portiere di notte* (*The Night Porter*, 1973); and Fellini's *Casanova* (1977).

La condanna is very loosely based on a true story that had hit the Italian press in 1980: a schoolgirl (Simonetta Ronconi) had had a relationship with her geography teacher and subsequently denounced him for rape. The ensuing court case caused heated debate, with public opinion divided on whether or not the case constituted rape, especially as the teacher was sentenced and then subsequently pardoned. Bellocchio retains little of the original story beyond the ambiguous nature of the crime and the difference in age between the girl and the 'rapist.' Instead, he shifts the film into a Fagiolian frame, centring the film on the problematics surrounding men's relationship with women and focusing especially on issues relating to rationality and irrationality. He splits being and sexuality into two modes: the first – the Dionysian – is driven by the unconscious and the irrational, and it lies beyond the reach of rational control and will (this is the subversive sexuality already discussed with regard to Mad's performance in *La visione del Sabba*); the second – the Apollonian – is controlled by the law and behaves apparently correctly but is lacking in authenticity, passion, and beauty. *La condanna* argues that the first mode is authentic, and the second is a travesty of sexuality.

In the film, the first type of sexuality is represented by the Villa Farnese in which the 'rape' occurs, and the second by the courtroom in which the case against the 'rapist' takes place. Initially, Sandra (Claire Nebout) becomes trapped inside a museum (the Villa Farnese) after closing time and finds that an older man, the architect Colaianni (Vittorio Mezzogiorno), is locked in with her and is intent on having sex with her. She finally gives in to him and is shown – in a long still take – experiencing an orgasm, a sign that she has derived pleasure from the encounter. However, the following morning she discovers that the architect has the keys to the museum and therefore had choreographed the night's passion; they had not been equals after all. This poses the problem that will be the key to the arguments of the next part of the film: the place of power, consent, and rational 'law' in sexual relations.

In the second part of the film – which takes place in a courtroom – the dialogue between the architect and Sandra opens out to become a quartet of four voices: those of the judge, the judge's wife, Sandra, and the architect. However, the principal dialectic voices of this section are both male: the judge (scripted by Bellocchio) and the architect (scripted by Fagioli). Mirroring the Sciabola / Judge Ponticelli binary of *Salto nel vuoto*, the architect presents the case for the unconscious in sexual relations, while the judge defends the need for control. However, as the court case progresses, the judge's position is put into crisis, first by the architect and then by his own partner, who takes the architect's side. Although the judge finally sentences the architect to prison, he fails to put an end to his own doubts about the meaning of sexual relations.

The architect is tried for depriving Sandra of her liberty (he possessed the keys to the museum but did not let the girl out) and for violently forcing her to have a carnal relationship with him. According to the law, Sandra was therefore in a position of inferiority. In the courtroom scenes Sandra herself rewrites the seduction from the point of view of consciousness, portraying herself as a victim of a man who was physically and mentally stronger than she was and who insulted her, broke down her defences, and then possessed her. Sandra is torn in two. She is attracted to the Apollonian law, which protects her but effectively turns her into a victim and denies her the possibility of real sexual pleasure. However, she is also drawn to the unconscious, which enables her to experience orgasm but steals her will and liberty.

The relationship between the judge and his companion, Monica (Grazyna Szapolowska), takes the discourse on sex a step further. One night the judge, unable to sleep, gets up and goes to his study to look again at a reproduction of Leonardo da Vinci's *Madonna Litta* – the painting that the architect and Sandra together had admired in the museum prior to the rape or seduction. Monica follows him. Seeing her, the judge tries to force himself on her, to kiss her breast in imitation of Leonardo's child suckling the Madonna. Monica reprimands him, not for his violence but for its inauthenticity; his forcefulness comes not from unconscious desires but only from a desire to control her by *imitating* desire. This is a desire learnt from books, which the mise en scène emphasizes by situating the actors between heavy bookshelves. Monica then vocalizes her Fagiolian views on rape. She calls him a rapist because his disappointing sexual bond with her is violation ('Mi violenti ogni volta che mi deludi e mi deludi sempre' [You rape me every time you disappoint me, and you always disappoint me]). Paradoxically, her next move is to accuse him of being *unable* to be a rapist. In Monica's speech, the term *rapist* therefore assumes two opposing meanings, one negative and one positive, but neither is allied to its legal significance: in the first sense, a rapist is a man who deludes a woman sexually by failing to give her pleasure (which he should do by forcing her to orgasm), failing to be in touch with the unconscious, and failing to be 'mad' and overstep limits; in the second, 'positive,' sense, a rapist denotes a man who brings a woman pleasure by overstepping limits, using force on her, and controlling her pleasure. Monica accuses the judge of using the wrong kind of force, one that results from conscious will and not from an unconscious desire, which would instead enable them both to lose control. The judge will never find this kind of force while he lives and controls with his mind. According to Monica and Fagioli, he is thus incapable of understanding the paradoxical needs of a woman. We are clearly in very problematic territory; the film risks legitimizing rape.

Later, when the judge goes to see the architect in prison, the architect finally reveals the core of the paradox: women have a 'segreto che non ti danno mai spontaneamente. Bisogna costringerle. Però poi sono felici di essere violentate … ma ti denunciano, e forse hanno ragione' [secret they will never give you spontaneously. You need to force them. But then they're happy to be raped … but they denounce you, and perhaps they're right]. The film provocatively (and blatantly incorrectly) states that consent is never feasible within a genuine sexual relationship, a position articulated by the architect during the trial as follows:

Essere consensiente significa, mi pare, scegliere liberamente e consciente-mente di fare una certa azione, solo che nel rapporto sessuale libertà e coscienza, da un determinato momento in poi, perdono di importanza, anzi sono di ostacolo. La bellezza del rapporto sessuale sta proprio nel grado di incoscienza che l'uomo e la donna insieme riescono a raggiungere.

[Consenting means, I think, freely and consciously choosing to perform a certain action, except that, in the sexual relationship, from a determinate moment onwards, these things lose importance; in fact, they become an obstacle. The beauty of the sexual relationship lies precisely in the degree of unconsciousness that the man and woman together succeed in attaining.]

The judge's long speech at the end of the trial shows him opting for the side of the Law. He stresses the need to draw a line between the conscious and the unconscious and to stand on the side of the conscious because it is the only way of being able to pass judgment – a point with which Fagioli would certainly not agree. The judge knows that if one were to take the unconscious into account, the whole legal system, the law of the father, would collapse. He punishes the architect for having stood up against the Law. However, the film's position is that the judge pays too: he pays for his own normality and his rejection of the unconscious in his failure to connect with women.

In the third and final part of this film there is a shift to an allegorical mode, which replays the film's themes in their essentiality. The camera follows the judge as he stumbles on a hollow cavernous edifice built from great blocks of stone or marble. Inside he sees a farm girl sitting atop an outcrop, like a siren. Watching him, she slowly bends down and laps clear water with her tongue, like a wild animal. In the following scene he discovers her again, this time out in the fields during the harvest. He watches the woman pouring wine for her male companions while they slap and tease her sexually. When the menfolk leave her to return to work after lunch, the woman empties sacks of grain on the ground and lies on the grain, falling asleep beside the judge. The references to fertility (grain) and purity (water) are obvious. After her after-noon siesta the woman returns to the field, where a menacing combine harvester and four men approach her. The men appear to attack her, but when the judge intervenes, her words – the only words she utters in the film – are, 'Questa non è violenza' [This is not violence]. The judge is shocked and, realizing once again that he is missing something fundamental in his understanding of women, asks, 'È allora che cos'è?' [So what is it, then?] The woman's response is a long, knowing laugh. This silent, spontaneous woman and her mysterious laugh carry the meaning of the film. She is seen as an archaic creature linked with fertility and freedom. She is portrayed as free in her ways. In her acceptance of male violence in her search for pleasure she seems to represent the film's ideal of womanhood, and like Mad, this woman presents a problematic allegory of woman as the unconscious.

With the emphasis on the woman as something the man must recuperate if he is to be transformed and reach psychic wholeness, the woman becomes little more than a projection of what a man needs for his completion, despite Fagioli's theories that condemn projection as the establishing of an inauthentic relationship with the Other (Fagioli 2007). With its emphasis on sex as necessarily violent against women if it is to be authentic, La condanna produces a highly objectionable argument, which advocates violence against a woman because 'deep down she wants it.' While purporting to provide a new angle on sexuality, it only reiterates the age-old binaries of a passive woman – an object who undergoes violence – and an active man. The unswervingly male point of view that underlies both this film and La visione del Sabba will be examined again in chapter 5, as will be the question of whether or not Bellocchio's women can ever really rebel from such a position of on-screen inferiority.

Screening the 'I': Styles of Interiority

The 'model' of the psyche that emerges from Bellocchio's films is so strongly influenced by Fagioli's ideas that some of the films in the 1980s are almost impossible to grasp without some understanding of the concepts, especially the theories surrounding the recuperation of the irrational (whether as 'woman' or as 'child / mare calmo') and the discussions of transformation.

The psychological turn of 1979 affects not only the content of the films, which henceforward absorb psychoanalytical concepts, but also their style. Suddenly models of the psyche are screened through their symbolization in emblematic characters like Mad and Massimo, in the child in Salto nel vuoto, and in the silent farm girl in La condanna; allegorical narratives frame psychoanalytical concepts; paintings reveal obscure meanings. However, the shift also has important implications for other areas of cinematography, especially as these relate to space and time and to narrative ambiguity. It will be the task of the following subsections to explore how Bellocchio's films screen the inner 'I.'

The Oneiric and States of Hesitation

Before the watershed of 1979, dream sequences are absent from Belloc-chio's cinema, and only one film, the grotesque and highly symbolic *Nel nome del padre* (1971), incorporates any oneiric material at all.[14] This film, like Fellini's *La dolce vita*, satirizes an outbreak of apparitions of the Virgin Mary in Italy by showing a schoolboy who is masturbating while visualizing a beautiful statue of the Virgin that is moving towards him. However, as a single case of oneiric material in many years of film-making, it only serves to highlight just how infrequent was the use of oneiric material before 1979. Since that time, however, such material has become integral in Bellocchio's film-making and only two of the fifteen films made – *Enrico IV* (1984) and *La balia* (1999) – are wholly exempt from its presence. In *Vincere* (2009) the crucial wedding scene between Mussolini and Ida Dalser hesitates between dream and memory, allow-ing the film to avoid a final answer on whether or not it took place.

The oneiric signals a distinctive break between Bellocchio's early and mature film-making. It marks the introduction of a psychoanalytical model and a shift towards a deeper exploration of character psychol-ogy. It also implies a shift from an essentially literary and verbal matrix to a more cinematic one that relies heavily on the cinematic image for the communication of meaning. The oneiric serves two principal functions in Bellocchio's cinema, both of which are rooted in character subjectivity: first, it reveals the urges, desires, pain, and memories in the psyches of on-screen characters; and second, it recreates the sensa-tion of interiority by erasing boundaries between the 'real' (the outer) and the 'imagined' (the inner), conferring on his films the ambiguous and open-ended style that most characterizes them after 1979. Both of these functions of the oneiric have important implications for the devel-opment of the private and subjective within Bellocchio's cinema.

The unconscious material that is externalized in the dreams and onciric sequences in Bellocchio's cinema takes many forms, but gener-ally there is a shift from the more Freudian matrix of the films released in 1980 to a more obviously Fagiolian one by the mid-1980s. The first films to contain substantial oneiric material, *Vacanze in Val Trebbia* and *Salto nel vuoto*, are still broadly Freudian in the sense that – even though Fagiolian experiences are present – their focus is firmly on the relationship between a present trauma and the past suffering that caused it and has been repressed, returning only through dream. In *Vacanze in Val Trebbia*, for example, Marco witnesses various images of past suffering while he revisits the place of his childhood; projected onto the landscape are sequences from the deaths of Saint Sebastian and Christ – played by children – and other scenes of childhood guilt, like the stealing of apples from a farmer's tree. In *Salto nel vuoto* the oneiric world, unseen by the dreamers, again juxtaposes past and present; we see what the adult siblings are repressing, in other words, what they have lost by becoming adult – their vitality, rebelliousness, anti-conformity, and instinctive human warmth. The oneiric children who play in the apartment at night are freer than their adult counterparts and represent an attack on the bourgeois order. The precarious and threatened nature of their freedom is made clear in one of the final scenes where, dressed in adult clothes that are far too large for them, they hurl objects around the Ponticelli flat. This wearing of adult clothes is a warning of the future that lies before them. What they assume playfully in this scene and then cast off, leaving behind them as they depart, will become the same repressive clothes and role that they will be forced to assume later in life, when their casting off will, as the adult Ponticelli siblings know, become almost impossible.

Bellocchio's films after 1980, however, stop using dream to overtly juxtapose a character's past and present. The oneiric continues to be used to provide a privileged view inside the heads of characters, exteriorizing what by rights we should never be able to see, but later screenings, instead of expressing latent childhood memories, tend to centre on post-modern parallel worlds of narrative and psychological possibility, providing insight into other modes of being and spurs for character transformation. In *La visione del Sabba*, Davide's visions of Mad represent another possibility, or path, for sexuality outside the bourgeois sexuality that he knows: an overwhelming irrational sexuality that his own rationality threatens to destroy. In *Buongiorno, notte* (2003) the Aldo Moro whom Chiara sees walking freely around the apartment at night presents a parallel universe that she still has a chance to embrace, illustrating a possibility that history has tragically disallowed.

The schematic, and necessarily reductive, distinction between broadly Freudian and Fagiolian matrixes belies, however, an important constant in Bellocchio's treatment of the oneiric, one that is central to an understanding of both the model of the mind and the relationship between subjectivity and objectivity that is embraced in his films. This constant is what I will term the *hallucinatory mode*. The use of hallucination or visions – rather than self-contained dreams – permits the *co-existence* of past and present, here and there, and real and dream, and it sets up a hesitant relationship between states, presenting them as radically proximate.[15] This will have important consequences for the screening of interiority.

Salto nel vuoto is the first feature film to use the hallucinatory mode. The nocturnal appearances of the children seem too autonomous to be emanations of the sleeping judge or his sister; the camera never ties them definitively to either of the siblings, and they seem to emanate from the house itself.[16] The children's behaviour is not like that of creatures within a dream: they are shot naturalistically; their actions have none of the absurdity and dislocation of dream; they wander in rooms that are shot without the contortions of camera angle and mise en scène typical of the kind of dream found, for instance, in Salvador Dalì's sequence for Hitchcock's *Spellbound* (1945) or in Fellini's *8½* (1963). The oneiric here is not self-contained and bracketed off from the ongoing narrative. There are no external markers – such as a shot of the subject sleeping – that naturally draw attention to the presence of subjective material. Instead the oneiric material is an integral part of the film, so that dream and reality lie along the same narrative continuum (see Brook 2004a).

In *Salto nel vuoto* the oneiric apparitions are perfectly invisible to the real occupants of the house and seem to be exteriorized and to belong to the house itself. This is the same procedure used for *Buongiorno, notte*, almost twenty-five years later, when the images of Aldo Moro roaming the apartment at night are shot naturalistically, with an emphasis on the concreteness and autonomy of his physical presence: shot so as to be independent from Chiara's point of view, he takes a book from her sleeping hand as if he had concrete existence.

In both *Salto nel vuoto* and *Buongiorno, notte* the status of the oneiric occurrences is uncertain, although in the latter film the presence of a historical story (the real imprisonment of Moro, and his murder) anchors the meaning so that, for an Italian audience at least, the nocturnal wanderings of Moro will be seen as oneiric or fictional. In *Salto nel vuoto* the ambiguities are greater, owing to the absence of a historical real against which to measure them: the children hover between supernatural presences and psychic projections. They are hard to pin down as ghosts when their adult counterparts are still living, and their final destructive appearance seems real. Even Bellocchio struggles with their classification. In one interview he calls them 'fantasmi della casa' [house ghosts] (Biarese 1987, 23), and on other occasions calls them oneiric apparitions (Fanali 1980, 41) or refers to them as his own siblings (Bolzoni and Foglietti 2000, 52), suggesting that even for their author they hover between psychic projections and autobiographical memory. The key here, as it will be for many apparitions in the films that follow, is undecidability, a Todorovian hesitation between the real and the fantastic, an ambiguity arising from the concrete nature of cinematic representation in the face of what should rationally be psychic phenomena (Brook 2004a and 2007).

The hesitation between the real and the fantastic is a key to Bellocchio's films from 1979 and appears to be a deliberate procedure. The relationship between screenplay and film makes this clear. *La visione del Sabba*, for instance, hesitates between presenting Maddalena as a mad woman who believes she is a witch born in the seventeenth century (in which case the film is a psychological drama) and presenting her as witch who has really lived for almost four hundred years (in which case the film is fantasy). Although the screenplay supports the first reading, the film brings out the ambiguities and constructs fantasy as a possible reading.[17] The film does not resolve its mysteries and avoids the classic dream/reality dialectic, preferring to opt for a fusion among vision, dream, and reality:

> Si produce uno smarrimento che va sia contro l'ordine realistico che contro l'ordine onirico 'classicamente inteso.' Quando ho scritto e poi girato il film ero sempre combattuto tra l'esigenza di costruire una struttura 'classicheggiante' nella quale entrassero le tre componenti di cui parlavamo [visione, sogno, realtà] oppure di realizzare quello che di fatto ho realizzato; qualcosa né di confuso né di gratuito ma certo di contorto. (Bellocchio, cited in Bo and Cieli 1988, 241–2)

> [It produces a sense of confusion that goes against both the realistic order and the oneiric order as 'classically understood.' Both in writing and in shooting the film, I was constantly battling between the need to construct a structure in a 'classical style,' in which the three components about which we talked (vision, dream, and reality) would appear, and the need to create what I actually created in the end: something that is neither confused nor gratuitous but is certainly contorted.]

Il Principe di Homburg follows the same strategy, and in both the open-ing and the finale of the film, spectators are left unclear as to whether they are witnessing dream or reality; indeed, the whole film is infused with a suspended, nocturnal, dream-like atmosphere. Here again the film's editing has deliberately mixed the cards that the screenplay had put in place. The opening sequence of the film, which presents a dream that reveals the Prince's strong subconscious desires for glory, deep-ens the levels of ambiguity and inverisimilitude already present in the screenplay. The screenplay suggests a linear development for the open-ing sequence: Homburg dreams that he is crowned by the beautiful Princess Natalia in the presence of the Elector's entourage and picks up the Princess's dropped glove; then he wakes to find that he has the glove in his hand. In the film, scene 2 of the screenplay has been split in two, and the second part has been placed at the opening of the film, so that incomprehensibly Homburg already has the glove in his hand *before* he meets the Elector's party. The dream or dumbshow frame is therefore deliberately provided with a more ambiguous relation to the body of the narrative than exists in either Kleist's play or Bellocchio's own screenplay (although in both the glove functions as a mysterious symbol for a mixed plane of existence in which real and oneiric are porous and co-existent).

In the finale of the film, the changes wrought on the screenplay by the film reiterate the process of ambiguity set out in the film's open-ing. Rather than being crowned for his actions, as he is in the opening 'dream,' the Prince is condemned to death for insubordination against the Elector after disobeying his command during a battle. In the final scene Homburg is brought blindfolded to the site of his execution, but at the last minute he is pardoned and crowned by Natalia. Homburg's fate, and indeed the interpretation of the film, depends on whether the scene is to be read as dream or as real. The final words of the film, spoken by the Elector, 'Certo, un sogno, che altro?' [Certainly, a dream. What else?], leave the ending of the film hesitating between dream and reality. The image track suggests that Homburg has been pardoned, but the words on the soundtrack suggest that the pardoning is no more than a dream. Kleist's play, however, unambiguously sees Homburg pardoned, and Bellocchio's original screenplay has a final scene in which the preparations for the execution are dismantled, a scene cru-cially omitted from the film. By eliminating this scene, the film allows a neat framing of the story within the (hesitatingly) oneiric, which the addition of the clarifying final scene would have denied. The ambiguity of their portrayal means that the 'dreams' are presented as equally real and important to the narrative as is 'reality': they are the symbolic key to the film, and their symbols of laurel wreaths and coronation enable a presentation of the motivating forces in Homburg's unconscious that will guide his actions in the rest of the film.

The hesitation between states of real and of dream and the creation of *opere aperte* [open works] are therefore deliberate, with scenes rearranged or removed so as to conceal the shift from the real to the oneiric (*La visione del Sabba* and *Il Principe di Homburg*), or with oneiric material added that is not present in their screenplays (*Buongiorno, notte*). Moreover, Bellocchio permits few external or internal markers that would clearly identify oneiric sequences as such, and this is reflected in the near absence of conventionally presented, fully identifiable dreams. Instead, the hallucinatory mode dominates. Even where Bellocchio does use dreams, he quickly undermines their status: in *Buongiorno, notte*, external markers show the first oneiric sequences of both strand 1 and strand 2 as dreams, but later occurrences of the same type of material are far more ambiguously presented; Davide's initial dreams in *La visione del Sabba* are quickly supplemented by flashes and hallucinations, and, by the end, the real and the oneiric are wholly unmarked and indistinguishable. Moreover, oneiric material, which is by its nature subjective, is repeatedly presented as lying at the borders of objective reality, either as supernatural but concrete appearances (*Vacanze in Val Trebbia*, *Salto nel vuoto*, and *Buongiorno, notte*) or as pre-existent documentary material (*Buongiorno, notte*). Most of the oneiric material is therefore presented not as self-sufficient dreams – brief parentheses in a film's portrayal of reality – but as an integral part of the film, resulting in films in which there is no hermetic seal between the confines of natural and supernatural, physical and mental, past and present, and here and there.

For Bellocchio then, dreams and hallucinations, in their ability to tell the truths of the psyche, are equal in importance to any more objective and naturalistic portrayal of the world, and so the spectator is not encouraged to see them as immaterial, inexistent, or even distinct from the real. Dream and reality are two interlocking states that are inseparable and, more importantly, between which it is unnecessary to distinguish artificially. The ambiguity and obscurity of Bellocchio's films in this period, and often currently, is therefore deliberately motivated and signals a shift into the private world of the individual, whereby subjectivity does not remain enclosed within the confines of an individual but is constantly in flux, colouring the objective world in a way that suggests that the world is forever the representation, or even emanation, of the individual.

Space and the Unconscious, or the House as Psyche:
Salto nel vuoto *and* Diavolo in corpo

'Space,' says Aitken and Zonn (1994), 'is the interaction between public and private.' In cinema, spatial relations are crucial to an understanding of self and society. The positioning of characters within certain spaces, and their relationship to that space as an opening or as an enclosure, is crucial to the construction of a character's place within society. At the same time, space can reflect the relationship of the character to his or her interiority, psyche, and inner world. The spatial positioning of characters is therefore decisive in the construing of films in relation to the political, the public, and the private.

Bellocchio's cinema is a cinema of interiors. His use of space, perhaps more than any other aspect of his cinema, reveals just how much (even in the political films) the psychological, the inner, and the unconscious actually dominate. Even when political material is approached, the spaces used to contain it are almost always tight and restricted: houses, small town squares, lecture theatres. There is no sense of an all-embracing panorama on society. Bellocchio's cinema has none of the epic status of the films of Sergei Eisenstein or Richard Attenborough, where wide spaces permit a focus on the choral, on the mass. Bellocchio concentrates instead on the domestic, which is characteristic of melodrama, not epic cinema. Even his portrayal of the student movement in 'Discutiamo, discutiamo,' as previously noted, takes place within the four windowless walls of a lecture theatre; most other films that treat the contestation stage instead the more dramatic street battles between students and police or show mass demonstrations. The use of an enclosed lecture theatre cannot fail to hint that the students are cut off from the outside, that their demands cannot really be heard outside these walls, and that ultimately they are isolated and few in number.

Bellocchio's cinema prior to 1980 already has a strong sense of the interior, typically imprisoning its protagonist within an institutional, or in any case limited, space: in *I pugni in tasca* and *La Cina è vicina*, the space was the provincial town with its enclosed buildings and domestic interiors; in *Nel nome del padre*, it was the claustrophobic, prison-like boarding school; in *Marcia trionfale*, it was the army barracks; and in

'Discutiamo, discutiamo,' it was the university classroom. Of the feature films made before 1980, only *Sbatti il mostro in prima pagina* opens out onto the street, framing wide city spaces and crowds, especially in its footage of political demonstrations and street battles. Only Bellocchio's two political documentaries, together with this film, have significant levels of the kind of outdoor shooting that might be associated with an epic mode of film-making.[18] All three, however, as argued earlier, are films over which Bellocchio had significantly diminished control.

In the films of the Fagiolian years, spaces continue to be highly enclosed, and few exteriors are presented. They retain and intensify the claustrophobia embedded in Bellocchio's earliest films, a claustrophobia that represents the confinement and limitations of society, especially bourgeois society. With the waning of interest in the political, what few crowd scenes were ever used by Bellocchio virtually disappear. The most significant change during this period, however, regards the relationship of interior space to the psyche of the protagonists, a relationship that results in an increasing metaphorization of spatial coordinates.

Keys to the relationship between the inner world of protagonists and the society in which they find themselves are embedded particularly in the apertures that reveal or hide the dichotomy of inner and outer space. These apertures onto the outside, whether they be doors, windows, or television screens, imply a discourse on freedom and confinement, and they feature throughout Bellocchio's film-making. They come to the fore as symbols during the Fagiolian period of film-making, when Bellocchio was using Giuseppe Lanci as director of photography. *Salto nel vuoto*, *La condanna*, and *Diavolo in corpo*, for example, tell us a great deal about the psyche of their characters and its relation to the outside world through the films' constructing and deconstructing of boundaries.

Salto nel vuoto begins with a low-angle shot of an open window, taken from just below the window and from outside. This empty window, with its shutters pushed back, resembles a stage, into which Judge Ponticelli's face will appear moments later. The judge looks out and down curiously towards the camera or spectator below him, and only a subsequent eyeline match makes it clear that he is in fact looking not at us but at a bloodied sheet on the ground five storeys below. The bloodied sheet indicates the suicide of a girl who has thrown herself from one of these windows, a suicide that the judge is there to investigate. This window is thus the opening of the film and the closure of a life and represents both the temptations of the death instinct and the traumas of the relationship between inner and outer for someone who is trapped inside a life that does not open easily to the outside.

The motif of the window returns repeatedly throughout the film, and the double ending is choreographed around two different windows. The first is the one through which the judge (apparently) jumps to his death. The second is the window in the maid's house in Ostia, beneath which lies a symbolic sea. The two windows represent the two different ways of escaping the bourgeois control that the house represents: one negative, towards death; and one positive, towards life. For the judge, escape comes through an embracing of the death instinct that has haunted him daily; for his sister, Marta, it comes through her inner transformation.

In the portrait of the Ponticelli apartment the line between inside space and outside space is harshly defined. Repeatedly, the camera focuses on the judge locking the heavy door of the apartment behind him as he returns inside, shutting himself into his cage. The lighting – which so impressed Andrei Tarkovsky that he asked Giuseppe Lanci to work for him on *Nostalghia* (1983) – is unusual too, consisting primarily of natural light falling through the net-curtained windows of the apartment, lending the rooms their shadowy, enclosed atmosphere. The windows themselves look blind, showing little of what lies outside, beyond an occasional glimpse of some trees and the pavement below. They provide no real image of the outside world, a world that is already too far from the grasp of the Ponticelli siblings. What they do provide, however, is a space through which to discard things. On four occasions things are thrown through the windows onto the pavement below: scraps for the cats; Marta's clothes, sheets, and dolls that she hurls out when she loses control; domestic objects that are thrown onto the street by the 'oneiric' children when they wreck the house; and finally the judge's body. The apartment is more than just an apartment; it represents the psyche, a psyche that contains the phantasms from the past and that is trying to rid itself of the clutter of the present. What are ejected from the apartment or psyche through the window are indeed waste products: Marta's sexually repressive nun-like clothes and bedclothes; her childhood (represented by the toys); the apartment's bourgeois clutter; and finally the apartment's or psyche's great controller, her repressive brother. Only by the progressive removal of these things can Marta's psyche be healed.

The space inhabited by the judge's double, Sciabola, stands in contrast to all this. An artist, he lives on a barge moored on the Tiber. Sciabola's barge, unlike Ponticelli's house, is not fixed, and it can travel, thus representing the gypsy nature of its inhabitants (linking Sciabola with other social 'outsiders' in Bellocchio's films, like the gypsies in *Il sogno della farfalla*). Sciabola's space is open to the comings and goings of others, and he and his friends are usually out on the barge's deck, which is in constant dialogue with the city.[19] Even the cabin below has no obvious door and is easily entered by a simple set of stairs. The disposition of space in the film therefore creates a dichotomy between the limited, controlled, and claustrophobic space of the Ponticelli apartment and the open, moving space of Sciabola's world. The judge and his sister are locked into a limited bourgeois existence, whereas Sciabola's fiery life is open to a dynamic and even violent dialogue with others. The film is screening the battle of two psyches: the repressed bourgeois psyche and the liberated, but ambivalent and dangerous, psyche represented by Sciabola and his barge.

Six years later *Diavolo in corpo* puts spaces dramatically into play again – contrasting enclosed spaces, like the courtroom and its cage for prisoners, with open spaces, especially like the apartment in which the two young lovers meet. The geography of *Diavolo in corpo* mirrors that of *Salto nel vuoto*. Both films are set in Rome, and, in both, apartments designate private inner space. The River Tiber and the images of the sea reoccur and are again linked to the protagonists' psychic well-being. Like *Salto nel vuoto*, *Diavolo in corpo* begins with a suicide (this time, however, only an attempted one) and the opening scene is theatrical. An empty rooftop stage initiates the film, and long moments pass before a suicidal black girl steps out onto the roof tiles, threatening, in her incomprehensible language, to put an end to her life. However, even here a crucial spatial divergence is clear. *Diavolo in corpo* begins high on a rooftop in summer: it begins in the open, not just in an opening. This later film is more aware of public space, the outer, and the political. It moves beyond the house (whether barge or middle-class apartment) to encompass institutional spaces (school, courtroom, and prison).

It is worth exploring the film's opening scene further, given its significance for the relation between public and private. *Diavolo in corpo* begins with an establishing shot across Roman rooftops that captures a Rome which is not anonymous but recognizable and monumental (the Castel Sant'Angelo and the Roman hills behind are clearly in view). The rooftop area itself is divided into three zones: the top-floor classroom; the Dozza family terrace; and between them a tiled roof, an intermediate zone that unites and divides the two spaces. Giulia's space is within the Dozza family; Andrea's space is within the institution (a school that aurally spills out onto the roof space through the open windows, as a teacher's voice discourses on death in Giovanni Pascoli's poem 'La tovaglia' [The Tablecloth]).The black girl, as embodiment of the death instinct, occupies the middle space. The classroom seems to consist almost entirely of window, and these windows are all flung open, so that the space between Andrea (Federico Pitzalis) and Giulia Dozza (in her apartment opposite) is porous and filled with light.[20] Although the institutions of family and school will attempt to restrain these two young people within their respective frames and so maintain their respective places in society, the stage is set in the first scene for the interpenetration of their worlds. This open space is crucial for the development of the relationship between the two protagonists, allowing them to meet. It is across this divide, which represents different worlds in terms of age, experience, and gender, that the two come together.

In the ensuing film two locations embody their relationship: the Tiber and an empty apartment. Early in the narrative they row together down the Tiber. This trip, which recalls the idyllic boat ride of the lovers in Louis Malle's *Les amants* (*The Lovers*, 1958) and also the use of the river in *Salto nel vuoto*, represents liberation from social functions and restrictions. Here, a positive and natural sexuality can flourish, as suggested by the close-ups of Giulia where, because of an off-the-shoulder top she is wearing, she appears naked against the backdrop of the trees and the bank. They row down the river, overcoming rapids and laughing together, until they reach the coast. Here their boat rocks gently in the calm sea, a *mare calmo* that they have attained (it is implied) through their instinctive sexual harmony.

The empty apartment, which resembles the vacant apartment in which the lovers meet in Bertolucci's *Ultimo Tango a Parigi* (Nicastro 1992, 191), is again pure and initially devoid of bourgeois trappings. However, because Giulia will live here with her ex-terrorist husband after they marry, the site is under increasing surveillance and threat. Giulia's future mother-in-law is determined that the girl should marry her son and repeatedly enters the apartment in order to prevent a relationship between the girl and the young intruder, Andrea.

When Giulia and Andrea first arrive in this apartment, there is little apart from a bed. Gradually new objects begin to fill the space, brought there by Giulia's future mother-in-law. However, the couple still manages to maintain this as a space beyond bourgeois convention, a space dominated by bed and couch (and so by sexuality) and by its windows. These windows, opening onto the outdoors and filling the apartment with light, are so different from the veiled windows of the oppressive Ponticelli space. Giulia's attempt to maintain the apartment as hers, beyond the trappings of the bourgeoisie and far from the married life she will be expected to lead, results in her repeated attacks on those objects that come slowly to occupy this space. She deliberately smashes plates when her suspicious future mother-in-law visits, and at the end of the film she throws great quantities of cutlery around the floor and dances among them. Like Marta, who casts her sheets and clothes out the window, like Ale and his sister in *I pugni in tasca*, who hurl their murdered mother's possessions through that same frame, Giulia rejects the material objects and the confinement they suggest. She opts instead for an uninhibited sexual relationship and for the profound transformation that it brings.

The bare apartment and the boat – the couple's preferred *points de réunion* – are countered by the courtroom, with its cages for political prisoners, and by the prison itself. Both of these go beyond their clear political implications to suggest a symbolic reading whereby Giulia's fiancé is himself limited and confined. In his post-terrorist quest for normality, he is building a cage for Giulia, symbolized by his own confinement and by his mother's complicit and gradual filling of the apartment with 'things.'

Diavolo in corpo, like *Salto nel vuoto*, marks out space into dichotomies of inner and outer, free and confined, closed and open, blind and seeing, and cluttered and empty. This is the modus operandi of many of Bellocchio's films. In *La condanna* the museum stands for psychic space, and the public nature of its function during the day is reversed at night. This space, like *Salto nel vuoto*'s apartment, is literally cushioned from the world outside, with its semi-darkness, its silence, its long corridors, its DNA spirals into the depths,[21] its red womb-like room, and its paintings of newborn babies. It is both womb – as a creative space – and psyche. *Enrico IV, Buongiorno, notte,* and *Il regista di matrimoni* have a similar treatment of space. Physical space is thus psychological and symbolic, with enclosed space functioning metaphorically as a representation of the psyche, its transformations, and its growth. The enclosed space of apartments, museums, and even castles comes to function as an objective correlative for the inner selves of characters, challenging the invisibility of the psyche and rendering it visible.

Temporality and the Unconscious: Enrico IV *and the Chronotrap*

The manipulation of temporal coordinates, just like the manipulation of spatial ones, is crucial to the construction of an atmosphere of interiority. The creation of zones where time appears to slow or stop is part of Bellocchio's imposition of a cinema of subjectivity. His manipulation of both narrative and shot time in the films subsequent to 1980 is a significant factor in this work.

The model of the unconscious proposed by Bellocchio's cinema is one in which linear narrative time is replaced by the coexistence of past and present. His cinema is filled with what I will term *chronotraps*: spaces that trap the past and hold it alongside the present; spaces that exist in parallel with the contemporary world but are not quite of it. The use of this term is a nod to Michael Bakhtin's notion of chronotopos (Bakhtin 1982), which is used by Bernardi to describe the psychic spaces of *Salto nel vuoto* and some further films by Bellocchio (Bernardi 1998, 104). These chronotraps, together with the use of slow-motion and dilated shots, can be interpreted as a way of manipulating time – slowing it, making it reflective and reflexive, and creating the illusion that we are in the presence of the unconscious.

Chronotraps are a central feature of the temporal organization of a number of films made in the 1980s. In *Vacanze in Val Trebbia, Salto nel vuoto* and *Enrico IV* certain spaces assume a timelessness in which the present is porous to a past that erupts again and again into it, overlapping with it, at times becoming indistinguishable from it. In these films and others, even after the Fagiolian years, the unconscious mind is projected outwards into a concrete space – an apartment (*Salto nel vuoto; Buongiorno, notte*), a landscape (*Vacanze in Val Trebbia*), a castle (*Enrico IV; Il regista di matrimoni*), geographical spaces that the past and the present share.

The Ponticelli apartment in *Salto nel vuoto*, a deliberate analogy for the unconscious mind, represents the psyche in temporal terms, not just spatial terms. It is plunged into perpetual shadow, which deprives it of a sense of ongoing time (a weak light filters through the net curtains during both day and night, so that it is often unclear what time of day it is). The apartment has a present that seems outside of history and time owing to the radical invisibility of the world beyond; this sensation is intensified by the domination of the mise en scène by heavy Liberty-style furniture that belongs to the apartment's past (Bernardi 1998, 107). Into this enclosed and deeply protected space come the phantasms or projections of the past, which share the space with the living present. At night, while Marta and her brother sleep, children emerge from the cupboards and from under the judge's bed and tear around the house in the darkness, laughing and playing. These children are Marta when she was younger and other siblings, including a disturbed older brother. Like the spirits of *Vacanze in Val Trebbia*, the children seem eternal; they do not grow up or grow older. They seem instead to have become detached from the linearity of life. It is as if the siblings' childhood is closed off from the adult Marta and her brother and repressed so deeply that they cannot see it at all. It influences their behaviour, nonetheless. The mad child's swearing in the oneiric sequences is repeated in the 'real' of the film when Marta finally stands up to her brother, repeating swear words under her breath and, finally, when challenged, calling him a shit to his face.[22] The apartment is therefore modelled on the idea of a human mind, in which time is not linear but is in some way undefined, full of repetitions, contradictions, and always open ended. The past is not a past historic but can at any time take up its place again in the present.

In *Salto nel vuoto* and *Vacanze in Val Trebbia* the timelessness of the psyche results from the use of the hallucinatory mode. Rather than employing flashback, which creates stronger causal links and tends towards closure,[23] Bellocchio uses hallucination, which loosens the causal link, leaving the relationship between the times fluid, ambiguous, and often indefinable. Bellocchio – who uses flashback in only one of his feature films – explains his refusal to use flashback, in terms of the desire to maintain a certain illusiveness: 'Io ho sempre cercato di evitare l'aspetto esplicativo del cinema. Per me il flashback è un arricchimento del racconto attraverso la spiegazione di antefatti, e da parte mia ... c'è proprio il rifiuto della spiegazione' [I have always tried to avoid the explicative aspect of cinema. For me, flashback is an enrichment of the tale through the explanation of prior facts ... and on my part there is a denial of such explanation] (Malanga 1998, 124). For Bellocchio, the hallucination, as a more ambiguous device, replaces the flashback; it is a means of providing information as to the causes of behaviour while maintaining an enigma.

The key to the difference between the hallucination and the flashback lies in the simultaneity that characterizes their temporality. Whereas the flashback necessitates an abrupt break or juncture between past and present, the hallucination displays past and present as simultaneous or co-present, with no fracturing of temporal or narrative continuity. The past is projected onto the present, leading to a radical juxtaposition of time within the one – present – frame. Present time is thus prized open and made to include references to the past. Gilles Deleuze's notion (1989, 48) of the flashback's loop or closed circuit, whereby the present loops into the past and then leads back again to the present, therefore does not apply. The loop is replaced by the overlaying of images and consequently by a paradigm of time as a totality that contains and maintains the past within it.

The hallucination emphasizes the persistence of the past and memory within the ongoing present. In *Vacanze in Val Trebbia* the traumatic past, represented by the images of Christ and Saint Sebastian, is overlaid on the same spatial and temporal coordinates as the present. Only the final shots of the film put an end to the simultaneous hallucinatory mode, splitting time into a clearly separated past and present; the sepia-toned photograph of Marco Bellocchio as a child that closes the film finally introduces a past historic (Marco Bellocchio as a real child, photographed and archived), in place of a present perfect that lingers along the banks of the river.[24] It replaces the fragile and ambiguous simultaneity with a more stable time frame. The hallucinations or phantasms of *Salto nel vuoto* also draw attention to the simultaneity of time and, therefore, to the persistence of the Ponticelli past in the judge and his sister's present. In both films, the screening of the past in hallucinatory mode suggests some form of causality, but above all it emphasizes the continuation of a past that is literally *living*; its significance in the unconscious is not subordinate to the significance of the present.

The castle in *Enrico IV* – set at Rocchetta Mattei, a fake kitsch castle, actually built in 1850 but in medieval and Renaissance styles – is Bellocchio's most complex chronotrap. Bellocchio's film, based on Pirandello's eponymous drama of 1921, carries forward the interplay between the divergent levels of past and present that were already in place in Pirandello.[25] As in Pirandello's drama, the film's present describes the day of a visit to Enrico's castle by his great love, Matilda (Claudia Cardinale); her current lover, Belcredi; her daughter, Frida (Latou Chardons); a doctor; and Count De Nolli, Enrico's nephew. The past, however, is complex, being constituted of three intertwining strands: the first delineates the events of twenty years previous when during a fancy-dress cavalcade a young man fell from his horse, hit his head, and went mad, assuming from that day the name and identity of the emperor Henry IV; the second pertains to the twenty years subsequent to the fall, in which 'Enrico' lived out his role as the Emperor in a castle, attended by actors and visitors who played the requisite parts; and the third is the historical past that Enrico re-enacts – that of the real Holy Roman emperor who defied the Pope in the eleventh century. Bellocchio takes these strands and screens them through a mixture of flashback and hallucinatory modes. However, he distinguishes himself from the playwright by grafting a significant fourth strand to the past: Enrico's lost childhood.[26] Bellocchio insinuates this strand into the film by adding young playful children and toys (rocking horses, toy swords, and so on) to the castle and, especially, by showing how Enrico's childhood still lives on within him. There is a touching scene in which the Emperor admires a flock of wooden birds hanging from the ceiling of one of the rooms, their wings flapping gently. Enrico's eyes are wide with pleasure and excitement and, just like a child, he urges his counsellors to pull again the strings that make them fly. In a further scene Enrico's past comes back in an image that condenses various levels of temporality. He has just met and recognized Matilda – the woman who twenty years previously he had loved to the point of folly – and, deeply distressed by the encounter, he retreats to his room, climbs onto a life-size rocking horse, and rides it hard, with passion, as if it were real. The medium close-up, which frames the head of a rocking horse and Enrico's head and shoulders against the background of the castle window, creates the impression that Enrico is riding the horse not only as a child (after all, it is a rocking horse) but also as a young man (it is the horse from which he fell many years ago, which caused him to go mad), as a middle-aged man, and as a tragic, medieval emperor (he is dressed as such). This multilayered image and the castle itself portray a world in which past and present are complexly entangled, so that the distinction between them tends to vanish.

The editing and shooting reinforce this entanglement by a complex overlaying of hallucinations and – unique in Bellocchio's cinematography – the cutting in of flashbacks. The first sequence of the film screens a hallucination or projection that resembles those in *Vacanze in Val Trebbia*. A Mercedes car carrying Matilda, Frida, De Nolli, Belcredi, and the Doctor slowly gains on the castle. As their destination looms, the occupants of the car discuss Enrico's life, including the original fall from his horse. In what seems to be a space adjacent to the road, we glimpse, through the bushes, horses ridden by actors in medieval dress. At one point, we see Matilda's face within the car juxtaposed with the horses in the fields beyond. It is not clear whether some of the material is from the present (perhaps Enrico's 'servants' in full fancy dress, exercising horses in the fields) or whether it is all from the past (materialized as a kind of hallucination). The hesitation between the two readings allows this material to become at once highly subjective and objective: the galloping horses are part of Matilda's memory but also part of Belcredi's and Enrico's, and they almost seem to belong to the very land itself, just as the children did in *Vacanze in Val Trebbia*.

Even Bellocchio's use of flashback in the film blurs the boundaries between chronologies, in the way that flashbacks traditionally do not. Whereas most cinematic flashbacks draw the spectator from the present to a past acted out in an elsewhere, Bellocchio uses similar geography for both the present and the re-enactments of Enrico's fall twenty years previously, and this creates the impression that there is almost no spatial or psychic distance between the two events. With the halting of time and the hallucinatory moments, the castle and its territory act as a chronotrap, mingling different moments of the past with the present. In some senses, time has not moved on for twenty years – the hands on the prominent castle clock are stopped at 9:55, the time that marks the moment when Enrico went mad and first assumed the role of Emperor. In his rethinking of the play, Bellocchio rather emphatically emphasizes the clock (which is not part of the mise en scène of Pirandello's text) and has the Doctor add as part of his cure the return to time from timelessness: the Doctor not only arranges for the pictures of Frida and Enrico to come alive – as in Pirandello's play – but also simultaneously sets the castle clock chiming once again.

This tendency to shuffle time periods, to never box the past within a past remote, is very characteristic of Bellocchio's cinema, which seems perfectly at home with anachronisms. There are many examples of the commixture of past and present. In *La visione del Sabba*, for instance, time swings effortlessly between the present and a past dominated by witch-hunts and plague, where psychoanalysts are transformed into inquisitors and analysands become witches. In *L'ora di religione*, the character of Count Bulla, whom Ernesto meets at a party, seems to have emerged directly from an archaic world: his clothes and bearing are old-fashioned, and he resolves an argument by challenging Ernesto to a duel. In *Buongiorno, notte*, the seance scene, which shows politicians contacting spirits of the dead in order to discover Moro's whereabouts, has a deeply anachronistic quality, enhanced by the rich and suggestive photography; the apartment where Moro is held carries a sense of 'sospensione' [suspension] in 'questo triplice passaggio ... tra cella, anticella, appartamento' [this triple passage between cell, anti-cell, and apartment], and in the 'tempo interno' [inner time] associated with the emergence of the oneiric (Turco and Roberti 2004, 40–1). In *Il regista di matrimoni*, the Prince and his daughter, Princess Bona (Donatella Finocchiaro), are locked away in their Sicilian castle and seem to belong to a different, more ancient, world in which different rules of behaviour dominate and all clocks are stopped. In *Vincere* the same actor, Filippo Timi, plays both Benito Mussolini and his son. Bellocchio's cinema, moreover, often forges a sense of eternal or of endlessly repeated patterns, as in the children who seem never to grow old in *Vacanze in Val Trebbia* and *Salto nel vuoto* and the indestructible witch, Mad, in *La visione del Sabba*.

Each of these examples shows that after 1980, Bellocchio's cinema constructs a permeable and unsteady present in which the past is always ready to cohere. Henri Bergson's thesis on time, as reproposed by Deleuze (1989), seems relevant here. Deleuze's commentary on Bergson presents a past that is preserved in itself as past in general (in other words, as non-chronological), a past that co-exists with the present that it will be. Deleuze also notes that subjectivity is 'non-chronological time grasped in its foundation' (82). This seems to be precisely the paradigm of time that is manifest in Bellocchio's cinema. Its anachronism profoundly affects the narrative, revealing not only subjectivity but also the proximity of the psyche (as 'achronological') and cinema (as a medium that is capable, through mise en scène, anti-progression in the narrative, and cinematography, of profoundly mixing the chronological cards).

In Bellocchio's films of this period, the mixing of cards is not confined to the creation of chronotraps, zones in which outer space becomes the space of an inner psyche. There is a shift towards anti-narrative progression, especially through the extreme temporal dilation of shots and, to a much lesser extent, through the use of slow motion. Bertuzzi notes just how radical the transformation of the length of shot is from Bellocchio's early cinema to his cinema of the eighties; in *I pugni in tasca* there are roughly 800 shots, whereas in the Fagiolian *La condanna* there are 201, or only a quarter of the total in early films (Bertuzzi 1996, 120). The reduction in the number of shots is proportionate to a growth in shot length during this period.

Diavolo in corpo is perhaps the film that most strongly evidences this kind of shot dilation. In general, its pace is slow, and the ongoing plot is fragmented and lacking in narrative tension. In some sequences the slowing of the narrative is taken to an extreme, and the spectator, rather than being swept along by the plot, is positioned so as to observe the characters' inner emotions. In the opening scene, where an inarticulate black girl climbs onto a rooftop, a series of extremely dilated shots establish an intense non-verbal communication between the suicidal girl and Giulia, who is standing on the terrace just below. This seven-minute sequence contains only eighteen shots, and they alternate between the black girl, the students (including Andrea) in the schoolroom, and the terrace where Giulia is standing with her mother and a priest. Shot 10 lasts more than forty seconds and frames the black girl in medium close-up against the roof tiles as she looks desperately out of the frame towards us; shots 14 to 17 alternate dilated medium close-ups of Giulia with those of the black girl; shot 15, which frames the black girl, is a minute long. These shots are mainly devoid of speech, and when the black girl does at first speak, it is in her own language, incomprehensible to an Italian audience. These dilated shots are used in order to focus attention on the intense faces of the two girls, both of whom are crying. The centre of attention is on their non-verbal intuitive communication, on an emotional proximity that overcomes their spatial, racial, class, and linguistic distance.

Diavolo in corpo concludes with a strikingly dilated shot: a single motionless medium-close-up shot of almost two minutes' duration that frames Giulia's face and shoulders as she silently watches Andrea being interrogated on Sophocles' *Antigone* for his school examination. Once again, the shot focuses attention on the wordless communication of emotion. Instead of marrying her mediocre ex-terrorist fiancé, Giulia has escaped the destiny mapped out for her by others and has returned to Andrea, the boy she loves. The long steady shot catches the emotion of the moment, as her lips mime loving words to him, and she gazes at him until tears well up in her eyes. The steadiness of the shot, which reduces visual information to that provided by Giulia's face, allows the spectator to concentrate on what her presence and her behaviour means. It also encourages the spectator to absorb the complexity of the moment – not just emotionally but also in terms of the juxtaposition that takes place between, on the one hand, the visual image and Crivelli's emotional music for strings, both of which seem to represent pure emotion, and, on the other hand, the highly cerebral and academic verbal soundtrack, which is centred on Andrea's discussion of *Antigone*. (In its presentation of the woman as rebel, the play acts as a subterranean text in the film.)

Diavolo in corpo's dilated, lingering medium shots and close-ups are characteristic of Bellocchio's films made from the mid-eighties to the mid-nineties. Such shots, sign of a Bressonian approach, recur frequently and are generally associated with an intense attention to faces and body, especially those of the female protagonist:

> Il cinema del corpo, il discorso sugli sguardi e sui volti, l'espressione del corpo sono qualcosa che mi ha particolarmente coinvolto e comunque sfidato. La lunghezza dei primi piani fa parte della medesima ricerca: stare sul corpo, sullo sguardo attraverso un'intensità che si valorizza nel 'rimanere' lì il più a lungo possibile. (Bellocchio, cited in Bo and Cieli 1988, 392)

> [The cinema of the body, the discourse on gazes and faces, the expression of the body are things that have particularly concerned and challenged me. The duration of the close-ups is part of that same search: to stay on the body, on the gaze with an intensity that attains its value by 'remaining' there as long as possible.]

In *La visione del Sabba* the sex scene between Maddalena and Davide lasts for more than five minutes, consists of only seven shots, and begins and ends with close-ups on Maddalena's face that each last for over a minute; in *La condanna* the lover's sexual approach takes six minutes. 'Stare sul corpo'[Staying on the body], during the years in which Bellocchio worked with Fagioli, is an integral part of Bellocchio's style.

Since the break with Fagioli, Bellocchio's cinematic style has undergone a radical change with regard to the dilation of shots. *Il regista di matrimoni* is composed of just over nine hundred shots, more than four times that of *Il sogno della farfalla*, and so comes closer to reflecting trends in contemporary mainstream cinema. There is also a concomitant return to an alternating of shot / reaction shot and of classic two shots that Bellocchio had often rejected in the eighties. Moreover, his films now screen occasional sequences of flash cutting, with shots that are little longer than one second. In *Il regista di matrimoni* this occurs in both the fireworks scene and the scene in which Franco Elica first notices that every clock in the castle is stopped. In other words, the lingering dilated shot is no longer being used as a privileged tool for the exploration of the psyche.

The transformation in shot duration is due to more than Fagioli's influence, however. Mirco Garrone, who worked with Bellocchio from *Gli occhi, la bocca* to *La condanna*, was partly responsible for the dilated editing in these films. When Francesca Calvelli took over in 1994, shot time gradually sped up. The first film she edited, *Il sogno della farfalla*, mirrored previous films in terms of the number of shots (just over 250). However, her next film, *Il Principe di Homburg*, had some short sections of relatively fast cutting, despite the continuing presence of dilated shots. With Calvelli's third film for Bellocchio, *La balia* (which approaches 600 shots, almost triple those of his films of the early 1990s), the dilated shot definitively disappears. There is nothing in this film or in the following films that does not reflect the kind of shooting common in standard dramatic films of the period: a combination of shot / reaction shot and two shots; fast and flash cutting used for dramatic sequences; and the use of plan sequence. The break with Fagioli, the influence of Francesca Calvelli's editing style, and the outmodedness of slow-moving films and *temp morts* that had been ubiquitous in the intellectual auteur cinema of the sixties and seventies seem to have led to a very different conception of screen time.

The only way in which Bellocchio now continues to slow down time is through the use of slow-motion cinematography. Since the dilated shot disappeared with *La balia*, slow motion (which was rarely used in Bellocchio's cinema) has had a discrete presence, as if compensating in some way for the loss of dilation. Slow motion is used in his recent films to draw attention to subjectivity, and it shows subjectivity manipulating temporality. In *La balia*, for instance, a scene showing female inmates of a mental institution who are jumping down from trees is replayed identically later in the film, but in its second screening – captured in slow motion – the scene is subjective, revealing its inner, hidden, and real meaning. In this second screening, Dr Mori, a physician from the mental institution, is looking at socialist political posters that have been pasted illegally on the walls of a town. He has a flashback to three scenes in the mental institution, replayed in slow motion, including the scene in which the women jump from the tree. The eerie slow motion marks a moment of revelation: Mori makes a connection between the inmates of his institution and the socialist ferment outside its walls, which he suddenly realizes is led by the women. The slow motion marks the moment when he realizes just how rebellious and subversive these women are. The suppression of speech, a collateral effect of slow motion, further adds to the sense of this scene having been shifted from the outer, public sphere to the private one.

Slow motion reappears on a number of occasions in the following films, most notably perhaps in *L'ora di religione* when Ernesto watches two young girls pushing an old woman in a wheelchair at a party. Again, slow motion draws attention to the subjectivity of the protagonist's gaze. Ernesto, an artist, has just been criticized by his editor, Baldracchi, for his illustrations of the Pied Piper. Ernesto retorts that the problem is the artist's freedom with regard to the child's imagination. At that moment, a short slow-motion sequence shows the passage of the two little girls in front of Ernesto's eyes. The slow motion signals the importance of the moment to the protagonist: the two children stand as a kind of objective correlative for Ernesto's words, and also as a kind of warning. These children, who moments earlier were running freely around the heavily decorated, oppressive rooms, have now been bound to old age; their fantasy and play have been disrupted and replaced by obedience to their elders. The slow motion therefore acts not only as a signal of the importance of the scene to Ernesto but also as a key for the spectator to a sub-theme of the whole film – the imagination of children and its manipulation by adults. Like a motif, this theme winds around the story of Ernesto's young son, who is being 'encouraged' by his mother and other adult relatives to believe in God so that the family can further the cause of sanctifying the boy's grandmother. It is embedded too in the story of the Pied Piper of Hamelin – which appears at the beginning of the film, when Ernesto is illustrating the story, and in a later scene, when children are coerced by a priest to ascend a stairway on their knees. The theme appears too in the story of Saint Maria Goretti, which Baldracchi is keen for Ernesto to animate. Goretti died a 'martyr' at the age of eleven, defending her virginity against her cousin.

Chronotraps, shot dilation, and slow motion together work to disrupt narrative progression, to shift the spectator's attention away from plot and towards subjectivity, and to move from mechanical and linear time to an interior time based on simultaneity and near stasis. They are unmistakable signs of a model of the psyche as timeless or atemporal, a model that has already been seen in the two characters who figure the unconscious: Mad in *La visione del Sabba* and Massimo in *Il sogno della farfalla*. If Mad has lived for hundreds of years and fuses the time of the Inquisition with the modern, Massimo lives the eternal present of the unconscious, which is not structured in linear fashion. As the three 'witches' say to him, 'hai fermato il tempo per non morire e non hai avvenire' [you stopped time so as not to die, and you have no future] – a comment supported by Fagioli's own interpretation of Massimo (1992, 36) as 'lo sconosciuto; il presente eterno anche se irreale; non ha passato, non ha futuro' [the unknown; the eternal present, even if is unreal; it has no past, it has no future]. The most inner and private space that a human being possesses, in other words, is a place beyond the rules of linearity and mechanical change.

Conclusion

Cinema's lack of a stable subject pronoun – the *I* of a first-person narrator – and its innate tendency to confer on everything within the frame a sense of objectivity and reality unequalled in the arts, would suggest a medium that is profoundly at odds with the portrayal of subjectivity. However, after 1979, Bellocchio's cinema shows that the deepest recesses of the 'I' can in fact be at least partially screened. His cinema becomes highly manipulative of its spatial and temporal elements in order to create a sensation of being enclosed within a psyche, where past and present are contemporaneous, and where the outside seems very far away. His use of personification and analogy, whereby characters (like Mad and Massimo) and spaces (like apartments, castles, or a DNA-structured museum) come to stand for aspects of the psyche, is part of a similar search. His use, too, of oneiric cinematography, which creates high levels of narrative ambiguity and open-endedness, shows how the inner world and the outer world may be equal in significance; it also implies that interpretations of the films should be based not only on the logic of the conscious mind but also on the slippery and often illogical associations of the unconscious one.

The highly subjective cinema of the Fagioli years is not always successful. It is often heavy handed, slow, overly intellectual, and hard to follow. However, Bellocchio's apprenticeship to Fagioli and his research into the human mind in the eighties and nineties has left a legacy in his film-making of a subjective mode of cinematography that continues to make itself felt even when Bellocchio returns politics to centre stage in 2002 with *Buongiorno, notte*.

4 Bellocchio's Political Cinema from the Eighties to the Present

During the eighties, when the focus of Bellocchio's cinema was on interiority, Bellocchio's interest in politics did not, in fact, entirely disappear. Since 1980, five feature films explicitly or implicitly reference the politics of terrorism and the 1968 contestation, and one film, *Vincere*, treats Italian fascism. In 1982, *Gli occhi, la bocca*'s protagonist, Pippo Pallidissimi, is the exemplum of a failed rebel of the contestation who must learn to adapt to a new socio-political climate. In 1986, *Diavolo in corpo*'s love story takes place against the backdrop of the judicial trials of political terrorists in the eighties. In 1999, *La balia*, set in Italy at the beginning of the twentieth century, uses as a subplot a socialist uprising that has strong hints of the 1968 contestation.[1] In 2002, in *L'ora di religione*, one of the protagonist's brothers, Ettore Picciafuoco, is an ex-terrorist, a failed rebel who has re-integrated and is working in the heart of an institution (a mental home), which as a young man he presumably would have abhorred. In 2003, *Buongiorno, notte* rereads the kidnapping of the president of the Christian Democrats, Aldo Moro, by the extreme left-wing terrorist organization Brigate rosse [Red Brigades] (BR) in 1978. In 2009 Bellocchio screens the story of Mussolini's lover, Ida Dalser, and their son, Benito Albino, who were imprisoned in mental institutions when their presence became uncomfortable for *Il Duce*. In addition to these six films, Bellocchio made two political documentaries that treat the years of contestation and terrorism: *Sogni infranti* (Discussion on Deliriums, 1995) and *La religione della storia* (The Religion of History, 1998).

Six films and two substantial documentaries may seem quite enough to prove the presence of high levels of ongoing political commitment in Bellocchio's cinema, even during the *riflusso*. Indeed, the treatment of political terrorism emerges, apparently paradoxically, in Bellocchio's

Diavolo in corpo (1986), right at the heart of Bellocchio's quest for interiority through Fagioli and right in the middle of the *riflusso*. At the time of this film's release, even film-makers like Rosi and Moretti had stopped making films in which political commitment was fundamental. However, with the shift to psychological and subjective modes of film-making under Fagioli – which coincided with a general postmodern turn from *impegno* – discussions of Italy's political scenario, even where existent, were no longer foregrounded, and slipped into the narrative margins. Subjectivity, embedded so uncertainly and uneasily in early films like *La Cina è vicina*, where it interrupted and undermined political discourse, during the *riflusso* took up a stable position within the narrative as a filter through which to read and interpret all reality, including the political one.

By 1980 Bellocchio's cinema seemed to have shifted away from the idea that *objectivité absolue* is the key to political cinema, as expressed in one of his early articles for *Cahiers du cinéma* (1966a, 43). The aim of this chapter is to see what happens to the political when the ideal of *objectivité absolue* is abandoned and, instead, the personal is put to the fore. The focus will be on *Buongiorno, notte*, seen nevertheless in the context of *Diavolo in corpo* and other films in Bellocchio's corpus that more obliquely tackle the phenomenon of Italian terrorism, and on *Vincere*.

Italian Terrorism: *Buongiorno, notte*

The interest in Italian terrorism shown by Bellocchio's films dates back to 1986 when terrorism appeared at the margins of *Diavolo in corpo*; broad concern for political violence can be traced back even further, to 1969 and to Bellocchio's second feature film, *La Cina è vicina* (1967), where the extra-parliamentary Camillo and his petty provincial attacks on social democracy are scornfully portrayed. Political violence is indeed depicted negatively wherever it emerges in Bellocchio's films: in *La Cina è vicina*; in the impasse between police and students that closes 'Discutiamo, discutiamo'; in *Diavolo in corpo*; and in *Buongiorno, notte*. *Diavolo in corpo*, in fact, overturns the moral message at the centre of Raymond Radiguet's novel and Claude Autant-Lara's cinematic adaptation by reframing, within the context of a contemporary terrorist case, a story of a woman's unpatriotic affair with an adolescent while her husband is away fighting at the front during World War I.[2] In Bellocchio's film, the young woman (Giulia) escapes her dry marriage to a repentant left-wing terrorist by having a passionate affair with a schoolboy. The affair, which finally leads her to separate from her fiancé, is shown as positive and transforming, allowing her to gain the moral high ground and so avoid the punishment of death that is meted out to her character in the novel's plot. The positive construction of the sexual betrayal within the film relies at least in part on the negative construction of terrorists, or rather ex-terrorists, that the film conveys.

If political violence is repeatedly connoted as negative by Bellocchio, *Buongiorno, notte* is the first film in which he (seemingly) puts terroris-mat the heart of a film and builds up a theoretical discourse around it. He constructs this within a context that had altered substantially since the time of *Diavolo in corpo*. For a start, by 2003 terrorism had gone from being a contemporary problem, as it was in 1986 when the maxi-trials of terrorists – like those shown in the film – were taking place, to something which in large part now belonged to the history of the country and was in the process of being memorialized.[3] As O'Leary (2008, 36), notes, left-wing film-makers were inevitably drawn towards 'interrogat[ing] the legitimacy and understand[ing] the consequences of politically moti-vated violence emerging from within groups close to their own political position.' This process of rethinking was certainly behind the making of the two documentaries on Italian terrorism, which would then feed into *Buongiorno, notte*. However, the turn by Italian film-makers of the new millennium towards a reappraisal of their country's terrorist past must also be seen in the light of the rise of a new kind of global terror-ism, which is marked by the destruction of New York's Twin Towers on 11 September 2001 and which fuelled an increased interest in terrorism in Italy. Bellocchio, in fact, claims that he had originally wanted to make a film on contemporary global terrorism, before choosing instead to concentrate on the more familiar territory of Italy's home-grown politi-cal violence. A film on terrorism like *Buongiorno, notte* is therefore *both* memorialization of Italy's past *and* engagement with the fears and con-cerns of global contemporary society.

Buongiorno, notte appears to bring politics centre stage, especially when compared to *Diavolo in corpo* which relegates the political plot to just six scenes (one at the tombstone of Giulia's murdered father; three in the courtroom; one in the jail; and one in which Giulia watches a television broadcast by her ex-terrorist boyfriend, Giacomo. *Diavolo in corpo* forwards only a paltry discussion of politics; with the excep-tion of Giacomo's television appearance, the long political speeches that are characteristic of *La Cina è vicina* and 'Discutiamo, discutiamo' are absent. However, in *Buongiorno, notte* the plot focuses on the real kidnapping and murder of the secretary of the Christian Democrats, Aldo Moro, and carefully reconstructs the period; its account is based on real historical testimonies, especially those of ex-*brigatista* Anna Laura Braghetti in her autobiography, *Il prigioniero*, and of Sergio Flamigni in *Il mio sangue ricadrà su di voi* and *La tela del ragno*, and on newspapers and film footage from the time. Moreover, unlike *Diavolo in corpo*, whose political realism is highly circumscribed (surfacing only in the shots of the mass cages and prison environment, which themselves have high levels of symbolic meaning), the later film incorporates real political documents into its exegesis.[4] It makes significant usage of television footage from 16 March 1978, the date of the attack on Moro, and screens images of Via Fani taken just after the ambush as well as a long sequence from the Confederazione Generale Italiana del Lavoro (CGIL) demonstrations against the Red Brigades that took place in Rome later that evening. Early parts of the film also concentrate on 18 March, the date of the funeral of the three policemen and the two bodyguards who were killed in the ambush, and the date too of the first written communication from the Red Brigades. After focusing on the early days of the kidnapping – the nation's initial shock, the funerals, the first communications from the BR and from Moro – the narrative jumps forward to the last weeks of the internment, leaving aside the less dramatic developments in the middle of Moro's detainment. From these latter weeks, the film shows footage of Pope Paul VI's speech on 22 April, in which he would pronounce the damning words that Moro must be released 'senza condizioni' [without conditions], and a short news bulletin from 8 May that announces that the Democrazia Cristiana [Christian Democrats] (DC) will be meeting the following day (too late, as it happens, because Moro will already be dead). Finally, under the closing titles of the film, we see footage from the official state funeral of Moro: the ravaged faces of the political establishment in a grandiose ceremony at which Moro's body is absent, removed from the funeral by his family at his own request.

The television footage serves a variety of purposes.[5] It sketches for spectators some of the key facts of the fifty-five days of Moro's internment, perhaps with a foreign audience in mind (after all, this film received funding from the international production company Sky). It also establishes a 'real,' lending credibility to the film's reconstruction of the historical period. At first glance, this is an anti-Baudrillardian gesture: the television images are presented not as simulation but as real, an *objectivité absolue* with which the film's narrative must interact.

The film's realism does not just lie in its documentation; there is also the careful reconstruction of the apartment, which reflects the space of the real Montalcini flat and the events that occurred within it as outlined in Braghetti's account. The layout of the flat is broadly analogous to her descriptions, although it has been adapted to the needs of the crew and the filming. In the film, Moro is held in a space behind the bookshelves, a space somewhat narrower than the two metres by ninety centimetres described by Braghetti. There is also an antechamber, which she describes as large enough for just one person, but in the film it is widened to make space for filming a number of the *brigatisti* [members of the Red Brigades] contemporaneously, allowing them to meet and discuss just outside Moro's prison. Braghetti also describes the peephole into Moro's room – which figures prominently in the film – and talks about her looking through it (27).

Some of the events that take place within this space have also been lifted directly from Braghetti's written account: Primo's canaries (which in the book, however, belong to Braghetti), Chiara's bus ride to pick up Moro's medicines, the screenplay found in Moro's briefcase, and Chiara's attention to the household's domestic world.[6] Braghetti's record of the day of the kidnap is also reflected in the film. Like Braghetti, Chiara takes a few days off work at the time of the kidnapping, allegedly to go on holiday in the mountains, and uses an ultraviolet lamp to feign a tan (25). Braghetti recounts how she was alone in the apartment most of the morning, with the radio and television on, and how the deafening sound of the helicopters alerted her that the ambush had taken place (7).

This seeming attention to realism, to *objectivité absolue*, and the recreation of history are not, however, where either the focus or the political thrust of the film lies. Its politics in fact emerges only through the *overturning* of objectivity. The portrait of the *brigatisti* bears only the most superficial similarity to the real *brigatisti*, and the shift from realism is signalled immediately through the use of alternative names for them.[7] Germano Maccari and Anna Laura Braghetti are represented by Ernesto and Chiara, the official couple that buys and lives in the flat. Prospero Gallinari, a member of the Red Brigades who had just escaped prison before the Moro kidnapping and had gone into hiding in the Montalcini flat, becomes Primo. Mario Moretti, the head of the Red Brigades and an extreme hardliner, is represented by the fourth, and politically dominant, character in the film, Mariano, who is seen most often talking to Moro.

The film's portrayal of the three male terrorists in the flat is highly superficial and has been described by many critics – rightly – as two-dimensional and historically inaccurate. The group's political discussions are reduced to a minimum, replaced by short catchphrases like 'la classe operaia dirige tutto' [the working class controls everything], which imply that the *brigatisti* are not thinkers but simply parrots, repeating undigested communist propaganda. Whereas Braghetti's account points to the men's repeated in-depth discussions of both military strategy and political ideology, in the film only Mariano engages in any kind of debate, and even then, the import of his conversations is emblematic and reductive. Prior to the ambush we never see the *brigatisti* discussing the complicated military organization of an attack on a key political figure who is protected by bodyguards; instead, we see the men engaged in some do-it-yourself construction of the book-case behind which Moro will be detained.

The mutation is not casual; it implies the whole film's procedure, as, despite the initially apparent *objectivité absolue*, it shifts from a public world to a private domestic one, from ambitious plans to small ones, and from portraying extraordinary men to portraying very ordinary and normal men. There is some motivation for their domesticity in Braghetti's account, which she emphasizes, describing, for instance, how the house 'avvolta nella penombra' [wrapped in shadow] and 'la cucina profumata di cibo' [the kitchen fragrant with food] seemed 'così normale, così consuet[a]' [so normal, so everyday] (Braghetti 2003, 26). However, Bellocchio accentuates this domestic side. The film repeatedly draws attention to the little domestic routines and details of the house: the neat trays with their serviettes that carry Moro's meals (23), the folded clothes, the cooking, and the ironing.

The film situates the four *brigatisti* in perfectly conformist surroundings that ape those of a happy family: the communal meals, Chiara's wedding ring, the crucifix over the matrimonial bed, and the perpetually present television with its news bulletins and variety shows. This is not an avant-garde brigade but a surprisingly normal little group whose rebellion has not even brought about important changes in their own lives; ironically, they continue to conform to the conservative, bourgeois ideals they are wont to attack. There is a historical basis for conceiving the terrorists' behaviour as so obviously conformist: in order to ally suspicions, clandestine members of the Red Brigades were to wear conventional clothes and appear to lead tranquil lives (see Meade 1990, 122). However, Bellocchio's account, which is less interested in historical re-enactment, accentuates this role playing in order to make a different point.

The emphasis on domesticity is one of the key political critiques of the terrorists to arise from the film, and it stems from Bellocchio's analysis of terrorism in *Diavolo in corpo*. In the earlier film, the political critique is centred on Giacomo Pulcini's acceptance of a small, mundane existence after he quits terrorism. There are only two scenes in which this ex-terrorist speaks, and in both he embarks on self-congratulatory monologues in which he outlines his newly won attachment to normality. In the first of these scenes, set in the prison, Giacomo states baldly to his fiancée, Giulia, who has come to visit him, that he now longs for 'una vita normale' [a normal life] and wants to be 'la maggioranza' [in the majority]. He then recites to her a long poem that he has written, which is a hymn to conformity, Sunday lunches, tradition, the family, and the church. In his renunciation of violence, Giacomo has renounced any position of contestation at all and has abandoned resistance to bourgeois norms, which are seen here in terms of family, church, and bourgeois rituals. He has created a black-and-white binary distinction between violent rebellion and conformism and, having first chosen the former, now chooses the latter. Bellocchio condemns this, a condemnation that is implicit in the mise en scène and the photography of the scene in which Giacomo recites his poem to his fiancée: overexposed shots of a bare, elemental, white prison room are emblematic of sterility.

In both *Diavolo in corpo* and *Buongiorno, notte*, the attack on the terrorists' innate normality, represented by domesticity, is coupled with a condemnation of their lack of sexual passion. While Giacomo recites his hymn to normality, Giulia tries to stimulate him sexually, but he rejects her, irritatedly telling her that she is hurting him. This rejection is part of the Fagiolian discourse on his lack of instinct and vitality and on his consequent inability to meet her on an instinctive, sexual level. Both his political and moral choices are motivated by his mind and his will.

In *Buongiorno, notte*, the discourse on absent sexual relations is explored further. Enzo, the young man who courts the terrorist Chiara, accuses her of dressing like a nun (and her clothes throughout the film are deliberately intended to appear concealing). Later in the film, Aldo Moro criticizes the terrorists for adopting a brand of Marxism more extreme than his own Catholicism, especially in its treatment of the body: 'disprezza il corpo più di quanto facciamo noi cattolici' [it despises the body more than we Catholics do]. Despite the fact that Braghetti would marry Prospero Gallinari in 1981, in the film almost no physical affection occurs between Chiara and Primo (who represents Prospero) beyond the briefest of kisses during the fireworks of New Year's Eve, 1978. Moreover, sexual attraction never blossoms between the four young terrorists, despite their living in close quarters. Overhung by a crucifix, the large double bed becomes emblematic of this lack. Chiara sleeps in it beside Primo or Ernesto while they are off duty, but between the bodies lies a great gulf; on the single occasion in which Chiara's hand instinctively seeks out something or somebody across the covers, she touches Ernesto and instantly, apologetically, withdraws. Bellocchio condemns the *brigatisti* for suppressing their instinct, for refusing to enter into a real contact with the Other, and preferring instead to live by a cold and mechanical ideology that denies such contact.

The third line of attack against the terrorists, present in *Buongiorno, notte* (but absent in *Diavolo in corpo*), revolves around motifs of blindness and closure. In *Buongiorno, notte*, a dialectic is established between the television (which represents the real) and the reconstructed world of the four *brigatisti*. The film cuts between the television screen's grainy images and the crisp digital images of the *brigatisti* who watch and respond emotionally to these images. The television footage has been carefully selected and alternates between political news bulletins treating the Moro affair and mindless Italian variety shows, which imply the normality and superficiality – even stupidity – of the *brigatisti*.

This television footage supplies an 'outside' – a public world that interacts, and often significantly conflicts, with the hidden and private world behind the doors of 8 Via Montalcini. It is especially in this conflict between documentary image and fictional image that the third critique lies: despite the apparent objectivity of the footage, there is little neutrality or casualness in the choice of the excerpts or in the way in which they are inserted into the film. They are deliberately selected in order to forward the argument that the terrorists are blind to reality.

The film's reconstruction of the morning of 16 March is tense and exciting, an excitement with which it is hard for the spectator not to identify. In the highly choreographed build-up, accompanied by a rousing, apparently diegetic soundtrack that suggests the dawning of a monumental event, Chiara wakes and contemplates the coming day. She dramatically closes the apartment's curtains, hears a helicopter, and rushes to the television, changing channels until finally the news of the ambush breaks. In all of this, we are being asked to identify with Chiara – with her excitement and with her outburst of suppressed joy at the bulletin. The news confirms that her men, who are not back yet, have been successful. It breaks the tension that has been building in the events and on the musical soundtrack.

The first news bulletin, taken from Giancarlo Santalmassi's newsflash on RAI 2, is crucial in outlining the facts of the case: the ambush of two cars in Via Fani, the killing of Moro's bodyguards and three policemen. The second television sequence – spliced into the film after the *brigatisti* have returned to Via Montalcini and sequestered Moro – already gives a flavour of what is to come: a scission between the television images (representing the real) and the false reading of reality proposed by the Via Montalcini *brigatisti*. While the *brigatisti* attend only to their prize, the second television sequence shows a policeman's body shrouded in a sheet. An ominous gong on the soundtrack accompanies the chilling footage. After a brief reaction shot of Ernesto, who is watching these images attentively from the sofa, the television footage returns: jerkily the camera slides over the sheet, picks up the detail of a dead man's hand under the sheet, and from here follows a very red thread of blood (clearly coloured post-production) to a pistol abandoned on the road and to one of the two ambushed cars. As the gongs continue, it is clear that any identification that spectators may feel with the *brigatisti*'s successful ambush has been ruptured, and the film begins to take on a funereal tone. This footage is the first sign that the *brigatisti* have misread reality and failed to see how the brutal gunning down of five innocent men, five men from the very classes that the Red Brigades were claiming to defend, would affect public opinion. We hear the words of the BR's first communication, superimposed on the images of the dead policemen and guards. The BR state that with this act they have brought their attack to the 'cuore dello stato' [heart of the state].[8] However, image and soundtrack are deliberately at odds: the images of the bodies of ordinary policemen – not statesmen – strewn across the road do not represent the heart of the state.

The film's thesis that the Red Brigades are out of touch with what is really going on in society is compounded by the footage from a mass demonstration of unions that evening in Piazza San Giovanni, Rome. Luciano Lama, head of the most important national workers' union, the Confederazione Generale Italiana del Lavoro (CGIL), makes an impassioned speech in which he denounces the Red Brigades as murderers and criminals. In the crowd, red PCI flags and white DC flags intermingle. The unionized left, with which the Red Brigades had initially had significant links, thus officially denies their support. The presence of PCI flags among the crowd indicates that communists are not necessarily behind the terrorists either. The four *brigatisti* sit together in front of the television during the San Giovanni demonstration, incredulous and indignant that the crowd does not rebel against Lama. The film cuts the footage abruptly at the words pronounced by Lama: 'dobbiamo aprire gli occhi' [we must open our eyes].

As many critics have noted, motifs of blindness and sight are taken forward in the film through a rich tapestry of symbols centred on eyes and looking. The shot that follows Lama's call to 'open our eyes' is, ironically, of Chiara's eyes closing as she falls asleep. The very title of the film (*Buongiorno, notte*) refers to light and darkness; Chiara's name means 'light' or 'clarity'; and the film script found inside Moro's case is written by Enzo Passoscuro, whose surname means literally 'dark step.' Despite the triumphal music in the build-up to the attack, Chiara's actions are ones that the film does not condone: she is shown closing the curtains on all the windows of the house and shutting over the window grating. In these movements she is protecting herself and the other *brigatisti* so that they cannot be seen; however, more important for the message of the film, from this position they cannot see. The apartment's penumbra becomes a metaphor too for this. The emphasis on sight and looking reflects the discourses around terrorism in the post-9/11 climate and, therefore, slots the film into a contemporary context that plays on the kind of discourses forwarded by Jean Baudrillard (2002) and Slavoj Žižek (2002) at that time. It also draws on the discourse of blindness and isolation of the bourgeoisie that is forwarded in the mise en scène of films like Bellocchio's earlier *Salto nel vuoto*.

Buongiorno, notte forwards a reading that shows the *brigatisti* as conformist, lulled by normality, rigid and asexual, blind, manipulated by ideology, and unable to really connect with other human beings. It privileges not a recreation of the historical period, nor even simply a 'reflexive palimpsest' (O'Leary 2008), although it is also these, but instead it deliberately manipulates history in order to forward a particular and partial agenda that has to do with re-evaluating political terrorism. This political critique, however, still only represents a small part of what the film is about. Ultimately, the film does not in fact centre on either the *objectivité absolue* of a re-enaction of the fifty-four days or a critique of the terrorists but on the figure of Chiara, the female 'focalizer' for the tale and the character with whom we are called to identify. It is Chiara as focalizer who brings interiority into the heart of the film.

Maya Sansa's Chiara is not Anna Laura Braghetti. Although in the preparation for the film Sansa was asked to read Braghetti's biography and other material pertinent to the Moro affair, Bellocchio did not want her to meet Braghetti or other members of the terrorist organizations lest her portrayal be influenced by them;[9] in other words, Bellocchio was not looking for a realistic depiction of character. Moreover, in her talk at the University of Washington, Rome, Sansa claimed that Bellocchio conceived Chiara's character as an amalgam of Braghetti and Adriana Faranda, a member of the Red Brigades who was less directly involved in the Moro kidnapping. Faranda claims only to have acted as postman during Moro's detention, collecting the letters and communications written in Via Montalcini and ensuring they got to their destination (Drake 1996, 126).

Anna Laura Braghetti was an *irriducibile*; in other words, she did not disassociate herself from the Red Brigades or ask for pardon. Nor did she help the police with their enquiries until the beginning of the 1990s. After the murder of Aldo Moro she continued to be involved in Red Brigade campaigns, and at the moment of her arrest in May 1980 she was planning the murder of a senior member of the Italian judiciary, Giovanni de Matteo (Braghetti 2003, 155). Braghetti is therefore far from the sensitive Chiara of Bellocchio's film, whose desire to see Moro freed almost overwhelms her. Moreover, Bellocchio's Chiara is almost devoid of serious political consciousness. This makes her hard to reconcile with Braghetti, who had been involved in politics from the age of fourteen and had completed two years in the extra-parliamentary Lotta Continua movement before joining the BR alongside her then lover, Bruno Seghetti. At the time of the kidnapping, Braghetti had her own small pistol, which she would use a year later during an attack on a provincial office of the DC (Braghetti 2003, 29). This pistol, significantly, is never shown in the film. The militant, politically conscious Braghetti does not correspond to Chiara. Bellocchio has other ideas in mind when constructing her character.

Chiara emerges, in fact, from some hints of resistance expressed in the accounts of two female members of the Red Brigades. In Braghetti's written account, which is in itself a fictionalized reconstruction, she talks about her alienation with regard to the military and masculine aspects of the *brigatista* life. She claims that she did not have 'grandi rapporti con l'aspetto militare del sequestro' [a great relationship with the military aspect of the kidnapping] (28), and her account is full of her sense of difference and extraneousness as a woman: 'la guerra è una cosa dei maschi e, quando le femmine ci si trovano dentro, in un modo o nell'altro sono fuori posto' [war is a man's thing and, when women find themselves in it, in one way or another they are out of place] (29). Her account too seems to suggest that Braghetti felt alienated by the men's political discussions, finding them boring (43). In a key phrase, she says that if she had taken seriously even once this sense of extraneousness, she would have saved lives (29). It is here – in the lost potential for an alternative outcome – that Bellocchio finds the inspiration for his Chiara. He fuses these hints of resistance in Braghetti's autobiography with the resistance of Adriana Faranda, another female *brigatista* who, during the fifty-five days, repeatedly pleaded with Mario Moretti for Moro's release, but to no avail. Faranda believed that the Red Brigades were making a huge political mistake in annihilating Moro. During the Moro trials Faranda claimed to have been 'troubled by her conscience' in the wake of the killing, repeatedly claiming that the *brigatisti* had constructed a 'vision that did not correspond to reality' and that 'two rigidities had killed Moro: the militarist mentality and the intransigence of government' (Drake 1996, 124–5). How deeply rooted her regrets really were, when she too went on to commit further crimes, is questionable, but it is this *potential* for a different outcome, seen in both Faranda's and Braghetti's accounts, that Bellocchio uses as a basis for his resistant Chiara. The message appears to be that if Chiara/Braghetti/Faranda had followed her feminine instincts, Moro might not have died. Behind both their accounts lies the continuing influence of the Fagiolian model, with its emphasis on the importance and *possibility* of transformation and the refusal of the ineluctability of history. Bellocchio is aware of this:

Non potevo subire la tragedia di venticinque anni prima, non potevo accettare quella fatalità religiosa. Dovevo tradirla. Dovevo ribellarmi a quella cronaca inerte, indifferente e disperata. E Anna Laura Braghetti divenne in sceneggiatura un altro personaggio, Chiara appunto. L'infedeltà occupò sempre più spazio nella sceneggiatura e ancora più nel film. (Bellocchio 2003, 8)

[I couldn't suffer the tragedy of twenty-five years ago. I couldn't accept that religious fatality. I had to betray it. I had to rebel against that inert, indifferent, desperate account. And in the screenplay Anna Laura Braghetti became another person: Chiara. This lack of faithfulness occupied increasing space in the screenplay and even more in the film.]

This resisting Chiara is the entry point for a high level of subjective material in the film, and her presence allows a reassessment of some of the material that might be considered objective, like the unremitting focus on the *brigatista* apartment, which may initially seem a 'natural' emphasis for the film. Instead, the film's structuring of the story almost entirely within the parameters of this space is a structural tightness that does not reflect Braghetti's autobiography. The film begins with the entry of the *brigatisti* into the space of the apartment and ends with Moro's tragic exit from it, whereas Braghetti's narrative cuts to and fro between the Moro affair and Braghetti's life before and after the kidnap. This transformation in the temporality of the original text shifts attention firmly from the public and political to the private. In the scenes of the ambush, too, the shifting of attention from the military ambush to the inner space of the apartment (where Chiara is waiting for the men to return) marks a shifting from genres of adventure and police thriller towards character subjectivity.[10] Chiara dramatically closes the curtains and the window grating, isolating the house from the outside; Braghetti, however, went out into the street to wait for the returning cars. We are in a space that is typically Bellocchian: the apartment, with its blind windows and chiaroscuro, resembles the apartment or psyche of *Salto nel vuoto* and is connected to the outside only by a television.[11]

The emphases on closure and on the domestic are clearly shifting the film's discourse from a realistic reconstruction of events to a subjectivizing and emblematizing of them. Chiara's portrait becomes indeed a private, not a public, one. This is particularly evident in the importance that the film gives to her inner world of dreams.

Chiara's dreams begin on the night of the kidnap. That night, as she sleeps, we see black-and-white images of an empty bench covered in thick snow, a melancholic scene suggesting a forlorn absence and a deeply penetrating chill. The bench is Lenin's. The second dream, occurring the following night, again shows documentary images of a wintry landscape, with a close-up of a large flag flapping, placards showing Lenin's face, and a train traversing a snowy bridge. Eerie Russian music haunts the soundtrack. As the dream ends, a young girl, shot in close-up, looks gently but piercingly out of the screen towards Chiara and us, the spectators. Later in the film, just after the terrorists announce Moro's death sentence, Bellocchio repeats the motif of the documentary-style hallucination in a complex and emotional sequence in which images are rapidly intercut. Chiara has just been handed a letter that Moro has written to his wife. As she looks at the letter, we hear Moro's voice reading the words, beginning 'Mia dolcissima Noretta' [My dear sweet Nora], but his voice is interrupted by the overlaying of a second male voice, which is referred to in the screenplay (79) as the voice of Chiara's father. This second voice, one intimately connected to Chiara's past, reads a chilling letter from *Lettere dei condannati a morte della Resistenza* [*Letters by Resistance Fighters Condemned to Death*], in which a young man writes a letter to his lover on the eve his execution. Then, as a female singer shrills wordlessly on the Pink Floyd soundtrack, distressing black-and-white scenes of the execution of Resistance fighters (from Roberto Rossellini's *Paisà* [Paisan, 1946]) are inserted between shots of a devastated Aldo Moro in his cell and close-ups of the predatory eyes of the male *brigatisti* looking in at him. The sequence ends with images of Chiara's tear-stained face juxtaposed against the same poignant black-and-white close-up shot of the little Russian girl seen in the second dream, a girl who seems to interpellate Chiara, and us, from the frame.

There is nothing as personal, as subjective, perhaps, as dreams. Yet Chiara's first two dreams have as their referent the death of Lenin and the removal of his body to Moscow. They link the actions of the Red Brigades in kidnapping Moro with the death of the man who was a great symbol of communism and whose death was read, by many, as marking the end of the communist utopia. After the death of Lenin would come Stalin, whose regime would be found to be bloody and corrupt. These dreams imply the tragic nature of the Red Brigades' action from its very outset, and also their inability to bring about the utopia they seek, a utopia that is already geographically and historically distant. These dreams, paradoxically, make a political comment, and they do this by using 'real' documentary images. However, they also go inside Chiara's growing sadness. The little girl's poignant, watchful eyes in the close-up that ends the second sequence, presumably showing the sorrow of a young Russian child in response to Lenin's death, seem to mirror Chiara's eyes, mutely warning her, mutely and impotently watching over her as she sleeps – reminding us perhaps of the lost child that Chiara once was.

Chiara's final hallucination, though made up wholly of an intercutting of public documentary material with reaction shots of the *brigatisti* and Moro, also paradoxically gives us an insight into Chiara's tortured mind. The presence of her father's voice implies Bellocchio's intention to link the Resistance material to Chiara's personal past, to give a hint of where her political militancy came from; it suggests that Chiara grew up in the midst of supporters of the Resistance. However, by linking the death of the Resistance fighters with the death of Moro, this sequence shows how Chiara's action is a betrayal, not a continuation, of that in which she believed. The return of the little girl's gaze at the end of the sequence is therefore far more tragic this time: Chiara has betrayed the vital ideals of her childhood. This young face therefore condemns her.

What is intriguing about these dreams is that the material, without exception, seems public, intertextual, and political – not personal – having been selected from Russian documentary footage of the death of Lenin and Stalinist Russia and from the Italian neo-realist film *Paisà*. The use of public, rather than private, material in the oneiric sequences serves to show how the *brigatisti* have interiorized a political sphere that is geographically and even temporally distant and, in so doing, have deleted and replaced their personal thoughts and desires. This aligns with the Red Brigades' practice of controlling and suppressing personal emotions (including compassion for the victim) where these are in conflict with the Brigades' ideas or ideology. However, the oneiric sequences also show how the contextualising of public material within the sphere of the private can enable it to be read in a new way. No longer do these documentary images mean only what director Dziga Vertov originally expected them to mean (to record the sorrow surrounding the death of Lenin); through their recontextualization they come to express a complex set of the fears, doubts, hopes, and sorrows surrounding the death of Moro, emotions that (by never being definitely tied to Chiara's point of view) also implicate us, the spectators, in a kind of collective dream or nightmare.[12] The images of Aldo Moro walking free through the flat at night are far more than just an emanation of Chiara's desires. He appears to belong to the very house, as if he represents the desire of the spectator, the Italian nation, and Bellocchio himself to witness a *different* ending to this tragic episode – an escape from the ineluctability of history.[13] As in previous films, the oneiric material here creates a multiple layering. Past and present, public and private, individual and choral, real and hypothetical co-habit this space, implying that whatever divides them is highly penetrable and porous.

Through her dreams, through the absence of a gun, and through her domesticity and gentleness, Chiara's character is withdrawn from the objectivity of political cinema. Hers is not a portrait of a real terrorist. However, this withdrawal does not leave Chiara's character devoid of political import, despite the subjectivity that it conveys. The political import of her character re-emerges through a series of shots between her and Moro through the peephole. They show both extreme close-ups of her eye looking into the prison and reaction shots of what her eye looks at. Both action and reaction shots are iris shots, where the centre of the image is brightly lit and the surround falls into blackness, thus creating a dramatic chiaroscuro that reflects and essentializes the play of light and shadow elsewhere in the film. These shots represent her eye looking in on Moro as he sleeps, writes, or discusses politics with the male members of the Red Brigades, and they imply the partial and extraneous nature of her vision (she, unlike the men, never enters Moro's den and is only ever the onlooker to events). Paradoxically, the peephole shots allow her to centre in on Moro and see his humanity. However partial is her point of view, Chiara is the only one who *sees* a real Moro, and not a hollow symbol of Moro, as her comrades do. Chiara is the only one, too, who is shown as having her eyes (and ears) open to the world beyond the apartment. Only she is shown outside the apartment: on buses, at the newspaper stand, in a café, and at her workplace. These are all spaces in which she comes in contact with everyday opinions of the kidnapping. She brings back the news: people say that they are murderers.

The door to Moro's prison becomes a kind of mask that can be penetrated by the eye, revealing the inside and the unseen – mimicking the way cinema reveals the private and the unseen. However, what is strange about these shots is how Moro looks back. On a number of occasions he catches or almost catches Chiara's eye. These brief lookbacks at Chiara or us, the spectators, are unsettling. Not only does he almost catch Chiara's eye; he also almost catches ours because his brief glances towards Chiara are also glances towards the camera. This is especially so in one case, where Moro's eye appears in extreme closeup. These shots imply not only that we are intruding on his privacy but that he is intruding on ours. They suggest that he is interpellating not just Chiara – with a direct look that would force her to see his humanity – but us, too. They implicate us in the reaction against history, in the desire to see history changed.

This is not the first time that this implicating look has appeared in Bellocchio's cinema. In *La condanna* the dynamics of looking are established around the rape scene at the beginning of the film, where the camera's penetration into wholly private space is met by the character's look-back. After pursuing Sandra around the locked museum, the architect finally seduces her. At the point of orgasm the architect/rapist disappears mysteriously from both image and soundtrack; now we see only Sandra's body and hear only *her* breathing. The spectator or camera literally stands in for the lover at this moment and is lovingly interpellated by Sandra with her eyes, which look directly up at us, and with her arms, which reach towards us. Sandra catches our eye and therefore positions us as the lover or rapist, a shot that on one level mirrors the look-back of pornographic film-making and, on another, makes us directly complicit with the rape or seduction – thereby implicating us in all the arguments over power, consent, and rape that will take place later in the film. Sandra's look back at the camera breaks the illusion that she is in a private space and seems to acknowledge the very public nature of cinema making and cinema going. By acknowledging us with her eyes, she acknowledges the public space of every cinema that will screen her.

Another striking episode that plays on the look-back is found at the end of *Salto nel vuoto*. This exquisite sequence is chilling in the lightness of its touch, as it shows the judge's final moments inside his house before he jumps suddenly (and lightly) from the window to his death. Marta and her maid have just left for the seaside. The judge, alone, walks through this space, which is now wholly his own, wholly private. But what happens next is unexpected. The camera detaches from him and goes off on its own accord around the apartment, as if finally released from its perennial task of slavishly following the film's protagonists. It pans around the space gracefully, exploring the rooms and coming across the judge repeatedly, as if almost by accident. The judge seems irritated by its presence (which is also our presence) and gets up brusquely from the piano and from the toilet seat when it enters his space. Out in the corridor, with the camera now by his side, he mutters, 'È casa mia … faccio quello che mi pare, no?' [This is my house … I can do what I like, can't I?] This rhetorical question is addressed to the camera, since, while pronouncing it, he glances at it – and therefore at us – for approval. The spectator finds himself or herself implicitly agreeing that, yes, of course he can do what he likes. The judge then walks quickly away from us, towards the window, and lightly, almost imperceptibly, jumps out. In this extraordinary sequence we are positioned as voyeuristically and intrusively involved in the private world that the judge inhabits, almost as if we are persecuting him and certainly unwittingly giving our approval to his suicide. The suicide is almost a snub to the spectator.

In these three very different scenes, from *Salto nel vuoto*, *La condanna*, and *Buongiorno, notte*, the spectator is involved with crucial – although clearly very different – intensely private moments in a character's life. The look towards the camera on these occasions transgresses the illusion of privacy and appears to involve us directly with the character –

no longer as passive spectator but as active, even irritating, pursuer and accomplice (in the ending to *Salto nel vuoto*), as lover, rapist or voyeur (in *La condanna*), and as female terrorist with the choice before her of whether to free Moro or to let him die (in *Buongiorno, notte*). The interpellation of the spectator in this way, especially in *Buongiorno, notte*, is a deeply political move. Despite their plunging us into a very personal and intimate world, Moro's sudden glances back at Chiara (or us) align us with Chiara's choice in front of Moro. It implies an active spectator who must make the decision that Braghetti or Chiara does not make: to resist terrorism, to see the victim always and above all as a human being, and, importantly, to connect.

Despite its concentration on the individual, its focus on the inner space of the Montalcini apartment, its deliberately and stridently anti-historical and misleading portraits of the *brigatisti*, and its bifurcating false ending, *Buongiorno, notte* does have political messages and can be defined, at least in part, as a political film. The film shows that the *objectivité absolue* of the re-enacted and documented historical context is not enough to make the film political. It is the film's forwarding of a distinct and controversial political discourse on terrorism – which it associates negatively with normality, with an inability to make real connections with the Other (symbolized in the absence of sexual relationships), and with the *brigatisti's* inability to *see* the real – that begins to bring real political import to the film. However, the political nature of this film resides not just in these factors but also at the very heart of the film's interiority, in its discourse on the need for transformation. In *Buongiorno, notte's* call for the recognition of the humanity of the individual (addressed directly to the spectator through Moro's glance, and through Moro's wanderings about the flat that are unhooked from a point of view), the film is proposing political change through the assumption of personal responsibility.

Vincere: The Stripped Self

Vincere, released in 2009, uses a similar formula to that employed in *Buongiorno, notte*: taking a true story from Italy's recent past, it interweaves political and personal material. It uses documentary film footage from the Istituto Luce archive and other cinematic and written documents to supplement the personal and fictionalized story of a woman who claimed to be Mussolini's first wife, Ida Dalser, and their child, Benito Albino Mussolini, both of whom were imprisoned and died in mental

institutions during the fascist regime. The film interprets these two figures as victims of Mussolini's unrelenting quest for glory.

Vincere, like *Buongiorno, notte*, revisits a problematic political period in
Italy's past and relies in part on a realistic reconstruction of events. The
film is based not only on historical visual documents from the period
but also on the medical records that Bellocchio had seen at Pergine's
psychiatric hospital, on conversations with people at Sopramonte (Ida's
hometown), and especially on three sources published or released in
2005–2006. These three sources included the journalistic reconstruction of events found in Alfredo Pieroni's book *Il figlio segreto del Duce*,
in which Pieroni reconstructs the story based on clinical records, on
conversations, and on letters written by Ida and others; Marco Zeni's *La
moglie di Mussolini*, a more rigorous and well-documented book; and a
television documentary, *Il segreto di Mussolini*, by Fabrizio Laurenti and
Gianfranco Norelli that was broadcast on RAI 3 in January 2005 as the
culmination of three years of research. Pieroni, Zeni, Laurenti, and
Norelli all argue that despite the absence of concrete proof, Mussolini
and Ida were most probably married and that she and her son were
eliminated because their presence, and perhaps the threat of the big-
amy it implied, was an obstacle to Mussolini's reinvention of himself as
a family man especially during the 1920s.

The facts of the story told in the film closely reflect the original story,
at least as it is found in the documents used for the film (which do contain inaccuracies and contradictions). The film uses documents also to
track some of the key steps in the history of the period: from the assas-
sination of Archduke Franz Ferdinand (1914) to the Russian revolution
(1917), the March on Rome (1922), the Lateran Pact (1929), Mussolini's
famous 'Vincere' speech in which he announces his country's entry into
war (1940) and from which the film takes its title, and his final demise,
symbolized in the crushing of his statue at the end of the film (1945).
Some tinkering has been done to the facts, but it is relatively minor. For
instance, Ida's first passionate and bloody encounter with Mussolini in
Trent in 1907 appears to be Bellocchio's invention because Mussolini only
moved to Trent in 1909 and no record exists of them having met prior to
1913. Ida's capture is also dramatized in such a way that it contradicts
the sources; she was actually arrested on her way to a hotel in Trent
where she had arranged to meet her old acquaintance, and close ally of
Mussolini, the MP Pietro Fedele. In the film, this event is spectacular-
ized by setting the capture in the Roman-style colonnaded mausoleum
to Cesare Battisti outside the city (a building that was erected almost a

decade later, in 1935). As Battisti was a nationalist executed in Trent for fighting against the Austro-Hungarian Empire in the First World War, the new setting takes on a political tone: the mausoleum emphasizes the fascist pro-war and nationalist agenda, the city's changing historical identity, and the 'Romanizing' of even the northern landscape.

One key fact with which the film has to grapple is the marriage between Ida and Mussolini, about which there are still opposing critical views: there is no definitive proof that it occurred, but those who argue that it happened claim that the fascists destroyed the evidence. The film's screening of the wedding allows opposing readings to coexist, as the scene can be read either as a flashback (that is, as factual) or as a dream or delusion; the fact that the wedding scene is collocated outside the ongoing historical chronology of the story, being linked to the morning of Ida's capture more than ten years later (the wedding is presumed to have happened in 1914 [Zeni 2005]) and screened only through Ida's point of view, suggests that it has been subjectivized. Moreover, as Ida is lying in bed when the scene begins, and the scene itself is stylized and choreographed, one might suspect the presence of the oneiric. Ultimately, the film hesitates between the two readings, allowing for both.

The ideal of *objectivité absolue* is more marked in *Vincere* than it is in *Buongiorno, notte*, where, despite the socio-political reconstruction, the emphasis is ultimately on fictionality, subjectivity, the oneiric, and hypothetical worlds. In *Vincere* the reconstruction is closer to the sources, and even the cinematography endeavours to mirror the styles of the time (the dramatic titles that fly towards us fast and aggressively follow, Bellocchio claims, the styles of revolutionary futurism and Eisenstein [Bellocchio 2009]). Nonetheless, despite the more empirical approach, the emphasis is not directly on institutional politics. This is not the life of Mussolini or the rise of fascism, although such elements are sketched in; what counts are the consequences of the political on the personal and the interrelation between the two worlds. The individual, personal history, not the official political history, is the focus of the film, as seen in the employment of a female focalizer (Ida) and the use of a melodramatic cinema code.

The interlinking and opposition of political and private spheres is notable in the film, and the space of the cinema theatre becomes a dominant measure of how the political and social history and mores of a nation are aligned or juxtaposed with individuals within that history (this reflects the use of television in *Buongiorno, notte*). Not only are both Ida and Benito Albino, her son, frequently returned to this space, but the films and documents screened directly interact with their, and the audiences', personal stories; this fact is emphasized by the frequent silhouetting of audience members against the images projected on the screen. The interlinking of public and private material is also seen in the film's predilection for the kind of dissolves seen in early cinema where the historical document and the fictional reconstruction are juxtaposed and overlap.

The interlinking of public and private is also linked to the emergence of prominent gender discourse. In *Buongiorno, notte* the gendering of the private as female and the political as male was incomplete because, however much Chiara's character was depoliticized, domesticated, and brought within the feminized sphere of the personal, the men (both terrorists and Aldo Moro) were also domesticated, imprisoned within the walls of the apartment, and removed from the 'outer' world; in other words, the political sphere itself was 'feminized.' In *Vincere*, however, the gender split between the two worlds is stark. *Vincere* is literally the narrative of the making of a man, Mussolini, on the one hand, and the making of a woman, Ida Dalser, on the other, and the narrative leads to a definitive separation of the two worlds and a juxtaposing of the relative power and moral value that each sphere represents.

The film, with few exceptions, follows a rigorously linear, chronological narrative that traces the rise of the young Mussolini to power and ends with his destruction, framing his life only from his entry into politics. It partially subverts the conventional historical retellings, by placing Mussolini, albeit briefly, into the domestic sphere of melodrama until he is established fully as a political figure, at which point he leaves this sphere and enters the political world. Once established, his only further appearances in the ongoing melodrama of the private, domestic world he has left behind take place on newsreels. The black-and-white historical Mussolini, now far more powerful, opposes his former fictional self, played by Filippo Timi, and literally abandons Ida's world by being spirited into a different medium. The space of Mussolini as political figure expands geographically (Trent-Milan-Rome) in direct opposition to the contraction of Ida's space (Trent-Milan-Pergine); his narrative moves to Rome, the capital and seed of Italy's long national history, while Ida is forced into silence in the provinces. The black-and-white footage used for the film's opening titles presents the male public phallic world in essence: soaring industrial chimneys reach towards the sky and vie with the domination of Milan's Gothic cathedral spires; both industry and church appear as mighty and dominating institutional-ized Nietzchean male structures that will crush the female world.

The film's focus is not ultimately on the making of the male world of the dictator (which would have made the film more obviously politi-cal) but on the effects of it on the film's female protagonist and on her attempts to resist her fate. The real Ida Dalser, as briefly implied by the film's first image of Ida framed within the sophisticated Milanese beauty salon she owned, was a fashionable and independent young woman; born just outside Trent (which was in the Austro-Hungarian Empire at the time), she was educated in Paris and in 1913 opened her own salon in Milan. Her narrative is one of progressive loss, exclusion, and an enforced retreat from the public sphere, which she bitterly con-tests to the end. Ida is the classic Bellocchian Antigone, a rebel at sea in the fascist world where the part she needs to play (as a psychiatrist warns her towards the end of the film) is the good fascist housewife, silent and obedient. She is eliminated not just because she is a threat to Mussolini's self-construction but also because she is an element foreign to the political ideologies of institutionalized fascism – the obedient wife and mother, ready for self-sacrifice.

Ida's exclusion from the public and political world of Mussolini is set in place early in the film. In 1914, just after they first become lovers, she is shown entering the offices of the socialist newspaper *Avanti*, where Mussolini is a journalist. Close-ups of male hands holding the door of the meeting room closed against her symbolize her position as outsider. When she finally forces her way in – the only woman to enter this male political space – she appears on the upper balcony of the room, alone, reflecting her alterity and exclusion and briefly aligning her visually with the position of Jewish women in a synagogue. Ida is also progres-sively excluded from Mussolini's domestic, private world, as demon-strated in a tragic scene where she watches him playfully and lovingly kiss his young daughter, Edda (born to Rachele, the woman who Mus-solini would later marry, in 1910). Her exclusion becomes total, how-ever, only after she persists in repeatedly asserting her identity – as wife of Mussolini and bearer of his firstborn son – and she is forcibly taken to the mental institution in Pergine, near Trent.

The parallel, but opposing, forms of communication neatly divide the enforced private world that Ida inhabits from the public and political world in which Mussolini lives. Ida's texts are her letters – handwritten, suggesting the personal, but still political in that they are addressed to those in power (Mussolini, the Pope, the King) – and her scrawlings on the walls of her room in Pergine mental asylum. Both the letters and the scrawlings are without addressees. The pathetic scene in which she climbs high up on the bars of the asylum to try to get the letters outside results only in a nun carefully picking up each one from the courtyard into which they have fallen. Mussolini and those in political power, on the other hand, have the full force of the media and the propaganda machine behind them. While her words never get over the walls of the institution in which she is imprisoned, *their* words are ubiquitous. Words are graffitied on walls (the slogan 'Il Duce ha sempre ragione' [The Duce is always right] appears in the background of the shot in which Ida is being taken back to the mental institution from which she has escaped); we see the regime's words being typed across the cinema screen as they officially communicate Ida's house arrest in Sopramonte, and other words fly towards the audience in the form of graphic signs like 'AUDACIA!' [Audaciousness!]. Photographs, too, set up the contrast between the two worlds: the young Mussolini's official photograph is taken of him proudly posed in front of a black fascist flag, with a dagger between the skull's teeth; Ida's photograph is taken in the cold blue light of the mental institution's flash, her face – almost devoid of makeup – seems naked, she has lost her own clothes and wears the institution's shift, the signs of the attack are still fresh on her face, and the composition resembles a police photograph, rather than a portrait. While Mussolini actively and forcibly constructs his identity through his portrait, her portrait shows how her identity has been stripped from her. Like the written texts, these visual texts also have different addressees within the filmic: Ida's photograph will disappear, like her letters, into the hidden world behind the institution's walls; Mussolini's is destined to have wide and public circulation.

The public world is aligned with the power, strength, and violence of aggressive fascism and an obedient church, while the private world – aligned largely with the feminine – appears to fail to make an impact on it. Despite Ida's great strength of will and fighting character, she is silenced, her letters remain undelivered, and she dies without regaining her freedom or drawing attention to what Mussolini had done to her. However, Ida's final look-back at the camera subverts this pessimistic narrative at least in part and returns a small, but significant, element of power to the female and personal sphere. This long gaze towards the camera as Ida, captured again by the authorities, is taken back to the mental asylum implicates us as audience (as do the look-backs of Chiara, the Judge, and Sandra) and calls on us not to be complicit with the regime but to carry on the fight that Ida, imprisoned, is unable to do. This look also implies a link with the current political situation: at the time in which the film was researched and made, Berlusconi had just been returned to power, and in interviews Bellocchio (2009) has likened Italy under fascism to Italy under Berlusconi. The link between Berlusconi and Mussolini, frequently established in contemporary Italian culture (see Brook and Ross 2009), makes this look-back particularly pertinent; it throws into relief the graffiti on the wall behind Ida's car as she is driven away, which proclaims 'Il Duce ha sempre ragione,' as if to remind Italians that just because someone has the monopoly over politics and their communication, as did Mussolini and as does Berlusconi, this does not mean that their decisions are right and should go unchallenged. Therefore, despite the ultimately negative outcome for both Ida and her son, the film's political message suggests that she, and we, should not be silent. When Ida screams up at Mussolini from the courtyard below the office of *Il Popolo d'Italia*, a poster on the wall behind her shows a woman with her finger to her lips and the caption 'Tacere' [Be quiet]. The regime expects silence and succeeds finally in silencing those who rebel against it, but the film ultimately defends the importance of individuals' maintaining their individual identity and speaking out against a dominant political discourse, despite the consequences.

Overall, the political meaning of this film lies clearly, on the most obvious level, with its anti-fascism. It is a straightforward denouncement of fascism as a brutalizing of the Italian people, its violent male ethos damaging the populous, silencing and suppressing those who stand up against it, rendering mad others, and killing through brutal wars and violent attacks on adversaries like the socialists. The theme of blood and violence is clear: from Ida's first bloody encounter with Mussolini to the brutal suppression of the socialists in Sopramonte and the black-and-white documentary images of the destruction of buildings and lives in Italy during the Second World War that are screened at the end of the film. The violence is there too in the early sex scenes, where the focus, unusually for Bellocchio's films, is on the male body. Mussolini's body is shown as strong, muscular, and violent, and Ida's, in contrast, seems fragile. The clip that appears in *Vincere* of Giovanni Pastrone's *Maciste Alpino* (*The Warrior*, 1916) and the poster visible later in the film of Pastrone's *Cabiria* (1914) reminds us of Mussolini's fashioning of his body on the strongman figure of Maciste, who appears in both Pastrone's films and is associated with the protection and colonial expansion of Italy.

Fascism is described in the film as blind (as implied by the rather obvious scene of a group of blind children, followed – again rather obviously – by members of the church, crossing in front of Mussolini and Ida as the future Duce discusses his plans, and then dissolving into images of soldiers marching). This is the same discourse as that used in *Buongiorno, notte* to criticize terrorism. Fascism is also proposed, however, as a kind of thievery. One of the first sentences that Mussolini utters is, 'Non sono un ladro' [I'm not a thief], and this is precisely what Ida will later accuse him of: from her, his regime steals her son, her freedom, her civic identity, and finally her life. The regime's robbing of individual identity is one of the strongest messages that the film proposes. Ida's nudity is implicated in this discourse; her absolute nakedness before Mussolini when she has sold everything (so that he can found the newspaper out of which fascism will grow) is a sign of this. The message is repeated in the cold nudity of the women in the initial night scenes in Pergine's institution and in the nakedness of Ida's apparently make-up-less face (unusual for a star actress like Giovanna Mezzogiorno) when on 18 January 1927 she is interrogated and told that she has no proof of her identity as Mussolini's wife. The robbing of identity is repeated in the parallel, though underdeveloped, story of Benito Albino's fate. Bellocchio has moved further from the source material in presenting Mussolini's son as damaged by the privation of his life, his identity robbed from him, so that, devoid of a solid individual self, he becomes a parody, imitating his absent father while he descends into madness.

Although the film's criticism is, on the most obvious level, a criticism of fascism, *Vincere* is not restricted to an analysis of just one political period. As implied by Ida's final look-back, the film's criticism of the privation of identity by political regimes, the need for the individual to stand up against political systems, even where it may seem impossible or ill advised, and the dangers of conformism and silence (as implied by the Church's behaviour with its support of fascism and by the kind of self-sacrifice that keeps people from rebelling) have an importance that transcends a single political period to give a clear message that is relevant today.

Conclusion

Both *Buongiorno, notte* and *Vincere* demonstrate that *objectivité absolue* is not sufficient, or even essential, for creating political films. These films revisit significant moments in Italian national history and, while emphasizing the private over the public, ultimately present strong political viewpoints that show the inner, more secret, workings behind the public discourse of history, aligning political change with personal decisions and personal identity. While admitting the powerlessness of the individual (neither Ida nor Chiara actually brings about a transformation of history), both films nevertheless support the responsibility of individuals to rebel against systems such as terrorism and fascism that are based on the suppression of the individual. The real interest in Bellocchio's cinema after 1980 lies in this aligning of political change with personal transformation.

5   The Rebel 'I': Patriarchy and Parents

Chiara's character in *Buongiorno, notte* and Ida's in *Vincere* bring us to the heart of Bellocchio's cinema and signifies the point at which the individual, the 'I' as *eye*, becomes political. They become political not just in the narrower sense of interacting with the state and its political representatives, seen in the guise of Moro and Mussolini, but also in the broader sense because of their insertion into power structures and their position of resistance towards them.

The figure of the rebel, which Chiara exemplifies, dominates Bellocchio's cinema from its origins in the early sixties to the present. This chapter will trace the interaction between rebellious, resisting characters and two power structures that are fundamental to Bellocchio's films, the patriarchal and the familial; it will assess how and why the rebel rebels and whether they can ever really step outside the cage constructed from society's power structures.

The Woman as Rebel: Politics and Patriarchy

The generic nature of the political backdrop to *La balia*, released four years before *Buongiorno, notte*, hints that something beyond a political reconstruction of late-nineteenth-century socialism is going on, especially when it is compared to the detailed political material in some of Bellocchio's earlier films. *La balia* offers no precise indication of the year in which the film is set; the street battle that takes place towards the film's close is a local, vague, and generic affair; when the socialist agitators furtively paste up posters in the dark streets (a scene that cites Camillo's painting of the words *La Cina è vicina* on the walls of the PSU offices), the posters are illegible, their precise message obscured.

Moreover, although we know that the female protagonist, Annetta (Maya Sansa), has a subversive socialist lover, all we ever find out about him is in Annetta's highly evasive and vague phrase 'metteva disordine ... faceva politica' [he made trouble ... he did politics].

The direction being taken by the political material only becomes clear in the aestheticized uprising at the end of the film. In the uprising the dominant figure, sweeping through the streets with her red flag, is the 'mad' woman Maddalena (Jacqueline Lustig), symbol of an instinctive and generic rebellion against the norms of family and of the mental institution (two institutions that are closely aligned in the film through parallel montage linking the domestic world of the male protagonist, Mori, with the professional world in which he is a psychiatrist). The discourse presented in this film therefore goes beyond any historical reenactment of the socialist uprising to put forward instead the concept of revolt in much broader terms. Ultimately, it is a film in which rebellion takes on a universal significance rather than a narrow, historical one, becoming emblematic of a defence of socialism (against capitalism), a defence of individuality and instinct (against the regime of psychiatry), and a defence of women (against patriarchy). The presence of a sensual woman at the heart of the uprising seems to indicate a threat to the male-dominated bourgeois world and its privileges. It certainly appears to position the woman as a powerful, even indomitable, figure.

This rebel woman is a sister to a host of characters in Bellocchio's films: Elena in *La Cina è vicina*, Rosanna in *Marcia trionfale*, Marta in *Salto nel vuoto*, Giulia in *Diavolo in corpo*, Mad and Maddalena in *La visione del Sabba*, Sandra in *La condanna*, Chiara in *Buongiorno, notte*, Princess Bona in *Il regista di matrimoni*, and Ida Dalser in *Vincere*. These female protagonists, conspicuous presences in Bellocchio's cinema, especially since 1980, have a capacity for boldly asserting themselves against patriarchal power systems, which sets them apart from the vast majority of female characters in the history of Italian cinema. They are repeatedly cast as Antigone in their challenging of the laws of the father, a link made explicit in the final scene of *Diavolo in corpo*, in which the camera focuses long on Giulia's emotional face while her young lover discusses Sophocles' text for his final school exam. Giulia's journey in that film is one long rebellion. She stands up against her dead father by planning to marry, in Oedipal fashion, her father's would-be murderer, the (ex-) terrorist Giacomo. She also stands up against her lover's father – a psychoanalyst who wants to proscribe and cure her behaviour[1] – screaming 'NOOOO!' before rushing from the room. Giulia's 'no!' is the defiance of a woman against a man, a patient against an analyst, instinct against logic, and the powerless against the powerful. With it, she stands up for her own view of the world and refuses to conform to 'normality' and to be 'cured,' to adapt to a world that is itself sick. In this 'no!' the film defends the right of feminine instinct and otherness to exist and not be destroyed or rather 'cured' by male psychoanalysis.[2] It confirms this right in allowing her to escape the inevitable narrative of marriage that her social context has prepared for her; at the end of the film she rejects this cage, opting not for the strictures of marriage but for the freedom of love.

As Natalini (2005, 188) says, Giulia 'si rivolta contro ogni forma di autorità, attaccando il potere dei padri attraverso l'alleanza coi figli' [rebels against every form of authority, attacking the power of fathers through her alliance with their sons]. Moreover, this rebellion – based on the personal, the instinctive, and the sexual – permits transformation for the female character, at least on some levels. Giulia *does* free herself from the constricting norms that society has set out for her and chooses her own way; even if this leads her, almost inevitably, to slotting straight into another relationship with a man, it is a relationship in which she has substantially more control and satisfaction. Furthermore, her ability to bring about an inner, positive transformation is implicitly contrasted with the moral and social failure of her ex-terrorist fiancé; his political revolt did not change Italy for the better, and he has not changed himself for the better in his decision to conform to his own mediocrity. She at least, on a personal level, is capable of change.

Although the presence of these rebellious female characters is certainly significant, it would be naive to think that it really signals an aligning of these films against patriarchy. Although Rosanna finally leaves her abusive husband in *Marcia trionfale*, her future without his protection is terribly fragile. Chiara ultimately fails to convince her male comrades to free Aldo Moro and so fails to change the course of Italy's history. Ida Dalser loses her battle to assert her identity as Mussolini's wife and dies in a mental institution. Even where women do seem to gain their liberty – Princess Bona, Marta, and Giulia – the patriarchal gaze of the camera, and the place assigned to them in the narrative, demonstrates their limitation within, and delimitation by, an ideology; despite the apparently good intentions of the narrative storyline, they can never escape it.

Bellocchio's contact with Fagioli's ideas in the late 1970s led to the development of a fundamental paradox. While women came to the fore for the first time in Bellocchio's films as rebel protagonists who were capable of achieving a certain level of freedom and transformation – a level that set them apart from most women in Italian films of the period – simultaneously, the structure, style, and characterization of the films led to increasing objectification of lead female characters and to their essentializing in terms of a limited range of characteristics.

In narrative terms, in most of Bellocchio's films, especially during the Fagioli years female characters are very far from existing, either visually or structurally, as independent of male desire. Whereas the male characters have an existence and significance before, and implicitly after, meeting a woman, the role of the female characters within the films is bound up in their relationships with the male. Men fight battles and are film directors, actors, judges, and artists; women are condemned by repeated filmic narratives to do nothing of consequence when they are not frequenting the men in their lives. Bellocchio's female protagonists are nearly always less complete and independent than their male counterparts, and most of them clearly exist for a male other, rather than for themselves.

There are, however, some notable exceptions to this rule, which first appear, significantly, *after* the Fagiolian period. Annetta, the female protagonist of *La balia*, and Chiara, the terrorist in *Buongiorno, notte* (both played by Italo-Iranian actress Maya Sansa) are women who work and have a life of their own. The painterly establishing shot that opens *La balia*, framing Annetta in her own surroundings alongside her female companions, sets up her apartness and independence from male characters from the film's outset. She literally has to be collected from this landscape by the male to be brought into the narrative. Throughout the film she maintains this independence, sustaining a parallel life removed from the attentions of Mori (Fabrizio Bentivoglio), in whose house she has gone to work. He becomes aware of her apartness only at the end of the film when he follows her across Rome and so discovers her double life: she nurses not only his child but also her own, whom she has had brought to the city, unbeknownst to him. A similar separateness can be seen in the women who live inside the walls of *La balia*'s mental institution; they are shown as radically independent of their male keepers, escaping out at night to lead – or follow – political movements.

In *Buongiorno, notte*, Chiara also demonstrates a certain determined independence. Like Annetta, her relationships with men are not all-consuming, as are Maddalena's or Giulia's; her life and her narrative do not revolve around Eros. Instead, work, both at the ministry and as a member of the Red Brigades, clearly occupies her. However, the shift from Eros to *opera* is not conceived in positive terms within the diegesis of the film, because her work as terrorist is denied moral value. Nowhere is this clearer than in the scene in which the men return to Via Montalcini after the ambush. During the ambush Chiara was waiting at home. While she waits, a neighbour rings the bell; when Chiara opens the door, she promptly plants a newborn baby in her arms, asking her to look after it while she goes off to collect her son. The scene does not appear in Braghetti's autobiography and seems incongruous. It creates suspense, but it also goes beyond this, assuming a symbolic meaning that damns Chiara's position as 'working woman:' A shot shows the baby lying abandoned and helpless on the sofa while Chiara goes off to help the returning men. The baby, occupying the entire foreground of the shot, struggles mutely without her. Out of focus behind the baby, the terrorists struggle with the box containing Moro. The use of focus here is highly ideological: with the baby being at the centre of the spectator's attention, we are left looking at what Chiara has abandoned and what should, rightly, be the focus of her attention, not ours. Furthermore, the choice of Maya Sansa to play Chiara cannot but refer intertextually to her role as wet nurse in *La balia*; in this earlier film Sansa played a woman who would never abandon a child (her own or another's) for any reason, especially not to be involved in kidnap and execution. Therefore, although they gain significant independence from men, the two characters played by Sansa are still inscribed strongly inside patriarchy, with the requirement to play the good mother or be damned. There are parallels here with *Salto nel vuoto*: Marta manages to escape her brother's control without running to look for protection from another man, but she is healed or saved only by embracing a child in the film's finale; this posits her in the role of mother, a role denied to her earlier in the film by her role as a single and sexless spinster.

It is hard not to notice how, in these three films, incompletion in the erotic sphere[3] is compensated by completion in the maternal sphere. In *La balia*, Annetta, whose lover is in prison, embraces both the child in her care and her own baby; Marta, at the end of *Salto nel vuoto*, gets into the bed of her maid's young child and embraces him. Chiara, the only character to fail in both erotic and maternal spheres, damns herself morally by doing so. It appears that despite positing the woman as rebel, Bellocchio's films ultimately position her in narrow, traditional roles: she is mother or lover.

For all the repeated featuring of women rebels in Bellocchio's films, it is clear that in every film so far, with the exception of *Buongiorno, notte*, and *Vincere*, attention is ultimately focused on the male characters, who are more complex, more deeply interwoven within the narrative, and ultimately providers of the films' point of view. The male characters have complex relationships with others, relationships that the female characters lack, with many films structured around a triangle in which two men mirror one another and the woman is the third character, typically an object of desire. This pattern occurs in *Marcia trionfale* (Capitano Asciutto and Passeri; Rosanna), *Salto nel vuoto* (the judge and Sciabola; Marta), *La condanna* (the judge and the architect; Sandra), *Il Principe di Homburg* (the Prince and the Elector; the Princess), and to a lesser extent in *Il sogno della farfalla* (Massimo and his father; Massimo's girlfriend) and *Vincere* (Mussolini and Mussolini's son; Ida Dalser). What the pattern shows is that beyond their relationships with women, men also create significant, usually conflictual, relationships with other men. Women, however, are deprived of this complexity. Where they have relationships beyond romantic ones, these are almost exclusively within the frame of the family and are of only very slight importance to either narrative or character development: Wanda (*Gli occhi, la bocca*), Giulia (*Diavolo in corpo*), Princess Natalia (*Il Principe di Homburg*), and Princess Bona (*Il regista di matrimoni*) are shown with their families, but even then, in the case of each of the two princesses, the girl's relationship with her father is of far less importance that the relationship between the father and the second male protagonist (Homburg and Franco Elica, respectively). With the exception of Marta's friendship with her maid in *Salto nel vuoto* and the groups of 'mad' women in *La balia* and *Vincere*, there is almost no sign of the development of the female-female relationships that would, according to De Lauretis (1989, 20) serve to undermine patriarchy. In other words, what is conspicuously missing from Bellocchio's films is any real attempt to collocate female protagonists as the centre point of the narrative. Even when the female lead might appear to approach this role (Marta, Giulia, Annetta, Chiara, Ida), an analysis of the films shows that – with the significant exception of Chiara and Ida – the female character never acts as the focalizer for the narrative. The central conflicts still revolve around the male, and he is the subject through whose eyes we are asked to see.

Although the female leads, especially since 1980, are explored in terms of their emotions, their transformation, and their growth, women are repeatedly positioned as object rather than as subject, as *for the other* and not *for themselves*, acting as a projection of male ideals to which they conform.[4] The apparent freedom that the narrative metes out to women in order that they can be or become 'themselves' is highly problematic because these selves are repeatedly limited to a restricted range of behaviour: instinctive, vital, animalistic, sexual, and 'mad' (that is, outside male norms). Although these characteristics are shown to be positive, and indeed subversive, and young men may possess them too (see the analysis of *Pugni in tasca*'s Ale, below), they nevertheless amount to a stereotyping of women into essentialist roles that have little to do with logic, intelligence, intellect, analysis, and a whole range of other characteristics from which they are typically excluded. The pedestal is narrow indeed.

The stereotyping appears to have as much to do with male projection as with female transformation, and – with the emphasis on the animalistic, the instinctive, and the bodily – it is women's impact in terms of spectacle that until recently remains central in the films. Repeatedly, although particularly during the years of Fagioli's influence, Bellocchio's films construct their female leads as objects of desire, typically casting sensuous, young, curvaceous women. Moreover, in the two films in which the attractive female protagonists are constructed less obviously as objects of desire – *Salto nel vuoto* and *Buongiorno, notte* – the lack of glamorous sexuality is marked as negative and unnatural, a sign not of freedom from patriarchy but of repression on the part of family (*Salto nel vuoto*) or ideology (*Buongiorno, notte*). Bellocchio's films therefore support the idea of young women as *naturally* sensual and provocative. This natural sexuality, however, is not in fact 'natural' but is constructed through the use of revealing clothing, silks, kohl, lipstick, bright provocative clothing, and sensual movement (the dances of Giulia, Maddalena, and Sandra). When the woman is supposed to be read as most natural and most womanly, she is nevertheless least herself because she has become a spectacle of make-up and clothing, constructed not for herself but for the Other.

Of all Bellocchio's films, *Diavolo in corpo* is the one that perhaps most objectifies its female lead. In the final scenes of the film, when Giulia returns home from a nightclub and, as a storm crashes outside, dances among the cutlery strewn across the floor of the apartment, her red silk dressing gown is slightly open, revealing a glimpse of her naked body beneath. Her dance in the dressing gown, knife in hand, appears to be a relaxed, self-absorbed moment that nobody watches. As if no one were there, she laughs, sweeping the cutlery off the table with her hands and kicking it with her bare feet. But, however carefree and self-absorbed she seems, her point of reference is constantly the camera. Although repeatedly turning her back on the camera (or spectator) during the scene, and enforcing the impression that this dance is for herself alone, when her dressing gown falls open she is facing the camera, the knife high in hand. The scene is therefore voyeuristic and takes on elements of striptease. Giulia's slim but sensual body, the materials and nature of her clothing (low-cut blouses, sheets wrapped around her, and a dressing gown), her red lipstick, her lack of underwear, and her dancing all construct her as a woman to be consumed as an object of desire, a saleable product on an art-cinema circuit. Despite her apparent freedom and her refutation of psychoanalysis, convention, and finally marriage, she is bound by a camera lens that voyeuristically constructs her in terms of simplistic masculine ideals.

This camera and its relation to the female body is crucial, especially in Bellocchio's cinema during the Fagioli years. The progressive suppression of the classic Hollywood action shot / reaction shot in favour of long takes during the eighties and early nineties favours attention to the female body. This is particularly noticeable in the sex scenes, where the camera remains steady, immobile, almost impassive in front of the bodies, often focusing on the woman's face in close-up, or even extreme close-up. This 'stare sul corpo' is certainly not indifferent to a body's gender. The difference in camera proximity between the shots of female faces and the shots of male faces can, in fact, often be quite marked. In a scene in *La visione del Sabba* in which a group of male psychoanalysts are gathered around a table to interrogate Maddalena about her attack on the hunter and rapist, Maddalena's face is framed in a medium close-up that isolates her (in her red dress) against the window behind her. The reaction shots of the psychoanalyst who interrogates her, however, are medium shots, framing him alongside his dark-suited colleagues. The alternation of shots between those that isolate the woman in a medium close-up and shallow focus and those that place the man in a medium shot within a social context is striking, and it is through this kind of photography that Bellocchio's films establish the paradigm of the woman as the object to be gazed upon, not as the rebellious political subject that she may at first glance seem to be.

The objectification of women in Bellocchio's films – particularly during the eighties and nineties – is not casual. Instead, it can be seen as part of a discourse that posits women as projections, parts, or creations of men. This idea (discussed in chapter 3 herein) was developed by Fagioli in *Bambino, donna, e trasformazione dell'uomo*, a book that argued that *donna* and *bambino* were aspects of the male psyche that needed to be integrated (through sex) for man to be transformed. This age-old idea of woman as a creation of man is explicitly posited by architect Colaianni in *La condanna* when he compares Sandra to Goya's provocative *Maja desnuda*, and she slowly places her bare arms behind her head to fully and obediently assume the pose on the bed. She, as woman, is created by the man; she is isolated and objectified; she is literally shaped. The architect, still watching her, says:

> Io cerco sempre un'immagine – le curve, le morbidezze di una donna bella. Cerco sempre lo spessore in una donna che le opere d'arte non mi danno. Ora tu sei un'immagine immobile in questo letto come un quadro di Goya – il mio desiderio non vuole niente da te. Ho la spinta per darti la vita, violentarti per darti il movimento, come un bambino che nasce. Tu tenterai a distruggermi come fa un bambino che nasce … Io ti darò il mio corpo senza il quale non puoi vivere.

> [I always look for an image – the curves, the softness of a beautiful woman. I look for the depth in a woman that works of art do not give me. Now you are an immobile image in this bed, like a Goya painting – my desire wants nothing from you. I have the force to give you life, to rape you to give you movement, like a child being born. You will try to destroy me like a child being born … I will give you my body without which you cannot live.]

La condanna aligns sex and creativity. It is no coincidence that the 'rapist' is an architect and that the 'rape' takes place surrounded by art. Nor is it a coincidence that one of the rooms for the seduction is loosely hung with red drapes, thus resembling a womb, and at the same time is an artist's studio, complete with jars, a painter's implements, and scaffolding. Sex, which is both animalistic (the architect repeatedly tries to take Sandra from behind) and artistic (the artist's studio and the choreographed ritual of seduction), possesses a highly creative force, according to a Fagiolian analysis. However, this work of creation can only be set in motion by the man. Adam-like, the man moulds and makes. The woman is moulded and made; she is not creative on her own. (Although the implication is that neither is man creative when he is alone, the emphasis in Bellocchio's films and in Fagioli's work is on the partiality of the woman in relation to man, not on the partiality of man in relation to woman.) Women are thus repeatedly posited as art objects. The association of woman and art (Frida's role as a painting in

Enrico IV, Sandra associated with various art works in *La condanna*, and Diana linked to the sculpture of Gradiva in *L'ora di religione*) emphasizes the nature of woman as spectacle and as object to be gazed upon, and her position as not so much heroic Antigone but biblical Eve – forever a creation and derivative of man.

Ultimately, despite the repeated rebellion of the female leads and despite the sexual freedom they attain, the combination of their propensity to failure, and, especially during the Fagioli years, their objectified treatment, their limited and essentialized range of behaviours, and their off-centre position in relation to both plot and character development suggests that Bellocchio's women cannot defeat the rule of the father against which they pit themselves. The father, reasserting himself in the ideology behind a camera that moulds and makes, is ultimately the victor.

Rebellion in the Name of the Father and Family: *I pugni in tasca, Il Principe di Homburg,* and *L'ora di religione*

In order to fully understand the idea of rebellion that underlies Bellocchio's cinema, one needs to go back in time to his earliest films, where it first emerges. It is necessary, too, to shift away from the political and back to the private, back to relationships within the family, which provide a blueprint for how the adult will respond to power structures.

The family, which Bernardi (1998, 18) terms the 'punto d'inserimento dell'individuo nelle strutture autoritarie' [the point of insertion of the individual into authority structures], has been repeatedly scrutinized in Bellocchio's cinema ever since his first feature film, *I pugni in tasca*, in which the young protagonist, Ale, plots to annihilate the members of his family, starting with his mother. Murders of family members occur repeatedly in Bellocchio's films: matricide and fratricide in *I pugni in tasca*, the murder (albeit off-screen) of Giulia's father in *Diavolo in corpo*, the murder of the mother by her deranged son in *L'ora di religione* (also off-screen), and the Prince's (perhaps imagined) murder of his son-in-law in *Il regista di matrimoni*. Moreover, even where actual murders do not occur, they are willed: in *La Cina è vicina* Camillo's detonating of a bomb threatens the safety of his older brother, and in *Nel nome del padre* Franc shoots his mother in the mirror, splintering the image of her face into tiny glass shards. Patricide is taken to a symbolic level in a number of further films that treat the annihilation of a symbolic father figure: Capitano Asciutto in *Marcia trionfale* and Aldo Moro in *Buongiorno, notte*.

The killing of family members (whether real or symbolic) represents the principal act of individual violence in Bellocchio's films,[5] implying a deep resentment of this most central of Italian institutions.

Italy has always been a country in which family is paramount. Ginsborg (1990b, 29), for instance, describes the primacy of the family and its links to Catholicism, a religion that sees the family as a safeguard against the power of the state and that lays great emphasis 'on the internal morality of the family: on its indissolubility, its piety, [and] the ability of parents to educate their children in a Christian manner.' The attack on the family, like the attack on other institutions such as the school and the army, is bound up partly with the ideas that were current in the late sixties and early seventies, a time when the gap between parents and their children deepened and a new teen culture formed around the notion of differentiation and distance between teenager and adult. During the sixties the idea of the family was strongly contested, and the family came to be seen as an authoritarian structure, a repository – especially in its bourgeois form – of hypocrisy, pettiness, and abuse of power.

In Bellocchio's films the family is unremittingly targeted as the epitome of all authority structures. The negative dynamics that exist between self and institution, described in chapter 2, are only a reflection of the dynamics that already exist within the family structure, where the relationship between self and other is first formed and then maintained in all its negativity. Bellocchio's films attack the bourgeois family as a pathological entity that corrupts the full range of interpersonal relationships within it.

I pugni in tasca is fundamental as far as the portrayal of family is concerned. It narrates the story of a middle-class family living isolated in the mountains in the north of Italy. Ale, the protagonist, is an epileptic adolescent who decides to take it into his own hands to clear up the mess that his family has become (one of the original titles for the film was 'Igiene familiare' [Family Hygiene]), and he sets about eliminating its members so that his older brother – the only sane member of the family – can have a normal life. Ale first kills his mother, by pushing her off a cliff into a riverbed below; he then kills a retarded brother by drugging him and drowning him in the bath. At the end of the film he himself expires during a violent epileptic fit that strikes him down while, alone in his bedroom, he is miming the aria that concludes act 1 of Verdi's *La Traviata*. His sister, who can hear his agony, chooses not to save him.

The film establishes the family unit as decayed. Ale suffers from epilepsy, his brother Leone is retarded, his sister, Giulia (Paola Pitagora), is emotionally fragile, and the mother is blind. The bonds between them are rotten, too, especially those of Ale and Giulia, who flirt with incest. Only the older brother, Augusto (Marino Masè), who is in charge of them, is exempt from mental illness and leads a normal life. The enclosed and claustrophobic villa, standing apart from the town (which represents an easy and carefree normality), is home to the worst pathologies of the bourgeois family.

The family meals are at the fulcrum of Bellocchio's satirical attack; they represent the point in the day when every family member is present and, therefore, provide a setting in which the full range of interrelationships can be scrutinized. Two meals, in particular, are recorded by the camera. The first of these establishes the routine and 'normal' nature of the abnormality of this family. The scene, complete with the attentions of a maid, the saying of grace, and the fine table settings, presents a veneer of civilization that is thin indeed. The action of the scene contradicts its middle-class setting. For a start, the father is absent, and the head of the table is occupied instead by Augusto, the elder brother and a father figure whose very presence draws attention to the absence of the real authority figure. The mother is blind and out of touch with what is going on around her. A white cat – homely but also uncanny – jumps lightly up onto the table and eats from the mother's plate without her noticing. Revealed in an under-table shot (the kind of low-angle subversive shot discussed in chapter 2 in relation to *La Cina è vicina*), Ale's feet incestuously approach and touch his sister's legs. The dialogue is minimal and seems to consist only of brief gunshots of irritation, mirrored in Silvano Agosti's fast and erratic editing style that alternates quick and often peculiarly angled close-ups and extreme close-ups of faces. In the sequence in which Ale's feet touch Giulia, the dialogue is reduced to little more than a series of short, imperative exhortations:

GIULIA: Smettila! (to Ale, who is touching her legs)
ALE: Ma dai!
GIULIA: Eh?!
ALE: Piantala! (Giulia has grabbed his leg under the table)
GIULIA: Ma va'!

[GIULIA: Stop it! (to Ale, who is touching her legs)
ALE: Oh, come on!
GIULIA: Eh?!
ALE: Stop it! (Giulia has grabbed his leg under the table)
GIULIA: Come off it!]

The whole scene is predicated on a dialectic between order and disorder, rationality and instinct, and moral norms and their overturning. Pasolini's acute analysis of the film situates it within a discourse on rationality and irrationality that helps frame the issues at stake:

> La caratteristica del mondo borghese, come dice con grande chiarezza Goldmann sulla strada di Lukács, non era l'irrazionalismo, come noi credevamo, ma il razionalismo. È il razionalismo la caratteristica principale del mondo borghese, l'irrazionalismo era una forma di lotta antiborghese, di quelli che Lukács, e sulla sua scia Goldmann, chiama gli individui problematici, gli scrittori, i poeti. (Cited in Bellocchio 1967a, 13)

> [The characteristic of the bourgeois world, as Goldman, following Lukács, said with such clarity, was not irrationality as once we believed, but rationality. It is rationality that is the principal characteristic of the bourgeois world; irrationality was a form of anti-bourgeois struggle on the part of those whom Lukács – and Goldman, following his example – calls the problematic individuals, writers, poets.]

Ale's character is marked by an irrationality and instinctiveness that his epilepsy alone cannot explain. In this dinner scene the camera twice follows his hand as it makes a disconnected and inexplicable gesture, moving across the sideboard and back. His sudden fits of irritation, peculiar gestures, and spontaneous laughter, and the way in which the film situates him with regard to animals (the cat is close to him on the table, and he adores chinchillas), all help to forge a portrait of a highly instinctual adolescent, who is the polar opposite of the regulation, rationality, and carefulness of the Catholic bourgeoisie, which is represented by the scene's mise en scène. In a theme that will develop in Bellocchio's later cinema, here we see instinct crushed by the structures of 'normal' and bourgeois life.

The mother is to blame, at least in part, for the decadent nature of this nuclear family. Her blindness is emblematic of her inability to understand her children; it signals her separateness, her self-containment, and ultimately the coldness of her nature. When an argument breaks out between the siblings at the table during the second dinner scene, she can only ask, 'Che succede?' [What's going on?]. She fails to act and interact, and this inability to give her children what they need on an emotional level is ultimately the cause of Ale's matricide.

The damaged relationship between mother and son is emblematized in the scene in which Ale, suddenly and spontaneously, rests his head on his mother's knee and says, 'Sono infelice' [I'm unhappy]. His mother responds in a gentle voice, 'Che cosa hai?' [What's wrong?], stroking his hair maternally. For a second, it seems that the long years of failed communication between the two are at an end. However, this empathy is brutally reversed by her next, wholly inappropriate, words, 'Vuoi una caramella?' [Do you want a sweet?] Ale recoils and abruptly leaves the room; he realizes in an instant that his mother is, and will always be, completely out of touch with him, still treating him as a little boy when he is now a troubled young man. She does not understand that he needs a very different kind of attention. Bellocchio remarks:

> Perché quando un ragazzo ha diciotto-diciannove anni, la madre non ci vede più, non lo capisce più, non gli serve più. Perché di solito non è riuscita ad aggiornarsi con le nuove esigenze del figlio, a riconoscere nella sua giovinezza la propria, a credere di essere stata giovane e di aver avuto comuni problemi. Così la ... morte [della madre di *I pugni in tasca*] è soltanto fisiologica, perché era già morta molto prima. (Aprà, Martelli, et al. 1965)

> [Because when a boy is eighteen or nineteen years old, his mother does not see him any more, does not understand him anymore, is no use to him. Because usually she has not managed to keep up with the new needs of her son, to recognize in his youth her own, to believe that she was once young and that she had the same kinds of problems. Therefore, the death [of the mother in *I pugni in tasca*] is only physiological, because she was already dead a long time ago.]

Ale kills his mother by pushing her over a cliff and thus rids himself of a woman whose presence is only a daily reminder of what she is not. At the ensuing funeral the contrast between what the mother was for her children and what she should have been is deliberately emphasized. The image of her cold dead face, lying within the coffin and swaddled in cloth like a medieval painting, is contrasted with the pious discourse of a priest whose face we never see. In a mixture of Latin and local dialect this priest (dubbed by Bellocchio) lauds the qualities of the *mater dolorosa*: 'La mamma, si sa, è la più vicina, la più ansiosa, la più partecipante' [Our mums are, we know, the closest to us, the most concerned for us, the most involved]. His warm homily contrasts ironically with the face of the mother, which in death seems to be little different than her face was in life: still detached, cold, unloving, and lacking in maternal qualities. Her children, who are each filmed in close-up as they bend down into the coffin to kiss her face, can barely bring themselves to touch her.

The cold, unfeeling, and unknowing mother is a figure that returns frequently in Bellocchio's films. In *Nel nome del padre* Franc's mother (played marvellously by Laura Betti) is a vampish, hysterical woman who understands nothing of her son; the boy is so angry with her that he shoots her image in the mirror. In *Il gabbiano* the mother (again played by Betti) inhabits the glamorous world of the stage, surrounded by her admirers and lovers, but she excludes her son and dismisses him as bothersome and irrelevant; in a bitter scene in which he stages his play in front of her, she responds with boredom and incomprehension, waving the play away with sarcastic comments to make her friends laugh. Twenty years later, in *La balia*, the narrative hinges on the contrast between the middle-class mother's inability to bond with her newborn infant and the unschooled nanny's instinctive understanding of the child's needs.

Released just three years after *La balia, L'ora di religione* elaborates most thoroughly the figure of the remote mother and her child's detachment from her. This mother, 'finta martire e reale assassina' [fake martyr and real assassin] (Cruciani 2003, 19), had been murdered by her deranged, blaspheming son in an action that repeats the matricide of *I pugni in tasca*. When another of her sons, Ernesto, visits his aunt to try to understand better why the family is trying to canonize his mother, he is met by the paraphernalia of the myth-making process. A surreal image of his mother's smiling face has been hung across the French windows in his aunt's house, so that it flaps mysteriously. This vast image, a photographic print, is framed so that it engulfs the entire cinema screen, smiling ambiguously out at the camera and thus the spectator. The framing emphasizes the immensity of the mother; her face fills the screen, overwhelming the son's head as he gazes up at her; his head is reduced by contrast to a black shadow. The mother's smile is strangely indifferent. Ernesto looks up into this image, but like a Madonna, the giant image does not look back at him; instead, it smiles out at us, ignoring him. It is precisely this inability of the mother to look back that is most strongly attacked in all these films. The inability of the mother to see, recognize, and love her sons is at the root of the fault line in the mother-son relationship: in *I pugni in tasca* the mother is literally blind, and in *L'ora di religione* she see everything (by looking into the camera) except her own son, who stands beneath her.

Throughout Bellocchio's films the mother is a key figure representing lack and creating a state of Fagiolian hankering [*bramosia*] in her many sons. The seemingly anachronistic notion of making a film in 2002 about the canonization of a murdered mother is in fact not as strange as it seems. In *L'ora di religione*, Bellocchio is underlining the continued centrality of the mother in Italian society, showing how she is still conceived in terms of Catholic symbology, even in a more secular Italy – in other words, in terms of the ideas of sacrifice and saintly maternity that conjoin in the figure of the Madonna. The kitsch photo shoot of their mother's 'martyrdom,' which Ernesto sees being filmed as he climbs the stairs towards Aunt Maria, is the epitome of this empty symbol. A camera operator directs a woman to look heavenward and feign a 'sorriso da santa' [saintly smile], while her 'son' buries a knife in her breast. This saintly image is divorced from reality because Ernesto's real mother was not a self-sacrificing *mater dolorosa* but a selfish, self-absorbed, and distant woman. She looms large in the life of the sons, but like Ale's blind mother, or the two mothers played by Laura Betti, she is impotent and useless to them, causing them to suffer harshly. The mother is implicitly to blame for the madness of two of her sons in *I pugni in tasca*, and of one in *L'ora di religione*, a blame that becomes more evident in Bellocchio's documentary on mental illness, *Matti da slegare [Fit to Be Untied]*.[6]

In *I pugni in tasca* the bad mother is present, but impotent. The father is absent, and his role and his chair at the table have been filled by another male, the older brother who controls and organizes the family. With the impotence and uselessness of the figure of the mother, Bellocchio's families become highly patriarchal. Fathers and, where fathers are absent, father figures[7] represent the locus of power and surveillance; unlike the mother, they watch their sons. They are also, ultimately, the protectors of the corrupt family unit. When, in *Il Principe di Homburg*, Princess Natalia believes the patriarchal Elector to have been killed in battle, her reaction is immediately to fear for her safety in the absence of the protector: 'E adesso chi ci protegge da questo mondo di nemici?' [And now who will protect us from this world of enemies?] In *L'ora di religione*, Aunt Maria, in her defence of the canonization of the mother, tells Ernesto that the family needs a father – a father, godfather, or patron saint; a father who will protect, provide an identity for the family, prevent it from slipping into nothingness, and, in practical terms, provide for the future of the only grandchild, Leonardo:[8]

> La famiglia Picciafuoco non conta più nulla, è la realtà, è la verità. Perché non ha un protettore ... senza un protettore, un padre, un patrono, un padrino battesimale, non sei niente. Qualunque padre, purché sia un padre: la massoneria, l'Opus Dei, l'Istituto Gramsci, il Circolo della Caccia, i Terziari Francescani, l'Associazione mutilati e orfani di guerra ... Per ritrovare il padre la famiglia Picciafuoco deve assolutamente conquistare un titolo che le restituisca dignità, prestigio, riconoscibilità ... questo titolo è la santificazione di tua madre.

> [The Picciafuoco family doesn't count for anything anymore. That's the reality, the truth. Because it doesn't have a protector ... without a protector, a father, a patron, a godfather, you are nothing. Any father will do, as long as it's a father: Freemasonry, Opus Dei, the Gramsci Institute, the Hunting Association, the Franciscan Tertiary, the Association of cripples and orphans of war ... To regain the father, the Picciafuoco family absolutely must gain a title that will restore dignity, prestige, recognizability ... this title is the sanctification of your mother.]

The figure of the father is thus central to the power of a family unit in society. Without it, the family loses its dominance.

In Bellocchio's earlier films, father and father figures, like the mother, are cold. However, they are also powerful and often violent and ruthless. Angelo Transeunti's father in the aptly named *Nel nome del padre* and Capitano Asciutto in *Marcia trionfale* are sadistic men, physically violent and obsessed with order and control.[9] They attempt to dominate their sons, and they succeed; both boys end up interiorizing their father's characters. Later, during the Fagioli period, the violence of the early fathers disappears and is replaced by a cool and abstract rationality (which was already latent, however, in the earlier fathers with their love of order and discipline). Massimo's father in *Il sogno della farfalla* and Andrea's in *Diavolo in corpo*, as university lecturer and psychoanalyst respectively, both belong to this category.

Il Principe di Homburg, the first film made by Bellocchio after the break with Fagioli, and a film that marks a borderline between the highly negative portrayal of the father in the earlier films and the more tolerant portrayal after 1998 (with the exception, that is, of *Vincere*, where the despotic father returns in the guise of Mussolini), perhaps best illus-

trates the role of the father in his films. An adaptation of Heinrich von
Kleist's play *Prinz Friedrich von Homburg* (1811), it recounts the story of
the young Prince of Homburg (Andrea Di Stefano), a romantic, som-
nambulant character who enters into an Oedipal conflict with the stern
Elector (Toni Bertorelli) when he fails to follow military orders during
a battle.

The film opens with the Prince drifting into the gardens of Fehrbellin
Castle on the night before battle. He appears to dream that the Elector
and his entourage approach him in the darkness and, taking a laurel
wreath from his hands, pass it to the young Princess Natalia (Barbara
Bobulova), who places it on the Prince's head, crowning him. When
the Prince awakens, he is troubled to find a woman's glove in his hand.
He remembers his 'dream'[10] but not the face of the mysterious woman
who, in fleeing from him, had dropped it. Later that night the Prince is
summoned to an army council. The plan for the morrow's battle is set
out, but the Prince of Homburg, distracted by the presence of Natalia,
who he recognizes from his dream, does not listen. When the battle
begins the next day, Homburg only faintly remembers the orders and
disregards them, attacking the enemy army as he sees fit. His attack is
successful, and the battle is won, but on his return to Fehrbellin he is
court-martialled and sentenced to death as a traitor. He has disobeyed
the Elector. At first Homburg cannot believe that this man will not
forgive him, but slowly he realizes the gravity of his act. The Elector
writes to Homburg, saying that if he thinks the sentence unjust, it will
be waived and he will be set free. The Prince, however, cannot bring
himself to call the Elector unjust; he refuses this offer and prepares to
die, believing that his death will celebrate the sacred law of war that he
violated on the battlefields. In the final scene Homburg is blindfolded
and brought out to be executed. This scene returns to that of the opening dream, providing a circular frame: Homburg's blindfold is taken
from his eyes; before him stands not the firing squad but the smiling
Elector, Natalia, and the whole entourage of the first 'dream.' Natalia
steps towards him and once again places the laurel wreath on his head,
as the assemblage exclaims, 'Viva il Principe di Homburg!' The aston-
ished Homburg asks, 'È un sogno?' [Is it a dream?] and the final words
of the film are Colonel Kottwitz's cool reply, 'Certo, che altro?' [Cer-
tainly, what else?]

The central theme of the film is the conflict between the Prince and the
Elector, the latter acting as a father figure and referred to by the Prince
in the opening 'dream' as *father* (although he is actually Homburg's

uncle). The Elector or father represents the law, rationality, and justice. The Prince or son, dressed in billowing Romantic shirts and clearly a dreamer, represents the instinctual, irrational, and impulsive. Homburg is also an individualist, signalling the kind of subjectivity that developed across Europe during the Romantic period. Bellocchio sets the film in Heinrich von Kleist's lifetime (during the Napoleonic wars) and not in 1675, the time in Kleist's original script, which allows him to draw this parallel between romanticism and the rise of individualism.[11]

In *Il Principe di Homburg* the dialectic established between father and son is complex, rendering problematic the definitive assignment of the moral right to either side. The two figures are, however, still strongly differentiated. The scene that best illustrates the divergence between the positions of father and son is the one that immediately precedes the battle of Fehrbellin. The military hierarchy is gathered in the castle to discuss the plan of battle, while outside the castle walls can be heard the boom of ongoing war. This scene establishes two planes of interest, one centred on the father (public, military, and rational) and one on the son (private, emotional, and irrational) and avails of the large, uncluttered castle room through which to shift the cameras' positions and so set up a complex interrelation of shots.

The public plane is dominated by Field Marshal Dörfling's dictation of the Elector's battle plan to the assembled men; the private plane, however, is dominated by a series of looks, established through action and reaction shots, between Homburg and Princess Natalia when he recognizes her as the woman in the dream and approaches her. This private plane is accompanied by Crivelli's sumptuous romantic score (absent from the public plane).

The two planes then fuse in the metaphor of a trumpet. In the public military discourse, a reference to a trumpet forms part of the battle plan, because Homburg has been ordered not to enter battle until it sounds; in Homburg's private discourse, the trumpet becomes instead a cipher for his burgeoning love of Natalia. He repeats the Field Marshal's words in a triumphant whisper, thus transporting them into his private world: 'Dopodiché farà suonare la tromba!' [After which the trumpet will sound!] The screenplay designates these words to be spoken with 'una sicurezza quasi infantile' [an almost infantile certainty] (Bellocchio 1997, 56). The Prince's private world is infantile and feminized. This infantile world is at loggerheads with the adult world of the father, and ultimately the scene presents us with the idea, to which Bellocchio's films so frequently return, that these two worlds – private, instinctive, and emotional versus public, law-based, and rational – cannot easily coexist. Although both seem to mingle in this space and in the symbol of the trumpet, two devices draw attention to their conflict. First, different shooting techniques are used for the world of the 'son' – close-ups and medium close-ups in shallow focus, which tend to isolate both Homburg and the Princess from their surroundings – than for the frame of the military grouping – wider, more embracing, medium to medium long shots. Second, Crivelli's emotional music is used for the shots in which Homburg and Natalia fall in love, but not for the shots in which the military world is framed. Finally, the different voice timbres, from Homburg's intimate semi-whispers to the Elector's strong masculine voice, show how the two worlds do not belong together. In the following scene on the battlefield this will become even clearer. Here, Homburg ignores the Elector's commands, to which his contact with the emotional, instinctive, and infantile world has made him deaf, and risks his battalion's lives for his own impulsiveness and his dreams of glory.

Homburg, like Bellocchio's Enrico IV, belongs to the generation of those who want it all and want it now; the opening 'dream' reveals his lust for glory (the laurel wreath), power (the Elector's chain of office wound into the wreath), and love (Natalia). However, he lacks the self-discipline to turn this from empty dreaming into concrete reality. Bellocchio acknowledges that, in the film,

> è come se il padre rimproverasse al figlio una specie di incontinenza passionale … L'obbedienza non è solo una dimensione repressiva, di controllo, di castrazione, ma anche di padroneggiamento della propria passionalità. (Cruciani and Sante 2003, 12)

> [it is as if the father were reproving the son for a kind of incontinence of the passions. Obedience is not just a repressive dimension, one of control, of castration, but also one of gaining control over one's own passions.]

Ultimately, this film, although weighing both positions, stands close to the side of the father, for the first time, despite the film's rooting of the point of view in the son. Although the Elector is formidable and strict, gone is the sadistic despotism of the early fathers or father figures. This is part of a general trend in Bellocchio's cinema of shifting slowly towards more positive father figures (like Mori in *La balia*, Ernesto in *L'ora di religione*, Aldo Moro in *Buongiorno, notte*, and Franco Elica in *Il regista di matrimoni*).

However, the anger of the rebel sons and daughters never quite disappears. Ernesto's angry but partial retort to his aunt, in *L'ora di religione*, a reply that tails off into silence, is a sign of a continuing attack on the father's control: 'Perché se non si mandano in quel paese i padri e le madri, ma radicalmente, definitivamente . . .' [Because if we don't send the mothers and fathers to hell, radically, definitively . . .] In *Vincere*, Mussolini is portrayed as the epitome of the bad father. The theme is emblematized in a scene where the young Benito Albino stands alone before the marble statue of his father's head, with his little chest out and his arms crossed, imitating his father's pose, before knocking the cruel, hard, unseeing statue from its pedestal. The portrait of Mussolini that emerges from the film is based on Freud's 'Group Psychology and the Analysis of the Ego,' which posits the authoritarian dictator-type as a kind of Nietzschean superman, the primal father, who is completely narcissistic and unable to love others.

All the difficulties that Bellocchio's families face are rooted in the substitution, for passion, of a social convention that masks instinctive feelings and falsifies the bond between self and other, leaving it formalized (self and mother; self and family) or rooted in cool, power relationships (self and father). These family relations are formative and sketch out relationships between self and other that are therefore highly negative. They prepare characters for relationships with everything they contact – from lovers to wives to church and state – such that the relationships will be tense and difficult and will involve the characters in perpetual and unresolved conflict.

Conclusion

Bellocchio's protagonists are caught up in a battle against a society that lays down laws that are seen to reduce, limit, and damage the individuals who are required to follow them. The rebellion of his characters is a consistent and evolving part of his film-making. In Bellocchio's first and second films, *I pugni in tasca* and *La Cina è vicina*, characters try to overthrow power structures completely and through violent means: Ale tries angrily to annihilate his dysfunctional family; Camillo organizes the collective resistance of a small pocket of radicals, intent on overthrowing the political system in its entirety through petty sabotage and bombs, such as the one set off at the Partito Socialista Democratico Italiano headquarters. Ale has some success, but Camillo has none. *La Cina è vicina*, instead, shows the failure of revolution: either it is irrelevant and vain and fails to make an impact (Camillo), or it is simply reabsorbed by the class that it attacks (as in the case of the two proletarians Giovanna and Carlo). In his next films, 'Discutiamo, discutiamo' and *Nel nome del padre*, Bellocchio turns to the collective and eschews violence, in favour of characters adopting a verbal discourse against the bourgeois educational and ecclesiastical systems. Both attacks on the system fail. 'Discutiamo, discutiamo' concludes with the police repeatedly hitting the students with plastic truncheons; that neither side flinches or gives way suggests a deadlock. The rhythmic blows of the truncheons suggests a battle that will last forever, with neither side budging, giving way, or winning – an eternal deadlock of opposing forces. In *Nel nome del padre*, the school accepts and expects rebellion and simply absorbs it. The failure of rebellion – this time an individual one, however – is repeated in *Sbatti il mostro in prima pagina*: a young journalist's resistance against the editor of the newspaper fails. His attempt to bring the truth to light cannot succeed, because the system that he takes on is too big and powerful; it easily suppresses what it does not like. Rovedo's attack is naïve; the one cannot attack the many. The newspaper is a powerful entity that is backed by another powerful entity, the political establishment. In the end, the truth that Rovedo upholds is powerless. Truth is not a locus of power. Power and knowledge are radically divided.

The shift from a position of impotence, which dominates these early films, to a position of at least limited power comes only when the desire for change becomes focused on smaller, less complex, and more personal goals. In *Salto nel vuoto* Marta's rebellion results, on one level, in only a tiny change – she gains the freedom to go to the beach; on another level, however, it is a much more complete revolution as it destroys the external power structures kept in place by her brother *and* it undoes many of the internalizations of those structures. Up to the present, the rebellion of the individual against the system is paramount in Bellocchio's films, and in small ways it can be seen as successful. Ernesto slips out of his family's (and the church's) hold in *L'ora di religione*; Chiara, though she ultimately fails, envisages a transformation of history and another path for herself, which may help others to succeed, in *Buongiorno, notte*; Princess Bona escapes her marriage to a dull and unsuitable man in *Il regista di matrimoni*; and Ida, although failing to achieve her goals in her lifetime, has finally had her story told and has made contact with the 'outside,' as acknowledged in her final look towards the camera in *Vincere*.

The trajectory of Bellocchio's cinema making moves therefore from impotence in the face of power structures – which were envisaged initially as large abstract institutions outside the self (family, educational and ecclesiastic systems, and the state) and which were fought collectively in the early seventies – to the discovery of rebellion on an individual and private level, with smaller and more personal goals. As Bellocchio says:

> Mi interessa compiere una ricerca più intima, più profonda nell'individuo. Sia nell'*Ora di religione* che nel *Regista di matrimoni* racconto ancora la ribellione, ma la ribellione di un singolo uomo … Prende in mano la sua vita concretamente e agisce invece di arrendersi alla disperazione. Al centro della politica ora c'è la volontà dell'uomo, non più un ideale politico di massa. Tutto dipende dalle proprie scelte, dalla vita che uno fa, dal suo coraggio, dalla sua viltà. (Bellocchio, cited in Zu Fürstenberg 2005, 86)

> [I'm interested in carrying out a more intimate and profound excavation of the individual. In both *L'ora di religione* and *Il regista di matrimoni* I still recount a rebellion, but it is the rebellion of a single man … He takes control of his life concretely and acts, rather than giving in to desperation. At the centre of politics now there's a man's will, rather than a mass political ideal. Everything depends on one's choices, on the life that one lives, on one's courage, on one's cowardice.]

The rebellions of Bellocchio's protagonists are attempts to establish a free and private space outside the world of the superego and society's rules, a space that is implicitly, and sometimes explicitly, a rebellion against the rules of the father.

The model of the self and other is one marked by a very high level of negativity and struggle, and it is this fundamental relationship that is repeated again and again in relationships with the Other. It seems that self and Other are irremediably at loggerheads. From the relationship of the self with father to that with the Church (*L'ora di religione*), the educational establishment (*Nel nome del padre* and 'Discutiamo, discutiamo'), the mental institution (*Matti da slegare*, *La visione del Sabba*, *La balia*, and *Vincere*), the political establishment (tackled indirectly in *Sbatti il mostro in prima pagina* and directly in *Buongiorno, notte* and *Vincere*), and the prison (*Diavolo in corpo*), self and Other clash.

The struggle that lies at the very heart of Bellocchio's cinema is the battle against a negative relationship with the Other, a battle embodied repeatedly in the figure of the rebel, which so dominates his oeuvre. The rebel, who is nearly always a protagonist in Bellocchio's films, is typically Dionysian, ruled by instinct and the unconscious and hitting out against rationality and consciousness as embodied in the father, the institution, and the father-text.

6   Tradition and Its Discontents

In this final chapter I will be exploring how a director who maintained a rebellious and often individualistic attitude towards society, its traditions, and its institutions deals with artistic traditions in his own work, especially the cinematic and the literary. The focus of this chapter will be Bellocchio's adaptations from the classics of European literature, particularly Pirandello's *Enrico IV* and *La balia*. However, the chapter will also explore Bellocchio's use of citation and will discuss two further films – *L'ora di religione* and *Il regista di matrimoni* – which involve their protagonists in complex and bitter battles for control against a pre-existing artistic or literary model.

Adaptations and Citations: Pirandello, Manzoni, and the Overturning of the Father-Text

In the course of his career thus far, Bellocchio has adapted the works of Luigi Pirandello (*Enrico IV, La balia, L'uomo dal fiore in bocca* [The Man with the Flower in his Mouth]), Heinrich von Kleist (*Il Principe di Homburg*), Anton Chekhov (*Il gabbiano*), and Raymond Radiguet (on which *Diavolo in corpo* is very loosely based) – a highly Eurocentric selection of texts, focusing largely on canonical theatre and literature of the late nineteenth and early twentieth century, that are in line with Bellocchio's literary predilections, as will be shown.

Bellocchio's adaptations have usually been commissioned (especially by RAI), but he has nevertheless been given some free rein to adapt a text of his choice, and the texts adapted are almost without exception from authors and texts that he considers seminal to him. He claims that *The Seagull* and *The Prince of Homburg* influenced him strongly for

many years and that he saw himself reflected in the two male characters of Chekhov's play, Trigorin and Konstantin – especially the former
(Tassone 1980, 43). His fascination for Pirandello emerges from their
shared interest in madness and acting. In *La Cina è vicina*, for instance,
Camillo's self-scrutiny before a mirror has a decidedly Pirandellian flavour; like the protagonist of *Uno, nessuno, e centomila* [*One, No One and
One Hundred Thousand*] (1926), who observes his reflection in a mirror
in order to try to see himself as others might, Camillo carefully observes
himself act prior to making his speech.

Bellocchio's adaptation of three of Pirandello's texts for the screen is
particularly significant. One adaptation, *L'uomo dal fiore in bocca*, is a
thirty-six-minute short film made on a low budget for RAI television in
1992. The other two, *Enrico IV* and *La balia*, are significant feature films,
again with RAI funding. All three form part of the national network's
ongoing program of adapting canonical works for television.

Written in 1921, *Enrico IV* is one of Luigi Pirandello's best-known
plays, and it was commissioned by RAI for film in 1984. Bellocchio's
version screens most of the key elements of Pirandello's plot: the
cavalcade, Enrico's fall from his horse and the ensuing madness (all
screened in flashback),[1] the visit to the castle on the part of Matilda
and her entourage, Enrico's reception of his guests, his confession of
sanity to his privy counsellors, the Doctor's cure, and the final stab-
bing of Belcredi. However, although the plot broadly mirrors the original throughout act 1, it diverges from it radically towards the end of
act 2 when Frida goes temporarily missing. In Pirandello's version, the
girl soon returns, dressed exactly as her mother had been twenty years
before, and ready to take up her position in the niche and her part in the
family plot to cure Enrico through a sudden shock. In Bellocchio's version, when the girl disappears, she changes into her mother's clothes,
but instead of returning to her family, she slips into Enrico's room and
lies down on his bed. Enrico spots her, and she, now resembling the
woman Enrico once loved, tries to kiss him. Although she then returns
to the family and takes up her position in the niche, the meaning of
the ensuing shock treatment has been completely transformed; it has
been emptied of its shock value because Enrico already knows of the
girl's existence. Moreover, Frida's gesture indicates the possibility of a
kind of healing for Enrico that the Doctor's ridiculous shock treatment
can never offer. The film then closes in a radically different way from
that of the original. When the Doctor floods the room with electric light,
revealing the living sculptures in the niches, Enrico still gets a fright

and in his confusion grabs Frida, as in Pirandello's version. However, when Belcredi – Enrico's lifelong rival – becomes involved, Enrico stabs him with a toy sword. Fake blood spurts out, and Belcredi, though shocked, is not wounded. In the final scene the visitors leave, and the 'Emperor' and his privy counsellors pick up and put away the props: the fake paintings, the fake stones, and the toy sword. They turn out the lights, and the final word said by Enrico is a simple and plain 'Andiamo' [Let's go].

Bellocchio's version does not show an equivalence in meaning that might be considered the hallmark of that so debatable a term, *the faithful adaptation*. The divergence in the plot at the end of act 2 and again at the end of act 3 signals a far greater shift on the level of both form and content than is called for by the conversion of 'a diegetic text (one that narrates or tells) into a mimetic one (one that represents or shows)' (Marcus 1993, 15). Many of the changes do result directly from the transformation of literary codes into cinematic codes. Pirandello's play becomes more cinematic, with greater attention to the image and the addition of some outdoor scenes, such as the long car journey towards the castle that opens the film, and the cavalcade enacted on a hillside. There has been substantial cutting of the original text: some of the text is made redundant by the images, and most of the longer intellectual monologues have disappeared or been severely reduced. The language changes, becoming more 'spoken,' simplified, and succinct. A musical soundtrack, which is crucial to the medium of film but was not foreseen in Pirandello's play, has also been added. However, what Bellocchio is doing is far greater than the necessary processes of reworking the play in a new medium. The points at which the plot splits radically from the original indicate significant divergences, especially for the role of Frida and for Enrico's character, which is transformed from that of a sane madman to a child-adult brandishing a toy sword. In addition, Bellocchio draws in a political discourse on class and develops a polemic against the Catholic Church, which are absent from Pirandello's play.

One of the most important shifts lies with the figure of Frida. In the film *Enrico IV*, certain characters come forward while others recede. Belcredi recedes, becoming a rather mild and unnoteworthy gentleman, and is no longer the grotesque figure of fun of Pirandello's play. Frida and her relationship with Enrico, however, come forward. In Pirandello's play, Frida's role is secondary and instrumental, and she has few lines; she exists largely to provide a mirror of her mother's youth in order to heighten the pathos of her mother's aging, and to act as a plot device, taking her part in the Doctor's plan. In Bellocchio's film, Frida is no longer secondary. Visually, she tends to dominate, attracting the camera lens and managing to steal the limelight from Matilda, played by Claudia Cardinale. Her character is transformed from a passive, frightened, and dominated girl to a woman who makes her own decisions and is capable of steering the plot. She goes off alone to explore the castle, insinuates herself into Enrico's apartment, and when he finds her there, brazenly kisses him. This act sabotages the shock treatment being prepared by the Doctor and positions her as a rebel against the norms of both the patriarchal family and the institution of psychiatry. Bellocchio's Frida is a woman who not only reflects the changes in the role of women between the 1920s and the 1980s but also portrays one of Bellocchio's rebel women, being a forerunner of Giulia in *Diavolo in corpo* and of Mad or Maddalena in *La visione del Sabba*.

Frida's kissing of Enrico, however, indicates a related concern that Bellocchio draws out: Enrico's sexuality. Pirandello's portrait of Enrico explains away Enrico's frustrated sexuality in terms of his unbounded love for Matilda and the ensuing romantic disappointment, after which we are lead to believe that he loves no more and turns for sex only to prostitutes. However, by having Enrico reject the advances of both Matilda and Frida (advances that are never explicitly made in Pirandello's version), Bellocchio draws attention to Enrico's inability to create a bond with a woman. The flashback to the cavalcade sees him prey to unrequited love for Matilda. However, this love is not shown favourably, as a sign of a real bond, but rather it signals the kind of projection against which Massimo Fagioli had warned. Enrico's failure to form a true bond in the past resurfaces in the present. In this light, Enrico's seemingly insignificant final word 'Andiamo,' in place of Pirandello's truly pessimistic 'Ora sì ... per forza ... qua insieme, qua insieme ... e per sempre' [Now yes ... perforce ... here together, here together ... and forever], gains a new significance. It implies a rejection of transformation. He has rejected the two women who might have opened up the possibility for a *real* cure, as opposed to the farcical cure proposed by the Doctor. He prefers to 'go away' with his infantile and impotent sword – a clear sexual symbol – rather than face the challenge of a real relationship. In this, Bellocchio's Enrico, seemingly so much less tragic than Pirandello's, is actually just as tragic: he is locked forever in his own unchanging psychic world, rejecting the transformation that would free him.

The brandishing of the toy sword presents another key shift between the two texts. Bellocchio's focus falls not on madness but on acting. Enrico is shown to be lucid from the start: we see him listening in carefully while Matilda rehearses her part as the historical figure Matilde of Tuscany, so that later, when he officially receives her in this disguise in his throne room, there can be no doubt that he recognizes her. For his portrayal of Enrico, Bellocchio claims to have stood 'contro la tradizione istrionesca dei Benassi, degli Albertazzi, dei Randone e di tutti quelli che finora ho visto in quel ruolo' [against the histrionic tradition of the Benassis, the Albertazzis, the Rondones, and all those who until now I have seen in that role] (Callari 1991, 415), choosing instead 'una follia apparentemente tranquilla, con tre o quattro momenti urlati, che non sono però i più folli' [a madness that is apparently tranquil, with three or four episodes of bellowing, which are not, however, as mad as they might be] (415). Bellocchio has claimed that Marcello Mastroianni's capacity for talking 'splendidamente sottovoce' [in a splendid undertone] (415) was behind the choice of a non-histrionic madman. Bellocchio catches the Emperor in his gentle melancholy and 'tran-tran quotidiano' [the routines of his daily life] (415), which are absent from Pirandello's more obviously tragic portrayal of the man. Bellocchio's Enrico, rather than playing a great emperor or madman, helps children with their homework, drinks caffé latte, and stabs with a toy blade. Bellocchio affirms that 'più che la follia, è la finzione che mi ha interessato nel tradurre in film il dramma pirandelliano' [it was pretence, more than madness, that interested me in translating Pirandello's play into film] (Nicastro 1992, 287).

Acting is also a Pirandellian concern, but Bellocchio draws the theme out, especially with regard to play. Whereas Pirandello's discourse on acting tends to have to do primarily with masking and the assumption of social roles – issues that reflect the highly codified Sicilian society in which Pirandello was formed – Bellocchio grafts a level of play and infantilism onto the discussion of acting. Many children live inside Bellocchio's castle, and we watch, for instance, as a girl plays in a huge pile of wool. The presence of these children, to whom Enrico is clearly attached, is positive on the one hand because they represent a certain naturalness that Matilda and Enrico have lost in their masking of self, but negative on the other hand in the sense that they indicate the childish, regressive world in which Enrico lives. This regressive world is marked too by the many toys that are strewn about in the mise en scène: there are the toy horses (which clearly reference Enrico's original fall), toy rocks, and the toy sword with which Enrico attacks Belcredi. These elements, far from referencing the Fagiolian idea of the first year of a child's life as *mare calmo*, seem instead to indicate how Enrico, in his closeted existence in the castle, is unable to grow emotionally and become an adult. He is aging without ever having left his childishness behind. His rejection of any kind of transformation of his inner state ensures that he remains trapped in a grappling and impotent infantilism.

Bellocchio's film is clearly shifting Pirandello's play into a psychological framework quite different from that of the original: the lack of growth and transformation is closer to a Fagiolian model than it is to a Pirandellian one, and the link between madness and acting is also part of a recurring discourse on mad people as actors, which will resurface in *La visione del Sabba* and *Vincere*. Moreover, as Gedda points out, the film can be read in relation to Bellocchio's arguments on fathers and sons, with Enrico as 'un padre mai completamente divenuto adulto' [a father who has never quite become an adult] (Gedda in Nicastro 1992, 325).

Bellocchio also draws a critique of society into his adaptation. The updating a play to the present is fairly common practice for adaptations of classic texts, but in this instance it allows Bellocchio to comment on a political period that runs from the 1960s to the 1980s, including the upheaval of the 1968 contestation. The cavalcade is set in the early to mid-sixties, and the post-cavalcade party cites Nadia's infamous striptease from Fellini's *La dolce vita* (1960) (Nicastro 1992, 285), revealing the frivolous decadence of a certain haut-bourgeoisie of the sixties that Fellini had caught so well. The return of these characters to the castle in the 1980s shows these same people during the *riflusso* and allows parallels to be drawn between the two worlds. Gedda comments that Bellocchio's *Enrico IV* reconstructs 'il cammino di una generazione di intellettuali sradicati, figli anagrafici del fascismo ... in un percorso ideologico caratterizzato dal protagonismo di fine anni Sessanta all'insegna tipicamente infantile del "tutto e subito"'(Nicastro 1992, 325) [the march of a generation of uprooted intellectuals ... sons born under fascism ... in an ideological itinerary characterized by the protagonism of the end of the seventies, under the typically infantile banner of 'everything and right away'].

This is the generation of the *riflusso*. By reducing the medieval history to little more than a pretext, the film reveals its focus on the contemporary world of post-war Italy. In particular, Bellocchio deliberately politicizes the position of the privy counsellors, who become representatives of the working class. In the luncheon scene in which they eat at a table, alongside Enrico, they have a brief and humorous discussion about their status as 'slaves.' Then one of them accuses another of having a 'mentalità sindacalista' [unionized mentality], while another retorts that this job is still better than working in a factory. Through this scene the film is making a small sardonic political point on the non-politicization of the generation that is coming of age in the eighties. These young people mock the unions and show no interest in fighting for their rights despite the fact that the masters – Enrico with his castle and Matilda in her Mercedes – still dominate. They are worlds apart from the rebellious and resistant young people of *La Cina è vicina* or 'Discutiamo, discutiamo.' Bellocchio takes the opportunity to gently mock the complacency of the eighties and its abandonment of the spirit that fights the fathers in an attempt to bring about change.

The film also uses the contemporary to vent concerns about the Catholic Church. In the throne room scene in which Enrico receives his guests, his rival, Belcredi, is nervously and noisily shifting coins about in his pocket. Enrico asks the man to empty his pockets, and the camera presents a close-up of a coin on which Pope John Paul II's head (rather than Pope Gregory VII's) and the year 1984 are clearly embossed. This reference to a contemporary pope allows the Canossa scene to be read in a rather different light. In this scene, presented in flashback, a furious Enrico stands out in the snow, bellows insults, and then hurls snowballs at an unmoving pope who is framed on a balcony above him. By reducing the medieval historical content almost to zero, Bellocchio shifts this scene from historical re-enaction to a timeless one that emblematizes the angry rebellion of one man against the Pope as a symbol of the power of the Catholic Church. The confusion of the identity of the Pope and the overlapping of past and present popes opens out a more general metaphorical side than is present in the play, and it can be seen as shifting the discourse on the Catholic Church within the discourse established by Bellocchio since the beginning of his film-making.

The emphasis on issues in contemporary society (the Church and the *riflusso*) and the sliding of the film within a psychological framework that draws on Fagioli make it clear that, however much this film might resemble 'teatro fotografato'[2] in its acting styles and mise en scène, it is far from any faithful aping of the original or father-text. Instead, it takes a pre-existent text and at crucial points bends it towards the director's personal concerns.

In *La balia,* made for RAI more than ten years later, Bellocchio detaches his film still further from the father-text; this detachment was facilitated by the nature of the original, a short story that, unlike a theatre play, needs expansion rather than contraction. This transformation is further facilitated by its status as a minor work. Whereas *Enrico IV* carries the weight of an extremely well-known canonical text, 'La balia' is only one of Pirandello's two hundred and fifty stories. *La balia*'s spectators are therefore unlikely to be making detailed comparisons with a so-called original. An examination of this second film reinforces the sense of the way in which Bellocchio works with Pirandello's texts.

The plot of Pirandello's short story is grotesque and tragic. The short story, written in 1913, opens in the Manfroni household in Sicily, as Mr and Mrs Manfroni receive a letter from their son-in-law in Rome, a socialist lawyer called Ennio Mori; in it he expresses a need for a wet nurse because his wife has failed to produce milk for the child. Mr Manfroni sees this as the perfect opportunity to revenge himself on Titta Marullo, a young man whom he had thrown out of his bakery for his revolutionary ideas; he arranges for Titta's young wife, Annicchia, to be sent to Rome to take on this humble role, forced to serve his own daughter. Annicchia, who has never set foot outside Sicily, accepts the proposal and is bundled on a ferry and a train and sent to Rome, leaving her two-month-old baby behind. Once in the Mori household she nurtures Mori's infant, now in her care, but suffers at the hand of Ersilia, Mori's wife, who is terribly jealous and repeatedly accuses her husband of being attracted to the girl. A few months later, Annicchia's husband, Titta, suddenly bursts into the house, furious, and announces the awful news that their baby is dead. Blamed for the death, the distraught Annicchia falls ill with a fever, and her milk runs dry. She is then expelled by Ersilia, who argues that the girl has no further purpose in the house. The short story ends with Annicchia having to move in with Mori's lecherous old secretary, Felicissimo, who assigns her the place of maid in his house in the expectation that she will also provide sexual favours. In the last paragraphs of the story, Mori dictates a socialist speech to Felicissimo; using the case of two babies born in different social circumstances, he proclaims the equality between people. Felicissimo chuckles as he writes, causing Mori to ask, in the final words of the story, 'Perché ride così?' [Why are you laughing like that?] The story thus ends on a tragic and ironic note: the wet nurse has been forced into prostitution, and Mori, ever the good socialist, fails to recognize how his grand theories fail to have an impact on reality.

Bellocchio's plot diverges substantially. His story opens with a double prologue, the first part of which is dedicated to Annetta who is shown in fields with her women folk, and the second to Mori – now a psychiatrist, not a socialist lawyer – who is shown visiting a rich patient. These prologues are followed by the development of two parallel plots. The main plot, centred on Mori's bourgeois house and household, narrates the birth of Mori's baby, his wife's failure to feed him or establish any relationship with him, and Mori's selection of a wet nurse. Annetta comes to Rome, nurses Mori's child, and is subjected to the jealousy of Mori's wife, Vittoria (Valeria Bruni Tedeschi). When Vittoria presents an ultimatum to Mori, saying that either Annetta leaves or she herself will go, Mori refuses to let Annetta go. His wife therefore departs, leaving Mori and the girl alone in the house. An intimacy, which is sensual without ever becoming openly sexual, develops between the two, as Mori teaches Annetta to read and write so that she can communicate with her imprisoned socialist lover. At the end of the film, however, Mori follows her in the street and discovers that she has brought her own child to Rome and has been nursing it at the same time as his child. Furious, he dismisses her immediately. When she returns to his house later that night and tries secretly to feed the child, she finds that the baby no longer needs her milk. Forgiven by Mori but no longer necessary in the role of wet nurse, Annetta leaves the household to return to the country.

The second, and secondary, plot of the film revolves around the institution of the mental hospital. Mori's work here as a psychiatrist brings him into contact with socialist subversives who play at being mad in order to escape imprisonment. Whereas Mori unquestioningly employs his medical methods, his young assistant, Nardi (played by Bellocchio's son, Pier Giorgio), becomes increasingly frustrated with their inability to cure their patients; he joins the socialist cause, which he believes can bring change, and eventually leaves the hospital. At the end of the film, Nardi and one of the female patients, Maddalena (Jacqueline Lustig), with whom he has fallen in love, stage an uprising in the centre of Rome, in which Annetta and Mori briefly get caught up before the denouement in which Mori discovers Annetta's secret. This second plot is wholly absent from Pirandello's original.

Bellocchio takes the rather grotesque, expressionist short story and retains only the bones of the plot. Very little of the original remains. For a start, although both versions are set in the early twentieth century, the two worlds stand apart geographically: the Sicilian flavour of the original disappears in a film that is set almost entirely in Rome, and in which Maya Sansa, who is not Sicilian, is required to assume only a gentle country accent. References to the island, its customs, and the Sicilian Manfroni family simply vanish. It is clearly not the short story's exoticism or backwardness that attracted the director. Furthermore, the grotesque style of the short story is substituted by a narrative style that approaches Chekhov and the realist, character-driven narrative of the late nineteenth century.

Essentially, Bellocchio takes the short story and remoulds it around his own themes in similar fashion to his reworking of *Enrico IV,* although in *La balia* the reworking is far more radical. Once again, Bellocchio shifts the role of a young woman into the foreground, and again the theme of transformation is insinuated into the fatalistic framework of the original. Moreover, the political themes that the short story harboured are drawn out and developed and come to stand in a metaphoric relation to the contestation of the late 1960s.

The figure of the *balia* is radically redrawn. Bellocchio's nanny, or wet nurse, is no longer the victim of 'una architettura rigida, fatalistica, veristica, nella quale vince un certo tipo di meschinità, di mediocrità tanto che la povera balia finisce a fare la prostituta e il suo figlio muore, secondo le regole di uno schema quasi zoliano che io non potevo accettare' (Bellocchio, cited in Malanga 1999, 6) [a rigid, fatalistic, veristic architecture, in which a certain kind of wickedness and mediocrity is victorious, so that the poor wet nurse ends up as a prostitute and her son dies, in line with the rules of an almost Zolian schema that I could not accept]. Bellocchio's *balia* is not the passive victim in an ineluctable tragedy in which she is passed from one set of male hands to another (from Mr Manfroni to Mori to Felicissimo). However shy and unschooled she is, like Frida she has a decisiveness that enables her to shape her own destiny. Annetta does not abandon her own child, as Mori demands, but brings him with her to Rome, enabling her to visit him each day. She becomes neither Mori's lover nor a prostitute but maintains her integrity and, as a positive character, avoids the narrative punishment that her predecessor, Annicchia, gets for acting as an agent of disruption. Instead, Annetta gently grows, patiently learning to read and write, and returns from her encounter with the bourgeoisie not only unscathed but also enriched.

A greater transformation is reserved for the male character, Mori. In Pirandello's version, Mori learns nothing from his encounter with the poor Sicilian girl, simply using the episode to support his arguments in the socialist circle; he passively allows his wife to sack the girl, and his old secretary to run off with her and ruin her. Bellocchio's Mori instead undergoes a slow process of awakening whereby he manages to prevent both his wife's madness and the *balia*'s tragic fate. In the film, Mori is no longer 'un vigliacco, un pupazzo, un imbecille, un buffone, come nel testo di Pirandello' [a coward, a puppet, an imbecile, a fool, as in Pirandello's text] (Bellocchio, cited in Malanga 1998, 125) but instead is

> un uomo problematico ma in grado di intuire che non può subire, più che l'isterismo, la pazzia della moglie; deve prendere posizione e cercare di difendere il bambino, e quindi difendere la balia … A suo modo è un eroe, con dei tentennamenti, ma senza passività. (Malanga 1998, 125)

> [a problematic man, but capable of intuiting that he can no longer bear the hysteria and madness of his wife; he must take a position to try and defend the child, and therefore defend the wet nurse … In his own way he is a hero, with waverings, but without passivity.]

Bellocchio's reinterpretation of the short story casts Mori deliberately as Pirandello's alter ego, a man who is, just like Pirandello was, forced to deal with his wife's pathological jealousy; it was the sign of a mental illness that would eventually lead, in Pirandello's case, to the woman's permanent hospitalization (Caesar 1998, 59–60). Bellocchio therefore reads Pirandello's short story as an expression of Pirandello's own crisis, with his alter ego, Mori, being a character 'che non riesce a risolvere il suo dramma personale, che è appunto quello di vivere con una donna – con cui ha avuto figli ecc. – e al tempo stesso impedire che questa donna impazzisca, come poi è avvenuta nella realtà' [who cannot manage to resolve his own personal drama, which is that of living with a woman – with whom he has had children, etc. – and, at the same time, preventing that woman going mad, as happened in reality] (Seta 2007).

In this reading, the prevention of madness becomes central. Bellocchio therefore expands the theme of madness and its cure, lodging it in both the film's plot (the madness within the house) and its subplot (the madness in the mental hospital). In the hospital Mori is shown controlling, but failing to cure, the mental patients in his care. If he is to save his wife, he must learn instead how to transform and cure their relationship. A key to this cure can be found in Mori's own advice to his patient (Michele Placido) at the beginning of the film: 'La vostra solitudine vi porterà alla rovina … è proprio questo vostro tenace isolamento che vi farà ammalare' [Your solitude will ruin you … it is exactly this, your tenacious isolation, that will make you ill]. The comment points to lack of communication and isolation as central components of mental illness, and it is precisely this lack of communication between husband and wife and their mutual isolation that allow Vittoria to become so disturbed. The blame, however, is not just theirs but belongs to a bourgeois society that encourages couples to marry from convention and fear rather than from love. The film presents the bourgeois family as an institution that in itself produces madness. In the letter sent by Annetta's socialist lover and read surreptitiously by Vittoria (who recognizes herself in it), the young man criticizes the bourgeois 'mogli obbedienti [che] si sono sposate per paura, per solitudine' [obedient wives (who) married out of fear, out of loneliness]. If Mori wants to rescue his wife from the madness inherent in the system, he must learn to go beyond what he does in the hospital, which is, as the rebellious Nardi points out, only to coldly 'osservare, classificare, riempire cartelle cliniche, accogliere tutti e non curare mai nessuno' [observe, classify, fill in clinical forms, take in everyone, and never cure anyone].

The film ends with Mori writing the reply that Annetta had asked him to write on her behalf to her lover: the reply of a woman to a man, written by a man. This divergence from the original plot (where Mori wrote a pious, blind, and hypocritical socialist tract) shows that Mori is beginning to understand what a woman might feel and what a genuine relationship between a man and a woman might be (and so, in some ways, this film continues the discourse of La condanna). He has after all glimpsed it in the liberatory love between Annetta and her subversive lover; he can see from the man's letter that they respect each other's individuality and have a profound and instinctive connection. His attempt to articulate a reply from a woman to a man harbours a seed of hope for his relationship with his wife and signals the possibility of breaking down the isolation between them, thus providing a key to preventing her madness. The film uses character transformation to break the ineluctability of the original text's fatalism.

The second major area where Bellocchio draws the plot closer to his own directorial and personal interests is the significant expansion of the short story's political elements. In the original, Mori is a socialist deputy, and Annicchia's husband is dismissed from his job and placed under house arrest for his subversive socialist ideas. Pirandello did not sympathize with the socialist movement, and neither character is portrayed favourably: Mori is a passive, ridiculous, uncomprehending, and hypocritical man; Annicchia's husband is wild and uncontrolled, a wife beater, and a power monger. In Bellocchio's film, Mori becomes less politicized, and the politicization is transferred instead to his young assistant, Nardi, a positive, if somewhat naive, character who wants to change the way things are; when he realizes he cannot do so through psychiatry, he becomes involved in a political movement. Annicchia's or Annetta's subversive husband is retained by Bellocchio, although we actually only see him once and then only very briefly. Nonetheless, he too becomes a positive character; he is not the rabid, violent man of the short story but a sensitive soul, capable of writing a warm, non-judgmental, and profound letter to the girl from whom he is separated. To the film Bellocchio adds the subversive female patients interned within the mental hospital. The focus is especially on Maddalena, a beautiful, silent girl who feigns madness in order to escape imprisonment for allegedly burning down a theatre. Again, she is portrayed as a positive character, as an intelligent and assertive leader who is sensitive, mysterious, and instinctive. Bellocchio also adds the scenes of socialist ferment: the pasting of posters on the wall, and the uprising that bursts onto the streets of Rome towards the film's end. However, as argued in chapter 5, the nature of the political additions to the text is generic and emblematic, and it signals that what interested Bellocchio here was not 'un discorso di ricostruzione storica, ma di interpretazione personale' [a discourse about historical reconstruction, but one of personal interpretation] (Malanga 1999, 7). The scenes become a sign of a generic revolt against bourgeois institutions, especially family and the institution of psychiatry; the latter is attacked here, as in *Enrico IV*, for failing to cure its patients.

Bellocchio's rewriting of Pirandello clearly shows what kind of procedure he employs when faced with the father-text, procedures that, to greater or lesser extents, are employed across the range of his adaptations. With the exception of his first adaptation, *Il gabbiano*, which he later criticizes as too literal, Bellocchio's relationship with the text to be adapted is one in which respect for the original is secondary to the process of drawing the text towards his own personal vision. He claims that his turn towards a personal adaptation is something he learned through the experience of *Il gabbiano*, admitting to Bernardi (1998, 7), a year after the release of that film, that only through it did he realize that 'anche su testi classici, bisogna avere il coraggio di essere meno rispettosi e cercare di disgregare anche schemi estremamente massicci, compatti, se si vuole fare del cinema' [even with classical texts one must have the courage to be less respectful and to try to disaggregate even very large and compact schemas if one wants to make cinema].[3]

Bellocchio's experience as adaptor is marked therefore by a progressive detachment from the literary originals. His adaptations imply a dialogue with the literary father, in which the father is persuaded to adopt the arguments of the son. The fraught Oedipal struggle can be seen as a reflection of the tendency in the eighties to see adaptation 'not as a flight from authorial self-assertion but rather as a challenge to appropriate another's voice and make it one's own' (Marcus 1993, 12).

Two recent films – *L'ora di religione* and *Il regista di matrimoni* – see Bellocchio working a pre-existent artistic piece into the texture of his own cinema, rather than making an official adaptation. These films are fascinating as they set up a dialogue with the original work of art that is far more explicit than anything Bellocchio does with the adaptations, simply because they present the spectator with a conflict between two versions of a work within the same film, explicitly showing how artists-protagonists (Ernesto and Franco Elica, respectively) deal with an original. In the adaptation we see a finished product, which refers only to a pre-existent version that lies beyond the filmic text, but in these two films we also see, explicitly, the process whereby an artist enters into dialogue with the past. In their treatment of the interrelationship of contemporary art and canonical pieces, they emphasize the ambivalence in Bellocchio's usage of canonical works. In both films, the protagonists are artists who must come to terms with their artistic inheritance.

L'ora di religione is a film whose protagonist, Ernesto, is a visual artist, and this allows Bellocchio to develop a substantial discourse on art. The film attacks art critics (the sardonic critic, Baldracchi, curbs Ernesto's artistic liberty), explores the temptations of fame (Baldracchi is compared to Mephistopheles, tempting Ernesto/Faust with glory [Bellocchio 2002, 34]), and explores the figure of the muse (in the guise of the beautiful and mysterious Diana, who helps reignite Ernesto's creativity). Part of the discussion centres on the relationship of the contemporary artist to the weight of artistic inheritance, as represented by the great monument of the Vittoriano, a huge white marble hymn to Italian nationhood that dominates central Rome. The building runs like a motif through the film. At the beginning, Ernesto is seen 'pencilling' over its image on his computer, and in two further scenes he drives past the building in a car. It finally comes to the fore when, on a visit to the mental institution at which his brother works, he is introduced to a genial madman, Curzio Sandali. Sandali is obsessed with the ugliness of the Vittoriano and claims that his attempts to destroy it (attempts beyond his powers) are the cause of his mental illness. He draws close to Ernesto and confidentially whispers, 'Io trovavo che quella bruttezza avesse inibito la fantasia degli architetti di tutto il mondo, gli avesse impauriti, terrorizzati' [I found that the ugliness of that building had inhibited the creativity of architects in the whole world, that it frightened them, terrorized them]. Curzio's point is that the force of a dominant work of art can be such that it prevents creativity and beauty from developing in its stead. It is only when, returning to his computer image of the Vittoriano towards the end of the film, Ernesto takes the figure of Gradiva and allows her to walk free of the building so that it crumbles behind her, leaving an open and florid space, that Ernesto's creative block is lifted, and the sleeping muse – Diana – rises from her sleep and embraces him.

A very similar relationship between dominant art object and contemporary creator develops in *Il regista di matrimoni*, as Franco Elica – also played by Sergio Castellito – battles with Alessandro Manzoni's canonical *I promessi sposi* (*The Betrothed*, 1827). Like Ernesto, Franco finds it difficult to get beyond the weight of the past and tradition and to create anew. Transposing the argument to the literary field, Manzoni becomes for Franco Elica what the Vittoriano was for Ernesto.[4]

In the film, Franco Elica, a minor Italian director, is working on a new adaptation of Manzoni's *I promessi sposi*. During the screen tests at the beginning of the film he is persecuted by hoards of willing actors who imitate characters from the novel. Most strikingly, a young girl – who bears an almost uncanny resemblance to the Lucia of Mario Camerini's 1941 film version of the book – appears unexpectedly in Franco's office and, without warning, launches into a passionate recitation of a crucial scene of the novel: the encounter of the young Lucia with the rich and feared Innominato [Unnameable]. In the novel, Lucia has been separated from her fiancé ever since a nobleman, Don Rodrigo, fell in love with her and decided to prevent her marriage; she is finally captured, not by Don Rodrigo but by the Innominato acting on his behalf. Lucia spends a frightening and eventful night in the Innominato's castle, during which time she so impresses the hardened man with her passion and religious zeal that he not only frees her but also promptly converts to Christianity. A hint of attraction hovers between the literary characters on that night, a hint which plants the seed of an alternative story (never told by Manzoni) of a Lucia who, instead of finally re-uniting with her young fiancé, Renzo, falls in love with this dangerous, complex, and mysterious older man. This seed of possible transformation of the story-line makes this scene literally a seminal one for Bellocchio's film.

In *Il regista di matrimoni*, Bellocchio battles with originals – both the novel and Camerini's influential film – in an attempt to overcome them. Not only is the director, Franco Elica, assailed by a Lucia who acts just like Camerini's protagonist, forcing him to recite the part of Camerini's Innominato word for word while black-and-white clips from the film are spliced into the scene, but he is also followed by two bodyguards who mirror the two henchmen employed by Don Rodrigo to bully resist-ers. However, Bellocchio's film is not an adaptation of either Manzoni's *I promessi sposi* or Camerini's film. There are few straightforward paral-lels between the plots or characterizations, nor could Bellocchio easily accept this, the most Catholic of novels, without major rewriting. What he does is takes a key moment of the plot – the meeting of Lucia with the Innominato – and transforms it so that it releases its potential. In Belloc-chio's version, Lucia (Princess Bona) falls in love with the Innominato (Franco Elica, whose role condenses the Innominato and Don Rodrigo, the man who blocks the engagement in Manzoni's tale). Princess Bona ends up seeing the folly of marrying her mediocre fiancé, whom she does not love, and she runs off with Franco. In effect, Bellocchio winds the plot of *I promessi sposi* into his film, while subverting it at two of its most central points: the love and final marriage of Lucia and Renzo and the conversion of the Innominato, which reflects the novel's pro-Catholic sentiment for which Bellocchio (Franco) shows only ironic detachment.

As a director, Franco Elica fails at first to extricate his film from the weight of the literary original and of Camerini's adaptation. While he is in his studio in Milan, the original texts repeatedly block Franco's creativity: actors burst into his office, citing Camerini, and seethe in the tightly framed, narrow corridors of the studio. Only when he flees to Sicily does the 'original' begin to lose its grip. Geographically, Sicily is as far as Bellocchio could have gone within Italy to get away from a novel based in the northern province of Lombardy. Although Franco continues to be pursued by Manzonian scenarios (the henchmen, and the wedding that threatens to close the tale as it does in the novel), his meeting with the betrothed Princess Bona and their nascent love allow Manzoni and Camerini to be finally overturned. Only at the end of the film, when Franco/Innominato rescues the princess, does he finally break completely free of the schema of the original. In Manzoni and Camerini, after braving all the obstacles, Lucia eventually escapes the fate laid down by Don Rodrigo and marries her fiancé under the benevolent eye of the Catholic Church. In Bellocchio's subversive version, it is Franco/Innominato/Don Rodrigo who runs off with the bride, snatching her from her father, the church, and her fiancé. The protagonist therefore beats the ineluctability of the original plot, transforming it – just as Ernesto in *L'ora di religione* beats the ineluctability of the Vittoriano when he draws Gradiva descending from the building, leaving its destruction in her wake.

These films reflect just how difficult is the relationship with the original in Bellocchio's cinema. They suggest that Bellocchio's relationship with his artistic roots is conflictual and fraught. This is borne out in a number of interviews where his discussions of his artistic heritage are defensive and contradictory. He has gone as far as to occasionally portray himself as a director without 'maestri e nemmeno allievi' [masters or even pupils] (Malanga 1998, 130), in other words as positioned somehow beyond, or outside, the cinematic tradition; somewhat surprisingly, critics have often supported this position (see Lodato 1977, 72, and Bertuzzi 1996, 31). He has also denied the citational aspect of his cinema, emphasizing the originality of his own creation of images over any images that his films may choose to cite:

> A differenza di altri cineasti, io non attribuisco mai ai quadri – e nemmeno ad altre cose – un significato specifico, stilistico in senso citazionista … In un mio film, non ci dev'essere mai un'immagine appesa al muro che viene prima dell'immagine che ho creato io. (Bellocchio, cited in Malanga 1998, 128)

> [Unlike other cineastes, I never attribute to paintings – or to other things – a meaning that is specific and stylistic, in the sense of being citational … In my films there must never be an image hung on a wall that comes before the image that I have created.]

It is clear, however, not just from Bellocchio's adaptations and reworkings, but also from the assimilation of various kinds of artistic texts into his cinema, right from the beginning of his career, that Bellocchio's is not the isolated voice he might sometimes want us to believe. Instead, his voice has always dialogued with cinematic, artistic, and literary masters, from Ingmar Bergman to Luis Buñuel, from William Shakespeare to Giovanni Pascoli, from Michelangelo to Gino Severini, creating palimpsestic and reflexive works.

Literature is a fundamental point of reference throughout Bellocchio's cinema. It lends itself to the narrative structure, and influences the characterization of films. *I pugni in tasca* and *La Cina è vicina* both incorporate aspects of distinctly nineteenth-century literary melodrama, and in the second film Vittorio's character is based in part on Guido Gozzano's Totò Merumeni, who slowly possesses the girl of the lower classes while the house sleeps (Bellocchio 1967b, 19). Literature also weaves its way into the films through frequent citation. References to late-nineteenth-century and early-twentieth-century poets, especially Giovanni Pascoli but also Giuseppe Giacosa and Lorenzo Stecchetti and others, abound.[5] Dante, Manzoni, Goethe, Shakespeare, and other canonical European works are frequently cited: the Faust myth is at the heart of *Nel nome del padre*'s macabre school play and provides a key to Angelo's character; in 'Discutiamo, discutiamo,' the University Chancellor declaims Victor Hugo; three Macbethean witches appear in *Il sogno della farfalla*; and in *L'ora di religione*, the presence of a character called Filippo Argenti, his name straight from Dante's *Inferno*, comments ironically on Church corruption. These are just some of the many instances in which literary texts are woven into Bellocchio's films. Theatre and opera too play a significant part, again with citations typically from nineteenth-century works.[6]

Art also has a strong presence, which is perhaps not surprising given Bellocchio's early interest in painting.[7] From the *Last Judgment* on the wall of the dining room in *Nel nome del padre* to Gino Severini's futurist painting in *Salto nel vuoto* to paintings by Leonardo and Goya in *La condanna* to the use of futurism in *Vincere*, works of art have had prominent places in the mise en scène of his films. Moreover, despite having berated others, such as Pasolini, for the practice (Malanga 1998, 126), at times Bellocchio uses paintings or painting styles as an inspiration for a pose or a costume in his mature cinema. The scene in *La visione del Sabba* in which Maddalena is tortured by the insertion of a needle into her 'diabolic point' (actually an old scar), for example, is described in the screenplay as being inspired by Rembrandt's *The Anatomy Lesson* of 1632 (Bellocchio 1987, 71).[8]

Finally, as far as the cinema tradition is concerned, influence from many directors, such as Robert Bresson, Luis Buñuel, Igmar Bergman, the early Luchino Visconti, Fellini, Antonioni, and Bertolucci, can be identified.[9] There are references, too, in either films or interviews to film-makers within a tradition of Italian *impegno* (Francesco Rosi, the Taviani brothers, and Ermanno Olmi), to Louis Malle, Polish directors Andrzej Wajda and Krzysztof Zanussi, and Andrei Tarkovsky.[10] Italian neo-realism, French nouvelle vague, Brazilian *cinema novo*, expressionist

German cinema (especially Fritz Lang), and New German Cinema (Werner Herzog, Alexander Kluge, and Wim Wenders) are all important reference points for Bellocchio.[11] These cinematic traditions are only rarely explicitly cited in his films, but they have nonetheless been deeply absorbed. *I pugni in tasca* has been likened to Sam Fuller's neo-fascism, a charge that Bellocchio did not wholly deny (Albano 2000, 22). *La Cina è vicina* has been compared to Joseph Losey's *The Servant* (1963), a link that seems more direct and plausible because the earlier film also describes the insinuation of the working class into an upper-middle-class household; in Losey's film a wealthy and spoilt Londoner employs a servant, played by Dirk Bogarde, who, over the course of the film, usurps power in the claustrophobic household. The French nouvelle vague can be seen in isolated instances in Bellocchio's cinema. The off-centre and low-angle shots in the early parts of *La Cina è vicina* can certainly be described as Godardian, and the quirkiness of some of the shooting in *I pugni in tasca* might also be seen as mirroring French techniques. There is a flavour of the nouvelle vague in the first shot of Ale jumping down from a tree, where he literally jumps into the frame (a shot of an empty garden), and in the sequence where Ale's sister is assailed on the road by boys on mopeds, in which repeated shots are taken of the same subject from slightly different angles. However, ultimately, there is little real stylistic experimentalism in Bellocchio's cinema that could be said to match the daring playfulness of Godard.

Bellocchio's difficult relationship with cinematic influences can best be seen, perhaps, in relation to two particular cases: Italian neo-realism and genre cinema. Michalczyk (1986, 15) claims that neo-realism acted as a cinematic father to the sons of the sixties and seventies, providing a model for them to follow or to resist. *I pugni in tasca*, Bellocchio's first feature, indeed suggests a certain continuity with the movement. As Bertuzzi (1996, 53) notes, the realism inherent in the location shooting, especially in the striking bleakness of the Apennine hills and the shots of Piacenza, continues the neo-realist legacy of capturing the physical world in its everyday grittiness, and there is an attention to the misfit and the socially marginal, characteristic of neo-realism. Yet, fundamentally, *I pugni in tasca* resists neo-realism. The bleak realist locations are far from being the focus of the film, and there is little in the cinematography – with its close-ups, zooms, and occasional light touches of experimentalism *à la nouvelle vague* – to suggest the neo-realist call for the kind of deep-focus, realist shots that were to signal the unbiased recording of a semi-documentary real. Nor does the film represent the neo-realist search for realism in external detail; instead, as in Antonioni's films, it suggests a quest for 'un'immagine interiore che andasse oltre' [an inner image that goes beyond] (Bertuzzi 1996, 31). Finally, the attention to the plight of the working and peasant class that is characteristic of the movement is absent from Bellocchio's films; the setting for both *I pugni in tasca* and the following feature, *La Cina è vicina*, is steadfastly bourgeois.

Despite admiring Rossellini and the early Visconti, Bellocchio clearly is at pains to detach himself from the movement, asserting in one interview that 'non c'era nulla di Neorealistico nel mio lavoro' [there was nothing neo-realistic in my work] (Bolzoni and Foglietti 2000, 50). He repudiates the parallels suggested by critics between his early films and Visconti's: *I pugni in tasca* had been linked to Visconti's *Ossessione* (*Obsession*, 1943), and *La Cina è vicina* to *Vaghe stelle dell'Orsa* (*Sandra of a Thousand Delights*, 1965) (Lodato 1977, 72). In fact, according to Bertuzzi (1996, 17), *I pugni in tasca* is the film that 'chiuse con aggressività i conti con i buoni sentimenti del Neorealismo' [aggressively shut the door on the do-goodism of neo-realism]. Bellocchio points instead to the influences of other forms of realism, such as the French masters (Jean Renoir and Jacques Becker), literary realists like Émile Zola, and, later on, cinéma vérité and contemporary political cinema from Brazil, Italy, and elsewhere. His critical position towards neo-realism arises especially from his uneasiness with what he calls its 'umanesimo sentimentale' [sentimental humanism] (Bellocchio 1967a, 55), and this, in its stressing of identification, contrasts with his own rather Brechtian and often ironic detachment from his characters and subject matter, certainly in his early films. Despite all this, Bellocchio retains an admiration for Rossellini, as his citation of *Paisà* in *Buongiorno, notte* suggests.

In Bellocchio's use of genres the overturning is even more apparent. With the exception of *Marcia trionfale* and *Sbatti il mostro in prima pagina*, the latter following the style of a *giallo* rather closely (a sordid murder, incompetent police, corruption, suspense, good guys and bad guys, stereotyped characters, and the dénouement in the film's finale), Bellocchio's films tend to subvert the genres that they incorporate. His widespread use of melodrama, for example, is far from any slavish emulation of the genre but, instead, implies a critical re-evaluation of it. Techniques of decentring, which have been discussed in relation to *La Cina è vicina*, allow him to establish a distance between spectator and character that breaks the identification that the genre aims to establish. In other films, genre is similarly overturned: Bellocchio drains much of the suspense from the courtroom drama (*La condanna* and *Diavolo in corpo*), for instance, and from the political thriller (*Buongiorno, notte*). Although the latter film does use some suspense (during both the lift scene and the scene where burglars try to break into the flat at night – neither of which are present in Braghetti's account), the focus is firmly on Chiara's gradual and profound rebellion rather than on Moro's plight and the terrorists' fear of capture. Other Italian political thrillers, such as Gillo Pontecorvo's *Operación Ogro* (*Ogro*, 1979), which charts the killing of Carrero Blanco by ETA in 1973, Giuseppe Ferrara's *Il caso Moro* (*The Moro Affair*, 1986), and the conspiracy thriller *Piazza delle cinque lune* (*Piazza of the Five Moons*) by Renzo Martinelli, have a much greater recourse to the kind of suspense typical of the political thriller.

It is clear that Bellocchio's reaction to genre cinema is to use it – consciously or unconsciously – to structure his films, while maintaining a certain distance. His use can therefore only be described as resistant. Any straightforward, non-distanced, and non-ironic use of genre – for example, that found in *Sbatti il mostro in prima pagina* – risks shifting the films away from the art-house status that Bellocchio is anxious to maintain.

Bellocchio's use of citation, styles, and genre demonstrates that far from being an isolated voice, his films are surprisingly self-reflexive and intertextual. As citation is one way of weaving one's own voice into the tradition, and the tradition into one's voice, such levels of citation could be a sign not only of conservation but also, necessarily, of a certain conservatism, especially when those works are as canonical as they typically are in Bellocchio's case. However, to suggest that Bellocchio's citation signals conservatism would be to miss two fundamental points: first, the citations (especially those of the sixties and early seventies) are primarily in an ironic key, and second, in later films the originals are often presented only to be radically overturned. Although, on one level, *La traviata*'s 'Sempre libera' provides a beautiful and dramatic ending to *I pugni in tasca*, on another level, its use is ironic, revealing melodrama to be ridiculous, simply a 'bene di consumo borghese' [an item of bourgeois consumption] (Chiaretti, in Bellocchio 1967b, 18). In *La Cina è vicina*, the literary citations are 'in chiave di farsa' [in a farcical key] according to the screenplay (18), and the film repeatedly desacralizes its own references to canonical Western culture: the final words of the crucified Christ ('Dio mio, Dio mio, perché mi hai abbandonato?' [My God, my God, why hast thou abandoned me?]) are used blasphemously by Vittorio, sitting atop a toilet and failing to defecate; and Gaetano

Donizetti's 'Raggio d'amore parea' contemporaneously blends tender-
ness and irony, being sung by the small, highly discordant, and mocking
little choir of children who are gathered, somewhat unwillingly, around
the bedside of Padre Comotti. This irony and farce in the use of citation,
especially in the early films, seems to signal that what we are seeing is
not a deep-seated middle-class conservatism underlying the apparently
rebellious nature of his films, but something more complex.

Bellocchio's use of genre, literary precedents, works of art, and filmic
precedents evidence one thing above all: that his films interact uneasily with the original, rebelling against it, attempting to break free of
the necessity of repeating what has been already said. They destroy
the original in order to be born. *Il regista di matrimoni*'s motif, based
on the phrase 'i morti comandano' [the dead command], is significant
in terms of the Oedipal struggle of director against father text. The message seems to be that the dead command and that bringing a new work
to life where the old work once stood is a Herculean task. In an interview Bellocchio expands on this, saying:

> Certamente 'i morti comandano ...' è anche il fatto di ossessionare la
> gioventù, l'adolescenza, con un'opera [*I promessi sposi*] che può essere di
> indubbio valore letterario, ma oggi imporla ha un significato di violenza
> culturale anche perché a quindici anni non è detto che ci siano i mezzi
> di maturità per comprenderla. (Bertone 2008)

> [Certainly, 'the dead command ...' and it's also the fact of obsessing young
> people and adolescents with a work [*I promessi sposi*] that may be of indu-
> bitable literary value, but imposing it today is an act of cultural violence
> because, among other things, a fifteen-year-old doesn't necessarily have
> the maturity to understand it.]

Bellocchio's suggestion that the imposition of the cultural texts of the
past is an act of violence that, as *L'ora di religione* and *Il regista di matrimoni* suggest, stifles creativity is a strong statement that implies the
need to read Bellocchio's adaptations and his use of citation in a very
different light. Rather than aping the high bourgeois culture of the
past, they instead show both a recognition of the place of this culture
in any creative attempt (it is always the 'already there') and an Oedipal
struggle to go beyond the weight of its influence, to stand against this
canonical culture that is transmitted wholesale from generation to generation, and to see that in every generation culture must be rethought

anew. This is certainly not a sign of a revolutionary in the grand sense. Bellocchio does not take that culture and throw it out wholesale, as Italian futurism, the Chinese Cultural Revolution, and other avant-garde movements have proposed. However, he does overturn culture, turn it inside out, show it reverence, but also irreverence, questioning the grand European father-culture that he has inherited.

Conclusions: Private Cinema in a Public Sphere

In the world of power the way to survive is to isolate oneself, not to rebel with the others. (Bellocchio, cited in Cattini and Ferrero 1976)

Although Bellocchio belongs to no school and claims to have neither masters nor pupils, his films are constantly in dialogue not only with the (mainly) European artistic works that precede them, as has been argued in this chapter, but also with many of the intellectual and social currents that have crossed Italian culture over more than forty years: left-wing political theory and psychoanalysis, and – to a lesser extent – postmodernism and second-wave feminism. His films also necessarily interact with the Italian and European cinema industry. While all of these currents and institutions are inscribed in his work, his films set up an uneasy, resistant relationship with them. He undermines, or at least questions, politics, for example, through the use of melodrama and subversive camera angles and, more recently, through their overturning in the emphasis on transformation in the private, not public, sphere. He stands against mainstream psychoanalytical trends by aligning his cinema with Massimo Fagioli, an analyst who rejected majority trends like Freudianism and was excluded from Italy's key psychoanalytical associations. Bellocchio also deliberately inscribes his film-making within auteur cinema against mainstream cinema codes. This suggests that on many levels Bellocchio's cinema deliberately tries to position itself a little apart, setting up an uneasy, resistant relationship with the outside, with the public sphere; this relationship affects almost all levels of his film-making – from the kind of production and distribution circuits he uses to the kind of psychoanalysis found in his films, the way he portrays women, his approach to political material, and his integrating and overturning of cinematic and cultural traditions.

The resistant relationship with the outside is at the heart of Bellocchio's filmic narratives, as argued in chapter 5, because, put simply, it sits at the centre of the depiction of character psychology. The most profoundly personal aspect of Bellocchio's characters – the psyche – is envisaged as rebellious towards what lies outside it – from the family home to the school, the university, the church, and the barracks. Bellocchio's films argue that the authentic self can *only* be in a position of opposition to the public world. To fail to rebel is to fail to respect the nature of our psyche. Interiority, in other words, is never wholly 'interior' – self-contained or self-reflexive – but is always in dialogue and is constantly influenced by the outside, typically negatively; this follows the Fagiolian model of the child's impact with the world through the mother who deludes the child, creating hankering, dissatisfaction, and hate. The positive power of the psyche, however, lies in the fact that the porous nature of the child's relationship with the outside means that the child is not just influenced by but also *influences*.

The focus of Bellocchio's films is therefore less on interiority itself. Instead, they focus on the *liminal zones* between the interior and the exterior, which emerge, for example, in the relationships between the sexes; the relationship between the individual and the collective; the relationship between oneiric, interior experiences and objective reality; and in the political look-back of characters who seek to gain their own transformation and the transformation of their spectators by making the personal political.

With the emphasis on borders or the liminal zones, the idea of the political or the public as an independent, circumscribed sphere captured through cinema by an *objectivité absolue* becomes obsolete; the public world is no longer a self-contained monad but is in a fluid, porous relationship with the private. After a period in the late 1960s and early 1970s in which Bellocchio's films battled with the notion of collective action, his cinema comes to reflect the idea that the assumption of personal responsibility is the key to social and political change; this belief in individual agency sees his films stepping beyond a postmodernist position that would see the individual as delimited and defined by external forces – of society, language, and culture – to a position in which the individual has power, however circumscribed. Transformation within can lead to some form of transformation without. The I has entered the political sphere.

Notes

1 Auteur and Autobiography

1 For a definition of *riflusso*, considered a period in which cultural production withdrew from a committed political stance, see Pertile 2003, 16–17.
2 The word *political* clearly has many meanings. A full definition of the meanings as far as this book is concerned will be given at the beginning of the subsequent chapter. Suffice to mention here that in the introduction the term is used in its narrower sense: 'relating to institutional politics.'
3 'My name is Marco Bellocchio, I guarantee auteur films one hundred per cent, and my liberty is in the producer's interest.'
4 Francesco Rosi (Gili 1976, 167) writes: 'La collaboration dans le cinéma ne signifie pas une marmite dans laquelle chacun essaye de mettre indifféremment ce qu'il possède, et puis on mélange et on obtient un "minestrone" qui s'appelle film. Non, ce n'est pas cela. La marmite a besoin d'un cuisinier précis qui prend toute la responsabilité, qui sait quels doivent être les ingrédients et comment ils doivent être dosés. C'est lui qui doit aller faire les courses, personnellement, parce qu'il sait ce qu'il doit acheter, il sait ce qu'il veut, il connaît déjà le goût que doit avoir ce "minestrone." Il doit le connaî[t]re dès le début, il doit tout savoir, tout prévoir.' [Collaboration in cinema is not about a pot into which each person tries to throw whatever he might have to hand and which is then stirred to obtain a 'minestrone' called film. No, that's not it. The pot needs a precise chef who will take full responsibility, who knows which ingredients to choose and how much of them to add. He should do the shopping personally because he knows what he needs to buy and what he wants. He already knows what the 'minestrone' should taste like. He must know this from the outset; he must know everything, must foresee everything.]

5 Many of the interviews with collaborators that are found in Malanga 1998
   point to this; in particular, see pages 192 and 205 for comments made by
   Crivelli on his work with Bellocchio. Castellito's comments about having
   influence over *L'ora di religione* can be found in Fusco 2001 on page 51 and
   in the interview with him that is incorporated in the Italian DVD of the
   film.
6 Retrospectively, Lou Castel would go on to attain a kind of alternative
   star status, but this was his first film; he had only just finished his training
   at the Centro Sperimentale (where he and Bellocchio had met). Paola
   Pitagora, who plays Giulia in the film, had worked in theatre and taken
   only some minor roles in television and cinema.
7 Bellocchio's films are typically made on a low to medium-sized budget, ·
   as is often the case with auteur cinema – particularly auteur cinema
   without a large international distribution. This naturally has affected the
   filmic products. Bellocchio has, for example, typically used well-respected
   European actors, like Michel Piccoli, rather than their more expensive
   Hollywood cousins. Choice of location is affected, too. Largely owing to
   financial constraints, *I pugni in tasca* was shot in Bellocchio's family home,
   and *Il Principe di Homburg* (*The Prince of Homburg*, 1997) was shot in Bulgaria. Budget considerations also affected the anti-spectacular filming
   of witchery in *La visione del Sabba* (*The Witches' Sabbath*, 1988). Bellocchio
   gives two reasons for the diminished spectacle in this film: his wish to
   'stare più sui personaggi, sulle loro psicologie' [focus more on the characters, on their psychology]; and, of a more practical nature, 'il trucco
   cinematografico comporta un impegno produttivo veramente grande,
   non solo finanziario ma anche di mentalità' [special effects call for a high
   level of productive commitment, not just financial but also in terms of
   mentality] (Spila 1987, 8).
8 Although Bellocchio was never required to use a particular actor, his
   choice of actors was limited in part to a pool which had to include foreign (often French) actors who had attained a certain box-office standing.
   Bellocchio comments: 'Il costo del film è tale perché esige degli interpreti
   da *box office*; per cui il regista invece che su 1.000 deve scegliere su 10, perché esige gli attori da *box office* – dovendo fare una coproduzione Francia
   e Italia – saranno 10, saranno 20; cioè la tua creatività deve concentrarsi,
   tra l'altro, su dei volti estremamente usurati, alcune volte … questo è il
   compromesso … Ma non è che li ho dovuti accettare … mi è data la libertà
   di scegliere.' (Zavaglia 1979, 34). [The film costs this amount because box-
   office actors are required; because of this, the director, rather than choosing from 1,000 actors has to choose from 10. Because box office actors are

necessary, when he has to make an Italo-French co-production, he'll have a choice of 10 or 20; in other words, one's creativity has to be concentrated on faces which are extremely worn out: sometimes … this is the compromise. However, it's not as if I have had to accept them … I do have the freedom to choose.]

9 This claim is perhaps somewhat exaggerated. We know, for instance, that Elda Tattoli suggested that Bellocchio use the voice of a fifty-year-old Emilian television actor, Raul Grassilli, to dub the young Lou Castel in *I pugni in tasca* (De Bernardinis 1998, 33).

10 Carlo Fuscagni, the head of film production for RAI Uno, Italy's first television channel, claims that 'quality films, the discovery and launching of new talent, and the choice of significant themes are the real objectives of RAI productions' (Fuscagni 1984, 45). The theory is often contradicted by the practice, however.

11 Perhaps unsurprisingly, given the support that Bellocchio has had from RAI, his cinema shows none of the hostility towards television that many of his Italian fellow directors have demonstrated: Fellini attacked the medium in *Ginger e Fred* (*Ginger and Fred*, 1986) and *Intervista* (1987); Maurizio Nichetti was caustic towards it in *Ladri di saponette* (*The Icicle Thief*, 1990); and Moretti satirized television's banality and omnipresence in *Caro diario* (1993) and *Il caimano* (2006).

12 Micciché (1995, 346-55) distinguishes between commercial *cinema civile* [civil cinema] and *cinema militante* [militant cinema]. He sees *cinema civile* as the 'volto pubblico e "spettacolare"' [public and 'spectacular' face] of a militant cinema made for parties, for unions, and rarely as a personal witnessing (348). He categorizes as *cinema civile* Bellocchio's *Sbatti il mostro in prima pagina*, Giuliano Montaldo's *Dio è con noi* (*God With Us / The Fifth Day of Peace*, 1969), Montaldo's *Sacco e Vanzetti* (*Sacco and Vanzetti*, 1971), Damiano Damiani's *Confessioni di un commissario di polizia al procuratore della Repubblica* (*Confessions of a Police Captain*, 1971), and Nanni Loy's *Detenuto in attesa di giudizio* (*Why*, 1971). As examples of *cinema militante* he cites Bernardo Bertolucci's documentary *I poveri muoiono prima* (*The Poor Die First*, 1971), Ugo Gregoretti's *Apollon: Una fabbrica occupata* (*Apollon: An Occupied Factory*, 1969/70), and Francesco Leonetti's *Processo politico* (*Political Trial*, 1970).

13 Luchino Visconti co-wrote almost all of his films with Suso Cecchi d'Amico, and both G.R. Aldo (his cinematographer) and Mario Serandrie worked with him until their respective deaths. Fellini worked with the composer Nino Rota and his scriptwriter Tonino Guerra throughout the key years of his film-making; he also recycled a series of actors, most

notably Giulietta Masina and Marcello Mastroianni, with whom his films then became associated.

14 Giagni does not have exclusive power over the production of the soundtracks. In a talk on 29 March 2007 at Temple University Rome, Bellocchio discussed the role also of Francesca Calvelli, his partner and editor, in the incorporation of Pink Floyd's music on the soundtrack.

15 It is worth mentioning that Bellocchio has a practice of casting family members in his films, usually in minor roles. The casting of his first wife, Gisella Burinato, in *Vacanze in Val Trebbia* implies a reference to their extra-filmic relationship, but this is not the case in *Nel nome del padre* (where she plays the little girl who sees miracles), nor in *Il gabbiano* (where she plays Mascia), nor in *Salto nel vuoto* (where she plays the maid). Similarly, the casting of Bellocchio's sisters, Letizia and Maria Luisa, and of his little daughter, Elena, in the shorts that were then edited together as *Sorelle* in 2006 has autobiographical meaning, but the casting of the same family members into the roles of aunts and a child in *L'ora di religione* does not – except in the widest sense (it is a nod to those spectators 'in the know' who will be aware of the director's extra-filmic family relationships). The presence of family members per se is not enough, therefore, to guarantee the formation of an autobiographical code.

16 The locations for Bellocchio's films are extremely circumscribed geographically. Most of the external scenes are shot either around Emilia-Romagna or in Rome and Lazio. Exceptions are limited to *Sbatti il mostro in prima pagina* (Milan), *Il sogno della farfalla* (Lake Iseo in Lombardy, and Greece), *Il Principe di Homburg* (Bulgaria), and *Il regista di matrimoni* (Sicily).

17 Detmers' laugh is the only part of her voice that is retained after dubbing. Bellocchio claims in a series of interviews to have been fascinated both by her laugh and by Lou Castel's in *I pugni in tasca,* to the extent of including, in the final version of both films, sequences in which the two characters had laughed spontaneously without being cued to do so (De Bernardinis 1998, 33).

18 Tormey writes: 'The relation between a work of art and the artist is contingent (never direct). The presence of an expressive quality in a work of art is never sufficient to guarantee the presence of an analogous feeling state in the artist. What the music expresses is logically independent of what the artist expresses. Musicians, and artists generally, don't express themselves in their work in any sense that is intelligible, consistent, and aesthetically relevant. Instead, we should see the work of art as a self-expressive object. This avoids the prevalent assumption that expression in art is either (a) a reference to something lying behind the work – a thought,

feeling, mood, attitude to which the work stands in some external relation or (b) a reference to something immediately presented to perception as an aesthetic "surface"' (1971, 121).

2 Bellocchio's Political Cinema in the Sixties and Seventies

1 Burns (2001, 4–5) proposes a tentative definition of the term *impegno*, linking it with the English terms *commitment* and *engagement*, but also with *undertaking, obligation, responsibility*, and *liability*, noting how it implicates a relationship between reader and writer and between writer and society. She disassociates the term from its 'instinctive association with a rather oppressive type of political literature, associated with neorealism and Soviet "socialist realism."'

2 *Postmodernism* is a difficult, much defined, but nevertheless almost indefinable term. However slippery the term is, one of the concept's core features is certainly its attack on notions of representability and reference. Roland Barthes, Jacques Derrida, and Jean Baudrillard have been foremost in undermining the idea that the word and the reproduced image represent the signified in itself.

3 Baudrillard defines *simulation* as 'the generation by models of a real without origin or reality: a hyperreal' (1994, 1).

4 Canova describes the withdrawal from socio-political cinema making in terms of a shift towards the three options that he considers open to Italian film-makers in the 1960s: 'la fuga' [escapism], 'il mascheramento' [masking], and 'l'irrisione' [scorn]. The first ('fuga'), he links to auteur cinema, which he sees as escaping from committed film-making towards television (for example, in the cinema of Rossellini), towards myth and the past (in Pasolini's *Edipo Re* [*Oedipus Rex*, 1967] and *Porcile* [*Pigpen*, 1969], and in Rosi's *C'era una volta* [*More Than a Miracle*, 1967]), or towards subjectivity (in the cinema of Fellini and Visconti). He links 'mascheramento' with genre cinema, and 'irrisione' with spy stories (2002, 13). For Canova, *impegno* is lacking in all three.

5 Umberto Eco's term, discussed in the eponymous book *Opera aperta* (first published in 1962), refers to works that eschew univocal signification in favour of a plurality of signification, which involves the reader in the creation of sense.

6 As the PCI became more integrated into the political system, its revolutionary outlook (which aimed to overthrow the bourgeoisie and replace it with the proletariat) became more moderate and reformist. The 'social democratizing' of both the PSI and the PCI during the 1960s left a void

open to the left of these parties. In this void the student movement and the organizations of the extra-parliamentary left, in which Bellocchio was involved, took root. For more details on the social-democratizing of the PSI and PCI, see Ginsborg (1990a, 254–97).

7 These dates were provided by Bellocchio in his interview (quoted in Moscati's *1969: Un anno bomba* [1998], 49–53) where he states, 'Il mio impegno politico va dalla primavera del '68 all'autunno del '69 e fu tutto interno dei marxisti-leninisti' [My political commitment goes from the spring of 1968 to the autumn of 1969 and was entirely with the Marxist-Leninists].

8 In an interview in 1978, Bellocchio says that, unlike the real Marxist-Leninists, who fascinated him and whom he considered to be serious and dedicated to their cause, the militants in *La Cina è vicina* 'erano proprio dei buffoncelli, figli della buona borghesia, tranne uno, ma comunque erano praticamente dei masturbatori che usavano il pensiero di Mao per fare i loro comodi' [were really little fools, sons of the good middle class, with the exception of one of them, but in any case they were basically masturbators who used Mao's ideas for their own convenience] (quoted in Bernardi 1978, 4).

9 Aprà and De Gregorio (in Nicastro 1992, 195) also note the de-centring of principal actions in the film, saying that they are continually 'spostate per intervento di azioni minori o collaterali' [shifted due to the intervention of minor or collateral actions].

10 For an excellent discussion of the contestation in the universities during this period, see Lumley 1990. He describes the kind of grievances that the students reported: courses were out of date, lecturers were old and old-fashioned, universities were cut off from society, and the style of education presumed passive students. He also describes the effects of government policy in this period, especially the Gui bill, which restricted entry into universities by fixing quotas (59).

11 The restricted budget and especially the restricted time available for filming certainly impinged on the choice of a Brechtian style. The availability of a lecture theatre in the Centro Sperimentale, the cheap fake beards and truncheons, and the use of a group of non-actor students from the University of La Sapienza in Rome radically reduced filming costs.

12 This statistic was written on the classroom board by one of the militants. However, although the argument itself holds (the universities were certainly mainly middle class at the beginning of the 1970s), Lumley's statistics (1990, 55) are probably more reliable. He claims that the number of working-class students increased from 14 per cent in 1960–1 to 21 per cent in 1967–8.

13 See, for instance, Nicastro (1992, 147), where Bellocchio claims that it was his 'esasperato individualismo' [exasperated individualism] that led him to take part; or Bellocchio's interview for *Close-up* in 1998 in which he says it was primarily his desire to find a new inspiration and avoid repeating himself that drew him into political militancy (Spagnoletti, Murri, and Cappellini 1999, 56).

14 *Paola* begins in the local offices of Servire il Popolo (the youth wing of the UCI [m-l]), where a political discussion among militants is recorded. The next sequence records the approach to Paola, and shots of the town through a car windscreen help to establish its poverty and neglect. The film troupe interviews people in the streets and houses there, and in dialect these poor families answer the angled questions, explaining that they have no electricity, water, or sewers and talking about infant illness and Paola's unfinished hospital that they so desperately need. After these long interviews, the film cuts back to the offices of the UCI (m-l) where the extra-parliamentary activists are discussing what should be done in the case of places like Paola; they declare that the right to a house is a basic right for all members of the proletariat. (Lou Castel, the protagonist of *I pugni in tasca* and himself a Marxist-Leninist militant, can be seen in the background to some of the shots.) Back in the streets, the camera records the occupation of houses (encouraged by the UCI [m-l]) and a march by the townspeople on 2 March 1969. The final sequence records the rhetorical speeches of the UCI [m-l] activists to the people of Paola, encouraging them to create a real communist party in place of the Partito Comunista Italiano.

15 The documentary is divided into three sections. The first (in black and white) acts as a preface to the marches and records the political debate amongst Marxist-Leninists within the closure of their committee room. The discussion reveals their disillusionment with the official communist party (the PCI), its revisionism, and its lack of revolutionary spirit. The debate concludes in upbeat fashion with clapping and the singing of the famous communist song *Bandiera rossa* [The Red Flag]. In the second part of the film, shot in colour, the camera moves outside the group's headquarters and into the streets of Milan. The film troupe goes first to the Alfa Romeo factory in Milan, where a voice over a loudspeaker encourages the workers: 'Mobilitarvi tutti per esprimere pubblicamente i vostri sentimenti di odio per la borghesia' [Mobilize yourselves to publicly express your feelings of hate towards the bourgeoisie]. Then, in a second sequence, the camera records students caught by UCI (m-l) pamphleteers as they leave their university building. These students are asked to join the workers

and peasants in the struggle. The second part of the film culminates with the Milan march, focusing on the UCI (m-l) activists who shout out slogans such as 'Marx-Engels-Lenin-Stalin-Mao Zedong' and walk in orderly fashion, wearing their neat red neckerchiefs, past Milan's great gothic cathedral. The third part of the film, also shot in colour, records the Labour Day march in the capital and the ensuing political rally. The film ends with the Roman crowd shouting 'Viva la dittatura del proletariato!' [Long live the proletarian dictatorship!] and waving copies of Mao Zedong's famous *Little Red Book*.

16 A comparison with the post-2000 re-emergence of documentary as a popular form shows just how radical this absence is. Michael Moore's *Bowling for Columbine* (2002) and Morgan Spurlock's *Super Size Me* (2004) see the films' directors appear in front of the camera to take an active and apparently single-handed swing at the big ideologies and corporations of the United States, creating themselves as modern heroes – eccentrics fighting alone for justice. In the era of the focus group, of direct channels of protest (especially through the Internet), and of reality television, the small isolated voice suddenly takes on disproportionate significance (the release of Moore's *Fahrenheit 9/11* was deliberately timed to swing the 2004 U.S. elections). This type of documentary is radically different to that which emerged in Italy in the late sixties and early seventies, where sociopolitical change was deeply linked to ideals of mass mobilization.

17 Bernardi (1998, 67) describes how the scenes from the film's present that were shot but not used showed Angelo as an 'industriale efficiente e illuminato' [an efficient and enlightened industrialist] and Franc as 'un intellettuale alle dipendenze di Angelo, che scrive articoli contro gli operai' [an intellectual who works for Angelo and writes articles against the workers].

3 The Dreaming 'I': Interiority and Massimo Fagioli's Model of the Unconscious

1 Michel David gives a detailed account of the beginnings of psychoanalysis in Italy in *La psicoanalisi nella cultura italiana* (1970).

2 See Silvia Vegetti Finzi (1986), whose chapter 'Introduzione della psicoanalisi in Italia' (254–65) traces the development of psychoanalysis in Italy until the mid-1980s. See also the Italian translation of Freedheim (1998), which carries additional material in an appendix relevant to the Italian situation.

3 Armando's *Storia della psicoanalisi in Italia dal 1971 al 1996* (1997), which is largely a pro-Fagiolian analysis of Fagioli's work rather than a general

history of psychoanalysis in Italy, outlines the reactions on the part of the press and provides an ample bibliography of newspaper articles relevant to the reception of Fagioli.

4 Bellocchio says his reason for this temporary separation was that he believed he may not have resolved his problems or that they were no longer necessary (Armando 1997, 377). However, he maintained throughout the 1980s that the seminars were positive.

5 Using the term *model* for Fagioli's ideas risks giving the impression that these ideas are more logical and coherent than they are. The word is therefore used only loosely here.

6 Despite Fagioli's vociferous attacks on the Freudian model, his theory nonetheless shares Freud's materialism (Fagioli's model of the baby's growth is rooted above all in the body) and Freud's construction of the child as a sexual being. Fagioli's theories of the unconscious in fact overlap with Freud's in a wide number of areas, especially with regard to the death instinct, fear of castration, the irrational, sadomasochism, repression, and transference between patient and analyst.

7 There is also a facile sexual metaphor lying behind the sword and sword-guarded characters. Ponticelli is never shown having a sexual relationship with anyone. The one woman whom he does invite to his house for dinner, instead of being seduced, finds herself taking out the rubbish when she leaves.

8 This ending is ambiguous and open ended, however. This final scene, in which the judge jumps, may be only Marta's dream. After all, she is shown asleep, and at the moment he jumps from the window she wakes with a start.

9 Fagioli's views on the place of the arts in enlightenment are contradictory. In *Bambino, donna, e trasformazione dell'uomo* he says first that literature is fundamental for a better understanding of the unconscious (207), but only a few pages later he categorizes literature alongside other intellectual pursuits and, in a Platonic mood, warns that it is one of the 'oscuri oggetti di desiderio, infidi, deludenti, pericolossimi perché ti uccidono se ti lasci andare a loro senza guardare' [obscure objects of desire, which are treacherous, deluding, and very dangerous because they'll kill you if you let yourself go to them with your eyes shut] (210). This ambivalence towards literature emerges in the film: Massimo's use of literature is construed as positive, representing his ability to express and know himself profoundly; his father's use of literature, however, is negative, showing literature first as a step in understanding but ultimately as an abstraction that separates its followers from a real connection with the world.

10 The witches therefore embody the negative aspects of character that Fagioli believes need to be eliminated in order for the *mare calmo* to take root. The fantasy of disappearance refers to Fagioli's theory as outlined in *Istinto di morte e conoscenza*, where he links it to a fear of the new that results in the desire to return to not-being, to darkness and the womb (Fagioli 1996). The hankering after something is the negative side of desire, in that it is linked to lack of satisfaction – the lack of satisfaction that comes when the mother does not respond to the child's early desires.

11 Mad is an image of the unconscious – just as Massimo would represent the unconscious in *Il sogno della farfalla* six years later. However, whereas Massimo is an image of an independent unconscious, Mad, representing the unconscious, is as much a projection of an aspect of Davide's psyche as she is either an independent character in her own right or an expression of the unconscious of a female character (Maddalena). The oneiric sequences in which Mad features are structured so that they appear not as Maddalena's memories or dreams but as projections of Davide's mind. In the first sequence of the film, for instance, we see Mad's soft body laid out on a board as the inquisitors prod it with needles in order to ascertain whether or not she is a witch. However, this scene (in which Davide, in the guise of an inquisitor, embraces her) is subsequently marked as Davide's dream, *not* Maddalena's; we see him waking from it. Moreover, when Davide first meets Maddalena in the flesh, there is also a case of psychic projection. As she stands before him in her provocative red dress, the point of view is that of Davide. The screen darkens, and her face spins around in the frame – a rather kitsch special effect – while she laughs sexily. The laugh, recorded in an intimate sound close-up and set against Crivelli's modernist score of plucking strings, creates the impression for the spectator of being positioned inside Davide's head. Seconds later, Maddalena is standing in front of him, expectantly, as if nothing whatsoever had happened. He has hallucinated her transformation. These two scenes show that Davide is the originator of the point of view for the film, and Mad is as much a representation of his own psyche as she is of Maddalena's.

12 The film can be seen in the context of the foregrounding of rape in films from the late seventies and eighties onwards. Jonathan Kaplan's *The Accused*, which was released only three years before *La condanna*, highlights (as Clover [1993, 76] notes) the issues of consent and the legal difficulties of prosecution, making the legal system the hero of the film. Clover claims that in this and other such films 'the focus has shifted from victim to lawyer, from questions of why men rape and how victims feel to questions of what constitutes evidence; from bedroom (or wherever) to

courtroom' (76). This is quite different from Bellocchio's approach, which, despite the courtroom scenes, concentrates not on evidence but on what happens in the bedroom: what constitutes rape, why it happens, and what it says about male-female relations.

13 This is not to say that Bellocchio's films had not dealt with sex previously. *I pugni in tasca* explored incest; *La Cina è vicina* highlighted political control over the female body through pregnancy and abortion; *Marcia trionfale* dealt with female objectivization and again with the control and surveillance of women by men. However, with the exception of *La Cina è vicina*, sex and sexual relations do not form the fulcrum around which the plot rotates. Neither do these earlier films show an interest in drawing female characters in depth; few actresses rise even to the status of co-protagonists. In *I pugni in tasca* Giulia (Paola Pitagora) has none of the complexity of the story's protagonist, Ale. *La Cina è vicina* is primarily choral, with the two women (Elena and Giovanna) playing important roles alongside Vittorio and his secretary, Carlo. In *Nel nome del padre* the two key characters (Angelo and Franc) are both male, and the film centres on an almost exclusively male world. *Sbatti il mostro in prima pagina* is dominated by the performance of Gian Maria Volonté as the newspaper editor. *Marcia trionfale* is again dominated by the male protagonist, Michele Placido, and set within the very male world of an army barracks; the role of Rosanna (Miou-Miou) as the sensual wife of the captain, although pre-empting the female roles of the later films, is still in a secondary position as sex object rather than subject.

14 The word *oneiric* is being used very broadly here to encompass not only dreams but also imaginings, hallucinations, and events that stand at the borders between imagination and the supernatural.

15 The word *hesitant* is being used here in the Todorovian sense. Todorov believes that the key to the fantastic is hesitation, the moment of uncertainty between two solutions, where the reader feels 'either he is the victim of an illusion of the senses, of a product of the imagination – and the laws of the world then remain what they are; or else the event has taken place, it is an integral part of reality – but then this reality is controlled by laws unknown to us' (Todorov 1973, 25).

16 Both the judge and Marta are shown asleep in their rooms when the children first appear – in the darkness behind Marta's face; in their second appearance, the children emerge from under the judge's bed while he sleeps; in the third appearance, the judge is asleep, but his sister is awake and singing a lullaby; and in the final appearance, Marta is out, and the judge is slumped against the door, barely conscious. It is worth pointing

out that the final appearance of the children does not seem initially to have been conceived of as oneiric, and indeed it differs from the other scenes in that the children are not Marta and her brothers; this time, although it is not clear where they come from, at the end of their performance the children retreat from the house into the lobby. However, their appearance is similar to that of the Ponticelli children, as is their wild Dionysian destructiveness. Moreover, nobody seems to take any notice of their presence. Bellocchio claims that the scene in which Placido and the children wreck the house was shot as a real scene, but when a critic subsequently suggested that this scene belonged to the judge's fantasies, Bellocchio agreed, although he admitted that this had not occurred to him previously (Perissinotto 1980, 10).

17 In the screenplay the story opens in the real, with a naturalistic car journey in which Claudio (Davide in the film), the psychoanalyst who is to examine Maddalena's case, is discussing with his wife whether Maddalena's tale is made up of real deliriums or it is just a pot of lies (9). In other words, the screenplay introduces the subject of witchcraft within the rationalist frame of psychoanalysis, not allowing for a reading that would hesitate between real and fantasy. The screenplay describes Claudio falling asleep in the car ('Claudio socchiude gli occhi, come se gli … fosse venuto sonno' [Claudio closes his eyes as if he … were overtaken by sleep] [10]) and dreaming the Inquisition torture sequences that include images of the witch Mad. In the screenplay it is clear that Bellocchio intended to use Claudio's dreams and hallucinations as the explanation for the fantastic sequences (although, in the final pages of the screenplay, this clarity vanishes). In the film, however, the story begins with images of a witches' sabbath as if they were real (and not part of Maddalena's or Davide's imaginings), and the dream sequences are not marked as such.

18 There are isolated street scenes of this kind in other films, most notably perhaps in *La balia*, where a highly choreographed socialist demonstration takes place on the streets of Rome, and in *Il regista di matrimoni*, where a religious parade engulfs the streets of a Sicilian town.

19 The barge is moored under the recognizable Vittorio Emanuele II Bridge (the sculptures on the bridge can clearly be seen in the background of many of the barge shots), which is a monument to the birth of Italian nationhood; its statues are called l'Unità d'Italia, la Libertà, l'Oppressione vinta, and la Fedeltà allo Statuto [The Unity of Italy; Liberty; Vanquished Oppression; and Loyalty to the Statutes]. The use of the bridge in the background to Sciabola's world appears ironic. It is also in a precursor of the more direct polemics against Rome's Vittoriano monument – another

monument to the nation – that will appear later in *L'ora di religione* (see chapter 6).

20 Bellocchio's cinematographer, Giuseppe Lanci, describes the use of light in this film as a turning point, breaking away from the darker worlds of his previous films. He explains that 'si trattava di portare la luce degli interni quasi allo stesso livello di quella degli esterni, non si dovevano sentire fratture tra la sovraesposizione dei tetti e la sottoesposizione dell'aula, e il fatto che fossimo in pieno agosto, quindi con una luce naturale fortissima, negli interni comportò una illuminazione insolita, realistica solo in apparenza o solo alla base, come del resto succede sempre nei film di Marco' [it was all about bringing the light of the interiors almost up to those of the exteriors. One shouldn't feel a break between the overexposed roofs and the underexposed classroom. The fact that we were shooting at the height of August, and therefore with a very strong natural light, meant that in the interiors there was unusual lighting, realistic only in appearance or in its origin, which, after all, is always the case in Marco's films] (Malanga 1998, 196).

21 In the opening scene the tour guide had discussed the DNA motif of the museum, thus revealing a key to reading the recurrence of spiral motifs in this part of the film. The guide, presumably referring to the villa's famous spiral staircase that Sandra and the architect later descend, says, 'Questo effetto straordinario di circolarità, soprattutto di movimento infinito … da sotto sembra che produca il DNA' [This extraordinary effect of circularity, and above all of infinite movement … seems, if you look at it from beneath, to produce DNA]. Biologically, DNA is at the very centre of human identity, and in this film a link is created between the staircases and the discourses on creation and reproduction that the film proposes.

22 The liberatory pleasure of swearing is also found in the later film *L'ora di religione*, where again it is a mad brother who swears (using, in this case, the strong and deeply blasphemous words *porco Dio*). In both films, swearing represents a rebellion against the established order. Marta's *stronzo* serves to bring her brother down off his pedestal, unmask him, and show him for what he really is, and it represents her first brave stand against him. In the oneiric sequences her mad brother's swearing against the priests is another hard stab against power and the institution, as are the words *porca Madonna, porco Dio* in *L'ora di religione*.

23 In *Flashbacks in Film* (1989) Turim argues that flashback is a causal form that tends towards closure. Drawing on Barthes's reading of Balzac's *Sarrasine* in *S/Z*, she indicates a number of reasons for using flashback: a flashback can initiate an enigma, binding the past to the present and

setting up a causal link between the two time frames; it can provide missing information; it can be used to develop an enigma and then to delay its
resolution (11–12).

24 In the film's closing sequence a naked boy – who earlier in the film had
been caught eating plums in a tree by a farmer and who is impossible to
collocate firmly in either the oneiric or the real – runs down a long cobbled
road towards the town of Bobbio. The final shot of the film then lingers on
a sepia-toned photograph of a young boy with curly hair, which – given
the evident age of the photograph and the resemblance to the adult Marco,
is likely to be interpreted by the spectator as being an image of the child
Bellocchio. If the beginning of the film collocates the film uneasily in autobiography (setting up an ambiguity between a universal 'marito' and a
concrete Marco Bellocchio), the film ends with a similar ambiguity. If this
is a photograph of the child Marco Bellocchio, it seems to nail the autobiographical references hard to the film; if this is not the case, then fictionality
comes to the fore. The status of the referentiality in the film hinges on this
final ambiguous image and must remain unresolved unless the spectator
decides to search for an answer in the extra-filmic.

25 The similarities and differences between Bellocchio's *Enrico IV* and Pirandello's play will be analysed in chapter 6.

26 This re-emphasis is not entirely a travesty of Pirandello. Even if Pirandello's emphasis is on themes of madness, mask, and acting, the doctor
in this play does point to the childlikeness of Enrico's behaviour when
he says, 'Bisogna intendere questa speciale psicologia dei pazzi, per
cui – guardi – si può essere anche sicuri che un pazzo nota, può notare
benissimo un travestimento davanti a lui; e assumerlo come tale; e sis-
signori, tuttavia, crederci; proprio come fanno i bambini, per cui è insieme
giuoco e realtà. Ho detto perciò puerile' [One needs to understand the
special psychology of mad people – see – one can be sure that a madman
notes, can note perfectly well, that what's in front of him is a charade, and
he takes it as such; and, yes sir, all the same, he believes in it, just as children do, for whom it is both a game and reality. That is why I said *puerile*].

4 Bellocchio's Political Cinema from the Eighties to the Present

1 In an interview with Daniela Turco in 2000 (65) Bellocchio makes this link
explicit when he speaks of the revolutionary female character, Maddalena,
in *La balia*: 'Per quanto riguarda lei io ho pensato proprio ad un tipo di
durezza rivoluzionaria come in qualche modo tutti noi, o almeno io, avevo
conosciuto nei tempi in cui la politica era al primo posto' [As far as she is

concerned, I had thought about a kind of revolutionary hardness like that which, in some way, all of us – or at least I – had known in those times when politics was foremost]. However, in an interview for *La Repubblica* in 1999 (Rombi 1999), he stresses the generic nature of the uprising in *La balia*, claiming that these images might be compared also to the concerns of immigrants from Kosovo.

2 Bellocchio (in Nicastro 1992, 292) gives historical referents for *Diavolo in corpo*. Colonello Mario Dozza died in 1979, a victim of terrorism. A *brigatista*, Giacomo Pulcini, was condemned to eight years and seven months for the killing, but he was released immediately as a result of the newly introduced law, the so-called *Legge sui pentiti* [Law on repentant prisoners].

3 The memorializing of Italian contestation and terrorism can be seen in numerous films made in the new millennium, including Renzo Martinelli's *Piazza delle cinque lune* (*Piazza of the Five Moons*, 2003) on the Moro killing, Guido Chiesa's *Lavorare con lentezza* (Go Slow, 2004), and Daniele Luchetti's *Mio fratello è figlio unico* (My Brother Is an Only Child, 2007).

4 Bellocchio's incorporation of television and documentary footage into his films has a long history and acts as a way of anchoring his films in the real, of breaking from subjectivity, and of presenting a broader and public picture. He says, for instance, 'Sento l'esigenza di riacchiappare il reale che sta veramente fuori di me, e con cui la mia vita privata non ha quasi mai avuto niente a che fare, di tirarlo dentro, nel discorso personale, per una specie di sfiducia nella forza di quest'ultimo. Così si spiegano queste sortite politiche … oppure altrimenti la necessità di mettere all'interno dei miei film delle sequenze di presa diretta con la realtà e la storia, come la morte del Papa in *Nel nome del padre* e i funerali di Fetrinelli o la faccia di Almirante in *Sbatti il mostro*' [I feel the need to grasp hold again of the real that is really outside me, and with which my private life has had almost nothing to do, to pull it inside, into the personal discourse. This is because of a kind of distrust of the strength of the latter. This explains the necessity of these political sorties … or the need to put sequences of direct recording of reality and history into my films, like the death of the Pope in *Nel nome del padre* and the funerals of Fetrinelli or the face of Almirante in *Sbatti il mostro*] (Bellocchio, cited in Nicastro 1992, 147).

5 Anna Laura Braghetti's testimony was crucial and played an important part in clarifying some of what went on behind the walls of 8 Via Montalcini. In particular, both her in-court testimony and her autobiography provide great detail on the layout of the apartment and its daily routines. Braghetti, one of the *irreducibili* of the Red Brigades, did not testify until

the fourth court case, known as Moro Quarter, which took place at the beginning of the 1990s. However, her testimony then was one of the most important of that final case. She told the court details about the layout of Moro's cell and the arrangements for buying the flat, and she claimed that, touched by Moro's plight, she had opposed the final death sentence (see Drake 1995, 122–6). In her autobiography she also displays a certain uneasiness at the time the death sentence was announced, although she continued to follow the *brigatista* line.

6 However, the title of the screenplay, its author, and its contents, as revealed later in the film through Enzo Passoscuro, are all invented.

7 The use of nicknames was true, however, to the workings of the BR; the Montalcini four took the names Camilla, Maurizio, Giuseppe, and Gulliver.

8 These words were common among the Red Brigades of the time and refer to their decision in 1977 to shift the focus from attacking capitalist bosses in the factories to targeting the state apparatus. Their targets were suddenly much more ambitious, and their aim was to unleash civil war (see Catanzaro 1991, 87–96).

9 Maya Sansa's comments in a talk given at the University of Washington, Rome, on 19 April 2007.

10 This is not to say, however, that there are no signs of the thriller genre. Since 2000, Bellocchio's films have incorporated suspense, and in this film there are significant signs of it: in the robbers knocking on the door of the apartment (not in Braghetti's account), in the arrest of Chiara's friend at the ministry (not in Braghetti's account, although many arrests were made in this period), and the whole build-up to the ambush.

11 The television, a ubiquitous item of consumerist culture, acts as an interruption of public space into the private (like the windows and doors in Bellocchio's films). Through this small rectangle enters the outside world, an outside world from which at times Bellocchio's characters in this period can seem to be radically cut off. In *Diavolo in corpo*, Giulia and Andrea are in the bedroom; the television is on, and Giulia's fiancé is there in medium close-up, looking straight out of the television as if entering the room. Giulia then flicks impatiently from channel to channel. The television serves to mark the contrast between an outer world, made up of cluttered, juxtaposed images and sounds, and the calm of the bedroom and a healthy relationship. It also contrasts the instinctive relationship between Giulia and Andrea (which takes place mainly, though not entirely, in the uncluttered apartment) with the relationship between Giulia and her fiancé (which is constantly marked by distance). Here the distance is the television, which transports him into the room only virtually, and

elsewhere, in the courtroom, he is behind bars. Televisions in Bellocchio's cinema are instrumental in the juxtaposition of private and public images. They can effectively split internal space into inner and outer, allowing the contrasts to play off each other. They can also serve further purposes; in particular, they allow the film to collocate itself within the present. In *Buongiorno, notte*, the television plays an important role in setting up a dialectic between the underground world of the Red Brigades in their hideout on Via Montalcini and the world of the establishment.

12 The oneiric sequences also provide a way of balancing the television documentary footage of the reaction on the part of the centre right and the Church with footage of the communist left, thus contrasting two ideologies on the same visual ground. They provide a way of constructing a bridge geographically between the communism of Italy and that of Russia, and temporally between the terrorism of 1978 and the Resistance of the 1940s. However, Bellocchio undermines any claim on the part of the Brigate rosse to be carrying on the work of the Resistance, by aligning the images of the execution of Resistance prisoners with the shots of Moro as prisoner. In the fourth oneiric insert, it is *Moro*'s letter that leads directly to the *Lettere dei condannati*, not the *brigatisti*'s ideology.

13 In a talk at Temple University, Rome (on 29 March 2007) Bellocchio mentions this escape from the ineluctability of history as being the only place in the film where Fagiolian ideas are still present.

5 The Rebel 'I': Patriarchy and Parents

1 The analyst's comment that psychoanalysis 'non ha certo il compito di trasformare il mondo ma piuttosto di aiutarLa ad adattarvi nei migliori dei modi' [certainly doesn't have a mission to change the world but rather to help you to adapt to it as well as you can] strikes to the heart of the Fagiolian critique of Freudianism.

2 The motif of the female analysand pitted against the male (Freudian) psychoanalyst or psychiatrist returns repeatedly in Bellocchio's films of this period: *Enrico IV, Diavolo in corpo, La visione del Sabba*, and *La balia*. In each case, the instinct of the female is supported against the logic of male science.

3 Annetta's partner (and father of her child) is in jail, and the relationship with Dr Mori, though sensual and even intimate, does not develop physically. Chiara has a 'husband' (invented so as to make her less suspicious), a boyfriend with whom she has almost no sexual intimacy, and a young suitor (with whom a relationship does not develop). In *Salto nel vuoto*

Marta's relationship with her brother is shown to be verging on incest, and her relationship with Sciabola, though intense, does not become a fully fledged sexual one.

4 Elsewhere in Bellocchio's opus there are some further signs of woman as the projection of a male character's psyche, as invented by him, rather than as having real existence. The most obvious example is that of the religious education teacher, Diana Sereni (Chiara Conti), in *L'ora di religione*. Diana takes a much less central role than Mad or Maddalena, despite being the principal love interest of the film, but like Mad, she seems almost to belong to the realm of the fantastic or to exist as a projection of Ernesto's desires. What renders her more a projection than a 'real' woman is that she lacks any civic status or any existence independent of her encounter with Ernesto. Her claim to real civic status – she presents herself as the religious education teacher – later transpires to be false, and instead her character's sole existence revolves around the seduction of Ernesto. Moreover, no one but Ernesto sees her. She enters both the school meeting room and Ernesto's apartment with ghostly ease, spaces to which she could not logically have access. This woman is either part of the family's plot to involve Ernesto in plans to make a saint of their mother, and as such is sent to implant religion in his soul, or a figment of his imagination. Or, more likely, she is both a figment and an element in a plot, for the film permits the ambiguity between the two readings to remain. It is also worth noting, however, that there is a case where the dominant gendering of projections is reversed. The male gypsy in *Il sogno della farfalla* can be read as a projection on the part of Anna (indeed, Anna seems to be aware of this when she says to him, 'Tu sei soltanto un'illusione' [You are only an illusion]). His appearance, both on the beach and later in the house, seems inexplicable and unmotivated. Like Mad, this gypsy represents the mysterious, the libido, the irrational, and all that Anna has repressed in herself. His appearance tells us that the irrational (associated by Fagioli with the figure of the 'donna') can also be projected and embodied in men (as it is in Sciabola in *Salto nel vuoto*).

5 Despite the comparatively non-violent nature of Bellocchio's cinema, there are also acts of real or symbolic mass violence, such as the police hitting students with plastic truncheons in 'Discutiamo, discutiamo'; the documentary footage of clashes between police and protesters, and the re-enactment of an attack on the newspaper offices at the beginning of *Sbatti il mostro in prima pagina*; and the aestheticized re-enactment of a battle at the beginning of *Il Principe di Homburg* (in which, however, due to heavy veils of smoke, little real violence is shown).

6 *Matti da slegare*, released in 1976, explicitly lays blame for the sons' ills at the feet of the mother (although it is also laid on the boys' poverty). Interviews with one of the boys, the mentally disturbed Marco, reveals the shocking extent of his neglect by his mother.

7 Actual fathers are often absent in Bellocchio's films, but substitute fathers play a central role. The protagonists of *I pugni in tasca, La Cina è vicina, Marcia trionfale, Il gabbiano, Salto nel vuoto, Enrico IV, Diavolo in corpo* (Giulia), *La condanna, Il Principe di Homburg, La balia,* and *Buongiorno, notte* have all lost their fathers.

8 The importance of this only child, as bearer of the family name, can also be seen to represent recent anxieties in Italy about the falling birth rate. Leonardo appears to be the only child born to the five brothers in *L'ora di religione*, and it is for him, ultimately, that the mother's sainthood is being attained. This reduction of numbers in the new generation, with the subsequent overprotection of the only child by the family, is an important subtext to the film and follows on from Moretti's *Caro diario* where Salina, one of the islands that Nanni visits, is dominated by only children.

9 Although the title of *Nel nome del padre* explicitly cites the father (indeed, both father and God), we see Angelo's father only once, in the opening scene. The film begins with a father and son imprisoned by the camera's framing within a long colonnaded portico, part – we soon discover – of the school buildings. The father is dragging the rebellious Angelo to the boarding school, and as they proceed, he beats the boy and roars at him to obey his father, demanding recognition and respect for his role ('Sono tuo padre! Rispettami!' [I'm your father! Respect me!]). Angelo does not answer back but, instead, angrily swipes at this brutal and domineering man. This is the last we see of the father, as the ensuing film takes place almost entirely within the walls of the school. Nonetheless, this scene, read in conjunction with the words of the film's title (*In the Name of the Father*) – words that pertain in this case not just to God, the Father, as in the Catholic blessing, but also to the earthly (authoritarian) figure – suggests the powerful presence of the paterfamilias lying behind the film's narrative. This film's title and its opening sequence hint at the ways in which the bonds that cement people together within the family are played out endlessly *beyond* the family in the individuals' relationships with the institutions. Angelo is leaving the conflict with the father behind him only to enter into an institution in which the conflict with the father will continue but will be transmuted onto a new, allegorical level. The scene immediately subsequent, in fact, shows a medium close-up of one of the school's prefects clapping his hands insistently and shouting an order ('Sveglia!'

[Wake up!]) at the boys. The physical beating of the hands repeats (in more acceptable and symbolic fashion) the father's hitting of his son with his hands. Also implied is that the awakening called for by the prefect will not be, for Angelo, the wakening into a new and better universe but into a universe dominated by the already known, by the (absent) father, and by his rules: respect, obedience, and deference.

10 See chapter 3 for a discussion of the nature of dream in the film. Both this scene and the final scene are suspended between dream and reality, making it hard to ever firmly say what happens or does not happen in this film.

11 Bellocchio has updated the set and costumes to Napoleonic times, presumably to draw out the discourse on Romantic individualism. However, the battle itself is still referred to as the battle of Fehrbellin and is still against Swedish troops. The history of the battle is clearly of little interest to Bellocchio (the battle scene is cursory and anti-spectacular), and he has mixed the two time frames with a disregard for historical accuracy. He is interested rather in the perennial and universal conflict of father and son.

6 Tradition and Its Discontents

1 In Pirandello's play the events of the cavalcade are briefly narrated by one of the characters. In Bellocchio's film, rather than have a character narrate the events, Bellocchio has them re-enacted, with Latou Chardons, who plays Frida, taking the part of Matilda as a young woman, so that the similarities between the two women are emphasized further. In the film, the scene of the cavalcade is expanded and assumes a more central position.

2 Robert Bresson's term *teatro fotografato* [photographed theatre] interested Bellocchio, and he claimed that, had it not been used in such a negative sense by the French director, he would have adopted it to categorize *La Cina è vicina*, as representative of the film's spoken and conceptual nature (Fofi 1967, 73).

3 The adaptation of *Il gabbiano* is much more literal than that of *Enrico IV*, and Bellocchio notes how parts of *Il gabbiano* are 'teatro filmato,' where the 'discorso cinematografico rischia di essere soffocato della bellezza letteraria del testo, che è affidato unicamente alla bravura degli interpreti, mentre i climi e le atmosfere restano inesorabilmente sullo sfondo' [cinematic discourse risks being suffocated by the literary beauty of the text, which is entrusted exclusively to the actors' abilities, while the climate and atmosphere remain inexorably in the background] (Bernardi 1998, 7).

4 It seems that Manzoni was a weighty presence for Bellocchio, too. Citations of Manzoni occur as early as *La Cina è vicina*: Vittorio is revealed as a 'bigotta e un docente liceale' [bigot and a schoolteacher] in his citing from Manzoni's *Risurrezione*, while serving breakfast to his girlfriend (Lodato 1977, 62). In *Nel nome del padre*, the nightmarish play that the boys stage also uses Manzoni's *I promessi sposi*.

5 In *La Cina è vicina*, Vittorio's religious aunts recite the words of poet and librettist Giuseppe Giacosa (1847–1906); in *Marcia trionfale*, Capitano Asciutto begs Passari to read him the Bolognese *poet maudit*, Lorenzo Stecchetti (1845–1916); in *Salto nel vuoto*, the relationship of the siblings, claims Bellocchio, is based in part on Giovanni Pascoli's morbid bond with his sister Mariù (Nicastro 1992, 365); in *Diavolo in corpo*, the film opens with the words of Pascoli's poem 'La tovaglia' [The Tablecloth]; in *L'ora di religione*, the poem read to Ernesto by Diana was written by Andrei Tarkovsky's father, Arsenyi; and *Buongiorno, notte*'s title is a miscitation of Emily Dickinson's bleak poem 'Good Morning, Midnight.' Darkness and light, and hope and desperation, are contrasted in her poem, so providing the central themes and motifs of the film.

6 Examples of theatre are as follows: in *Nel nome del padre*, the schoolboys stage a satirical play that sews together motifs from *I promessi sposi*, *Don Giovanni*, *Othello*, and *Faust* into a grotesque pastiche; in *Il gabbiano*, an avant-garde play written by the young playwright Constantin is performed to unappreciative family and friends; in *Vacanze in Val Trebbia*, children are seen re-enacting a piece from *Pinocchio*; in *Salto nel vuoto*, Sciabola belongs to an underground theatre troupe that we see rehearsing and play-acting; in *Gli occhi, la bocca*, the protagonist is a former successful actor who, at the film's close, dresses up as his dead brother in order to appear before his mother as a consoling vision; and in *La visione del Sabba*, Davide's arrival in the medieval town where Maddalena is being held is met with a rehearsal of a play about witch-hunts. *Il sogno della farfalla* is wholly dominated by theatre – the protagonist, Massimo, is an actor by profession and speaks only to recite from Shakespeare's *Macbeth* and Sophocles' *Oedipus at Colonus*, or to assume roles in *Il Principe di Homburg* and an unnamed biographical play written by his Bergmanian mother.

Examples of opera are as follows: in the ending of *I pugni in tasca*, Ale dies while listening to an aria from Verdi's *La traviata*; in *La Cina è vicina*, Donizetti's 'Raggio d'amore parea' from *Il furioso all'isola di San Domingo* is sung discordantly by little schoolchildren, and Verdi's *Don Carlos* is sung by Vittorio in the bath; and in *La balia*, Mori is coaxed into singing an aria from Ruggero Leoncavallo's *Pagiliacci*, 'Recitar, mentre preso dal delirio.'

In *Vincere*, 'Zitti, zitti, moviamo a vendetta' from Verdi's *Rigoletto*, sung by psychiatrists and guardians at the Venice asylum as they return from the opera, reflects the theme of silently removing the lover from the scene.

7 Tullio Masoni's *Marco Bellocchio: Quadri; Il pittore, il cineaste* (2003) discusses Bellocchio's painting (which he gave up when he went to train at the Centro Sperimentale) and the use of art in his films.

8 Apart from the case of Sandra's *Maja desnuda* in *La condanna*, discussed already in chapter 5, there are numerous other examples of this in Bellocchio's cinema. The settings of *Il Principe di Homburg* seem to be inspired by German Romantic painting, from Johann Heinrich Füssli to Caspar David Friedrich, for its greens and blues, and the costumes are derived from representations by Napoleonic painters (Bellocchio 1997, 168). In *L'ora di religione*, the reconstruction of the mother's 'martyrdom' is a parody of the religious painting of the Baroque. In *La balia* the beautiful rural opening scenes, with their soft, warm colours and pastoral feel, approximate Italian verismo paintings of the second half of the nineteenth century. In *Vincere* the fast editing, the launching of futurist slogans like '*Marciare non marcire*' [March, don't rot] across the screen, and the reconstruction of the futurist exhibition of 1917, with its backdrop of futurist paintings, all foreground the revolutionary, tradition-breaking rebellion of early-twentieth-century art, which the film reads as reflected in fascism until fascism became institutionalized and reverted to traditional modes in the 1920s.

9 The attraction to Bergman, Bellocchio claims, exists because 'mi ha sempre coinvolto fino in fondo nella sua disperazione, nel suo perdere Dio, e vivere l'angoscia per averlo perduto, per il racconto coinvolgente delle sue situazioni familiari, per la sua capacità di interrogarsi e interrogarci tutti quanti sulla disperazione' [he has always thoroughly drawn me with his desperation, his loss of God, and his living of the anguish for that loss, his engrossing tales of domestic situations, his capacity to interrogate himself and interrogate us all about desperation]. The use of one of Bergman's preferred actresses, Bibi Andersson, to play the cameo role of the mother in *Il sogno della farfalla* is a tribute to this director (Bellocchio, cited in Roberti et al 1994, 326). Buñuel, on the other hand, he admires as the 'l'esempio più riuscito di rottura con il realismo' [the most successful example of rupture with realism] (Mori 1994).

10 Of the Italian directors, Bertolucci is perhaps the most important. He and Bellocchio resemble one another especially in their intertwining of the political and the personal, the individual and the collective; their characters' rebellions against the status quo; the delving into the difficulties

surrounding sexual relationships; and their common fascination for the conflict of father and son (seen, especially in Bertolucci's *La strategia del ragno* and *Il conformista* [*The Conformist*, 1970]). Bellocchio's relationship with Bertolucci has been difficult, and Bellocchio has described it as one of 'stima and rivalità insieme' [both esteem and rivalry], admitting to having been envious of him after Bertolucci's successes with *Il conformista* and *Last Tango in Paris* (Malanga 1998, 130). Bresson is another key voice: Bellocchio had done a comparative study of Bresson and Antonioni for his thesis at the Slade School in London, and his selection of actors for their expressiveness rather than for their acting ability is something he shares with the French film director (Cattini and Ferrero 1976, 31). Bresson can therefore be seen to influence Bellocchio's idea of 'stare sul corpo,' which is behind the long takes in the eighties and nineties.

11 See Malanga 1998, 81–2, 86–7, 130–1, and Lodato 1977, 72–4, for discussions of influences on Bellocchio.

Filmography of Marco Bellocchio

1961 *La colpa e la pena* (short)
1961 *Abbasso il zio* (short)
1962 *Ginepro fatto uomo* (short)
1965 *I pugni in tasca*
1967 *La Cina è vicina*
1969 'Discutiamo, discutiamo' (short for *Amore e rabbia* by Carlo Lizzani)
1969 *Il popolo calabrese ha rialzato la testa* (or *Paola*) (documentary)
1969 *Viva il 1° maggio rosso e proletario* (documentary)
1971 *Nel nome del padre*
1972 *Sbatti il mostro in prima pagina*
1975 *Nessuno o tutti* (documentary)
1976 *Matti da slegare* (documentary)
1976 *Marcia trionfale*
1977 *Il gabbiano di Anton Cechov*
1978 *La macchina cinema* (documèntary)
1980 *Vacanze in Val Trebbia*
1980 *Salto nel vuoto*
1982 *Gli occhi, la bocca*
1984 *Enrico IV*
1984 *Impressions d'un Italien sur la corrida en France* (short)
1986 *Diavolo in corpo*
1988 *La visione del Sabba*
1991 *La condanna*
1992 *L'uomo dal fiore in bocca* (short)
1994 *Il sogno della farfalla*
1995 *Sogni infranti: Ragionamenti e deliri* (documentary)
1997 *Il Principe di Homburg*

1997 *Elena* (short)
1997 *Il gabbiano atto 1, scena seconda* (short)
1998 *La religione della storia* (documentary)
1999 *Un filo di passione* (short)
1999 *Sorelle* (short)
1999 *Nina* (short)
1999 *La balia*
2000 *L'affresco* (short)
2001 *Il maestro del coro* (short)
2002 *Appunti per un film su Zio Vanja* (short)
2002 *Oggi è una bella giornata* (short)
2002 *L'ora di religione (Il sorriso di mia madre)*
2002 *. . . Addio del passato* (documentary)
2003 *Buongiorno, notte*
2003 *La cavallina storna* (short)
2004 *La famiglia del vampiro* (short)
2004 *Sorelle (Il matrimonio)* (short)
2006 *Il regista di matrimoni*
2006 *Sorelle*
2009 *Vincere*

Bibliography

Materials on Marco Bellocchio

The following is not intended as a complete bibliography of materials on Marco Bellocchio, but contains only the works that were found to be of particular relevance to this study. An excellent record of the material written on Bellocchio can be found in Sara Leggi's bibliography in Adriano Aprà, ed., *Marco Bellocchio: Il cinema e i film* (Venice: Saggi Marsilio, 2005), 267–333; it covers a vast range of the material produced in Italy, but little of the material published abroad.

Albano, Vittorio. 2000. 'Marco Bellocchio.' In *Gente di cinema: Trent'anni di interviste*, 21–4. Palermo: Agis.

Aprà, Adriano, ed. 2005a. *Marco Bellocchio: Il cinema e i film.* Venice: Saggi Marsilio.

– 2005b. 'Tormenti, estasi, rigenerazioni: Una panoramica sull'opera di Marco Bellocchio.' In Aprà 2005a, 11–21.

Aprà, Adriano, Luigi Martelli, Maurizio Ponzi, and Stefano Roncoroni. 1965. 'Intervista con M.B.' *Filmcritica* 161 (September): 489–94.

Aste, Mario. 1998. 'Henry IV: From Pirandello's Play to Bellocchio's Film.' *Quaderni d'Italianistica*, 1998, 22, 109–21.

Arvat, Massimo. 1992. *Marco Bellocchio.* Turin: Quaderni del Museo Nazionale del Cinema.

Bandirali, Luca, and Stefano D'Amadio. 2004. *'Buongiorno, notte': Le ragioni e le immagini.* Lecce: Argo.

Bellocchio, Marco. 1963a. 'Bertolucci: Ben ti sta.' *Quaderni piacentini* 7/8 (February–March): 38–9.

– 1963b. 'Le quattro giornate di Napoli.' *Quaderni piacentini* 7/8 (February–March): 36–8.

- 1964a. L'epilessia. Unpublished screenplay for *Pugni in tasca*. Rome: SNC.
- 1966a. 'La révolution au cinéma.' *Cahiers du cinéma* 176 (March): 43.
- 1966b. 'La stérilité de la provocation.' *Cahiers du cinéma* 177 (April): 63.
- 1966c. 'Notes.' *Positif* 76 (June): 1–6.
- 1967a. *I pugni in tasca: Un film di Marco Bellocchio*. Screenplay. Ed. G. Gambetti. Milan: Garzanti.
- 1967b. *La Cina è vicina di Marco Bellocchio*. Screenplay. Ed. Tommaso Chiaretti. Bologna: Cappelli.
- 1987. Sabba. Unpublished screenplay of *La visione del sabba*. Rome: SNC.
- 1997. *Il Principe di Homburg di Heinrich von Kleist*. Screenplay. Ed. Giovanni Spagnoletti. Milan: Baldini & Castoldi.
- 2002. *L'ora di religione (il sorriso di mia madre): La sceneggiatura originale, le immagini, le differenze con il film*. Rome: Elleu Multimedia.
- 2003. *Buongiorno, notte*. Venice: Marsilio.
- 2006. *Il regista di matrimoni*. Venice: Marsilio.
- 2009. 'Marco Bellocchio, il paese conformista come durante il ventennio.' http://freedomlibertadiparola.blogspot.com/2009/05/marco-bellocchioil-paese-conformista.html (accessed 25 July 2009).
Bellocchio, Marco, and Sergio Bazzini. 1976. *Marcia trionfale*. Screenplay. Ed. Anna Maria Tatò. Turin: Einaudi.
Bellocchio, Marco, and Vicenzo Cerami. 1982. Gli occhi, la bocca. Unpublished screenplay, third version. Rome: SNC.
Bellocchio, Marco, and Daniela Ceselli. 1999. *La balia*. Screenplay. Rome: Gremese.
Bellocchio, Marco, and Massimo Fagioli. 1999. *La condanna*. Screenplay. Rome: Nuove Edizioni Romane.
Bellocchio, Marco, and Tonino Guerra. 1983. Enrico IV. Unpublished screenplay, second version. Rome: SNC.
Bellocchio, Marco, and Piero Natoli. 1980a. Salto nel vuoto. Unpublished screenplay. Rome: SNC.
- 1980b. *Salto nel vuoto*. Milan: Fetrinelli.
Bellocchio, Marco, and Enrico Palandri. 1986. Il diavolo in corpo. Unpublished screenplay. Rome: SNC.
Bernardi, Sandro. 1978. *Marco Bellocchio*. Florence: La Nuova Italia.
- 1998. *Marco Bellocchio*. Florence: La Nuova Italia.
Bertone, Vittorio. 2008. 'Marco Bellocchio: In Italia 'commandano i morti.' *Ilcibicida.com*, 10 May 2006, http//:www.ilcibicida.com/readarticle.php?article_id=62 (accessed 20 February 2009).
Bertuzzi, Laura. 1996. *Il cinema di Marco Bellocchio*. Perugia: Pontegobbo.
Biarese, Cesare, ed. 1987. 'Movimenti con rabbia.' *Cinecritica* X, no. 7 (Oct–Dec): 16–27.

Bini, Daniela. 1993. 'Enrico IV tra Pirandello e Bellocchio.' *Quaderni d'Italiani-stica*, Autumn, 14 (2): 1–11.

Bo, Fabio, and Silvana Cielo. 1988. 'Conversazione con Marco Bellocchio.' *Filmcritica* 384 (April–May): 239–46.

Bolzoni, Francesco, and Mario Foglietti. 2000. 'Marco Bellocchio: L'assolu-zione.' In *Le stagioni del cinema: Trenta registi si raccontano*, 43–60. Catanzaro: Rubbettino.

Bottiroli, Giovanni. 1986. 'Edipo senza volerlo: Una lettura psicoanalitica di *Diavolo in corpo* l'ultimo film di Marco Bellocchio.' *Segnocinema* 23 (November–December): 68.

Brook, Clodagh. 2004a. 'The Hallucinating Eye: Fellini and Bellocchio.' *Italianist*, no. 24: 64–76.

– 2005. 'Beyond the Controversy: Marco Bellocchio and Fagiolian Psycho-analysis.' *Italian Quarterly*, Winter, 55–66.

– 2007. 'The Oneiric in the Cinema of Marco Bellocchio.' *Italica* 84 (Summer–Autumn): 479–94.

Brunette, Peter. 1989. 'A Conversation with Marco Bellocchio.' *Film Quarterly* 1 (Autumn): 49–56.

Buffoni, Laura. 2005. 'À Rebours. I documentari di Bellocchio.' In Aprà 2005a, 107–26.

Callegari, Giovanna, and Nuccio Lodato, eds. 1979. *Marco Bellocchio: I pugni in tasca e La macchina cinema*. Pavia: Centro Stampa dell'Amministrazione provinciale di Pavia.

Camerino, Vincenzo. 1982. *Cinema e politica: Il 'film' di Marco Bellocchio*. Cavallino di Lecce: Capone editore.

Canova, Gianni, ed. 2002. *Storia del cinema italiano*. Vol 11 *(1965–1969)*. Venice: Marsilio.

Cattini, Alberto, and Adelio Ferrero. 1976. 'Conversazione con Marco Bel-locchio.' *Cinema & Cinema* 7–8 (April–September): 28–38.

Ceretto, Luisa, and Giancarlo Zappoli, eds. 2004. *Le forme della ribellione: Il cinema di Marco Bellocchio*. Turin: Lindau.

Codelli, Lorenzo. 2002. 'Entretien: Marco Bellocchio; le sourire de l'auteur.' *Positif* 496 (June): 22–8.

Comuzio, Ermanno. 2000. 'Della melodia ascolto il contrappunto: Le colonne sonore di Bellocchio.' In Rossi 2000, 39–44.

Costa, Antonio, ed. 2005. *Marco Bellocchio: I pugni in tasca*. Turin: Lindau.

Costantini, C. 1982. 'Ho sempre tanta voglia di ricominciare, ma non so da dove.' *Il Messaggero*, 3 September.

Cosulich, Callisto. 2000. 'Elogio dell'insicurezza.' In Rossi 2000, 23–7.

Cremonini, Giorgio. 1976. *Marco Bellocchio: Tra il 'personale' e il 'politico.'* Imola: Circolo del Cinema di Imola.

Cruciani, Mariella. 2003. 'Diventare uomini e donne: Il cinema di Marco Bellocchio.' *Cinecritica* 30–31 (April–September): 16–19.

Cruciani, Mariella, and Sante Cruciani. 2003. 'Marco Bellocchio: Il cinema di chi non si arrende.' *Cinecritica* 30–31 (April–September): 7–15.

De Bernardinis, Flavio. 1998. 'Doppiati e sdoppiati: Conversazione con Marco Bellocchio.' *Segnocinema* 91 (May–June): 32–4.

– 2005. 'Discutiamo, discutiamo. Sbatti il mostro in prima pagina.' In Aprà 2005a, 151–5.

De Giovanni, Neria. 1989. *La parola in regia: Enrico IV tra Luigi Pirandello e Marco Bellocchio.* Pisa: Giardini.

De Vincenti, Giorgio. 1991. 'Elogio del paradosso.' *Filmcritica*, no. 414, 213–16.

Di Francesco, F., D. Romenin, and N. Cappelletti. 1973. *Marco Bellocchio, Bernardo Bertolucci: Nuove proposte del cinema italiano.* Pordenone: Sagittario.

Di Marino, Bruno. 2005. 'Nel nome del padre.' In Aprà 2005a, 147–50.

Durst, Margarete, and Mario Pezzella. 2004. 'Discussione su "Buongiorno notte" di Marco Bellochio.' *Iride. Filosofia e discussione pubblica* 1 (April): 189–98.

Fanali, Rossella. 1980. 'Bellocchio e *Salto nel vuoto.*' *Cinema sessanta* 131 (January–February): 40–2.

Fofi, Goffredo. 1967. 'Vento dell'Est: Intervista a Marco Bellocchio.' *Ombre rosse* 2 (September): 65–76.

Fragapane, Giacomo Daniele, ed. 2003. *Appunti per un film su Zio Vanja: Un laboratorio digitale di Marco Bellocchio con gli studenti dell'indirizzo Spettacolo digitale.* Rome: Onyx.

Fusco, Maria Pia. 2001. 'Bellocchio affronta *L'ora di religione.*' *La Repubblica,* 3 May.

Gili, Jean A. 2002. 'La "religion" de Marco Bellocchio.' *Positif* 496 (June): 21.

Guastella, Daniele. 2003. 'L'omicidio, il lutto, la santificazione.' *Cinecritica* 30–31 (April–September): 20–35.

Iadanza, Antonella. 2001. 'Bellocchio senza "luce."' *Rivista del Cinematografo,* March, 52.

La Repubblica. 2002. 'Bellocchio: meglio che i partiti questa volta siano solo ospiti.' 13 September.

Lodato, Nuccio. 1977. *Marco Bellocchio.* Milan: Moizzi editore.

Lombardi, G. 2007. 'La passione secondo Marco Bellocchio: Gli ultimi giorni di Aldo Moro.' *Annali d'Italianistica,* no. 25: 397–408.

Malanga, Paola, ed. 1998. *Marco Bellocchio: Catalogo ragionato.* Milan: Olivares.

– 1999. 'Incontro con Marco Bellocchio e Daniela Ceselli.' In *La balia,* 5–20. Rome: Gremese.

Martini, Giacomo, ed. 2005. *Marco Bellocchio*. Modena: Regione Emilia Romagna.

Masoni, Tullio, ed. 2003. *Marco Bellocchio: Quadri; Il pittore, il cineasta*. Alessandria: Falsopiano.

Menarini, Roy. 1997. 'La morale e la politica: Intervista con Marco Bellocchio.' In Toni and Cristalli 1997, 37–9.

Minella, Maurizio Fantoni. 2004. 'Conversazione con Marco Bellocchio.' In *Non riconciliati: Politica e società nel cinema italiano dal neorealismo a oggi*. Turin: Utet, 219–24.

Mori, Anna Maria. 1984. 'Follia: È la maschera necessaria per vivere.' *La Repubblica*, 19 May.

– 1991. 'Bellocchio, la vita come Desiderio.' *La Repubblica*, 10 February.

– 1992. 'L'attore di Bellocchio ora rifiuta di parlare.' *La Repubblica*, 10 January.

– 1994. 'Bellocchio: Tutti zitti così ci si ribella oggi.' *La Repubblica*, 10 April.

Natalini, Fabrizio. 2005. 'Diavolo in corpo.' In Aprà 2005a, 185–89.

Neria, Giovanni, 1989. *La parola in regìa: Enrico IV tra Luigi Pirandello e Marco Bellocchio*. Verbania: Giardini.

Nicastro, Anita, ed. 1992. *Marco Bellocchio: Per un cinema d'autore*. Florence: Ferdinando Brancato.

O'Leary, Alan. 2008. 'Dead Man Walking: The Aldo Moro Kidnap and Palimpsest History in *Buongiorno, notte*.' *New Cinemas: Journal of Contemporary Film* 6, no. 1: 33–45.

Parigi, Stefania. 2005. 'La condanna.' In Aprà 2005a, 195–200.

Perissinotto, Maria Regina. 1980. 'Entretien avec Marco Bellocchio.' *Positif* 231 (June): 6–12.

Pescarolo, Leo. 1986. 'Lettera a Marco Bellocchio.' *La Repubblica*, 19 February.

Pezzotta, Alberto. 2005. 'Marcia Trionfale.' In Aprà 2005a, 156–60.

Roberti, Bruno, Francesco Suriano, and Daniela Turco. 1994. 'Lavorare sulla bellezza del 'niente': Conversazione con Marco Bellocchio.' *Filmcritica* 446–47 (June–July): 323–28.

Rombi, Roberto. 1999. 'Bellocchio: Pronto a stupire.' *La Repubblica*, 7 May.

Rossi, Giovanni Maria, ed. 2000. *Marco Bellocchio: La passione della ricerca*. Fiesole: Premio Fiesole ai Maestri del Cinema.

Seta, Albertina. 2007. 'Conversazione con Marco Bellocchio sul suo ultimo film, *La balia*.' *Pol.it*, http://www.psychiatryonline.it/ital/bellocchio1.htm (accessed 20 February 2008).

Spagnoletti, Giovanni, Serafino Murri, and Stefano Cappellini. 1999. 'Il dovere di non ripetersi.' *Close Up* 5 (November–January): 55–9.

Spila, Piero, ed. 1987. 'Intervista: Il travelling è un fatto inconscio.' *Cinecritica* 7 (October–December): 7–11.

Stefanutto-Rosa, Stefano. 1986. 'Il diavolo nel subconscio dello psicanalista selvaggio?' *Cinema Nuovo* 300 (March–April): 10–13.

Tassone, Aldo. 1980. 'Marco Bellocchio.' In *Parla il cinema italiano*, Vol 2, 7–44. Milan: Il Formichiere.

Turco, Daniela. 2000. 'Piccoli movimenti, piccoli passi: Conversazione con Marco Bellocchio.' *Filmcritica* 501–02 (January–February): 60–7.

Turco, Daniela, and Bruno Roberti. 2004. 'Buonanotte, giorno: Conversazione con Marco Bellocchio.' *Filmcritica* 541–42 (January–February): 37–46.

Vighi, Fabio. 2005. 'On the Real Limits of Self-Consciousness: Gazing Back at the Subversive Subject with Marco Bellocchio.' *Culture, Theory and Critique* 42, no. 2: 147–61.

Yacowar, M. 1989. 'The Bedevilled Flesh: Bellocchio's Radiquet.' *Literature Film Quarterly* 17, no. 3: 188–92.

Zalaffi, Nicoletta. 1973. 'Interview with Marco Bellocchio.' *Sight and Sound* 42, no. 4 (Autumn): 197–99 and 231.

Zu Fürstenberg, Nina. 2005. 'L'individuo al centro: Tutto il resto è frivolezza.' *Reset* 87 (January–February): 85–6.

General Bibliography

Aitken, Stuart C., and Leo E. Zonn, eds. 1994. *Place, Power, Situation and Spectacle: A Geography of Film*. Lanham (MD) and London: Rowman & Littlefield.

ANICA, ed. 1987. 'Il marketing del Film D'Essai: Identikit dello spettatore "specializzato" (Il nuovo cinefilo).' *Cinema d'oggi* 14 (August): 16–17.

Armando, Luigi Antonello. 1997. *Storia della psicoanalisi in Italia dal 1971 al 1996*. Rome: Nuove Edizioni Romane.

– 1999. *Percezione delirante: Idea della cura unità dell'esperienza; la formazione storica della teoria della nascita e gli scritti di Massimo Fagioli del 1962–1963*. Rome: Nuove Edizioni Romane.

Badaloni, Nicola. 1971. *Il Marxismo italiano degli anni sessanta*. Rome: Editori Riuniti.

Bakhtin, Mikhail M. 1982. 'Forms of Time and of the Chronotope in the Novel.' In *The Dialogic Imagination: Four Essays*, ed. Michael Holquist. Austin and London: University of Texas Press.

Barański, Zygmunt G., and Robert Lumley. 1990. *Culture and Conflict in Postwar Italy: Essays on Mass and Popular Culture*. Basingstoke and London: Macmillan.

Barbato, Tullio. 1980. *Il terrorismo in Italia negli anni settanta: Cronaca e documentazione*. Milan: Editrice Bibliografia.

Baudrillard, Jean. 1994. *Simulacra and Simulation*. Trans. Sheila Faria Glaser. Ann Arbor: University of Michigan Press.

– 2002. *The Spirit of Terrorism: And Requiem for the Twin Towers*. Trans. Chris Turner. London: Verso.

Bobbio, Norberto. 1996. *Left and Right: The Significance of a Political Distinction*. Trans. with introduction by Allan Cameron. Chicago: University of Chicago Press.

Bolzoni, Francesco, and Mario Foglietti. 2000. *Le stagioni del cinema: Trenta registi si raccontano*. Catanzaro: Rubbettino.

Bonsaver, G. 2004. 'The Rome Cell.' *Sight and Sound*, no. 14: 12, 28–9.

Braghetti, Anna Laura. 2003. *Il prigioniero*. Milan: Fetrinelli.

Branigan, Edward R. 1984. *Point of View in the Cinema: A Theory of Narration and Subjectivity in Classical Film*. New York: Mouton.

Brecht, Bertolt. 1995. *Brecht on Theatre: The Development of an Aesthetic*. Ed. and trans. John Willett. London: Methuen Drama.

– 2003. *Brecht on Art and Politics: Diaries, Letters and Essays*. Ed. Thomas Kuhn and Steve Giles. London: Methuen.

Brook, Clodagh. 2004b. 'Screening the Autobiographical.' In *Italian Cinema: New Directions*, ed. William Hope, 27–52. Oxford: Peter Lang.

Brook, Clodagh, and Charlotte Ross. 2009. 'Conclusions: Splinters of Resistance.' In *Resisting the Tide: Cultures of Opposition under Berlusconi (2001–2006)*, ed. Daniele Albertazzi, Clodagh Brook, Charlotte Ross, and Nina Rothenberg, 231–40. London: Continuum.

Brooke-Rose, Christine. 1988. *A Rhetoric of the Unreal: Studies in Narrative and Structure, Especially of the Fantastic*. Cambridge: Cambridge University Press.

Brown, David J., and Robert Merrill, eds. 1993. *Violent Persuasions: The Politics and Imagery of Terrorism*. Seattle: Bay Press.

Brown, Hilda Meldrum. 1998. *Heinrich von Kleist: The Ambiguity of Art and the Necessity of Form*. Oxford: Clarendon Press.

Brunetta, Gian Piero. 1993. *Storia del cinema italiano: Dal miracolo economico agli anni novanta, 1960–1993*, Vol 4. Rome: Riuniti.

Burns, Jennifer. 2001. *Fragments of Impegno: Interpretations of Commitment in Contemporary Italian Narrative, 1980–2000*. Leeds: Northern Universities Press.

Caesar, Ann Hallamore, 1998. *Characters and Authors in Luigi Pirandello*. Oxford: Clarendon Press.

Callari, Francesco. 1991. *Pirandello e il cinema: Con una raccolta completa degli scritti teorici e creativi*. Venice: Saggi Marsilio.

Camerino, Vicenzo. 1998. *Il cinema e il '68: Le sfide dell'immaginario*. Manduria: Barbieri.

Canova, Gianni, ed. 2002. *Storia del cinema italiano, 1965–69*. Venice: Saggi Marsilio.

Catanzaro, Raimondo. 1991. *The Red Brigades and Left-Wing Terrorism in Italy.* London: Pinter Publishers.

Clegg, Stewart R. 1989. *Frameworks of Power.* London: SAGE.

Clover, Carol J. 1993. 'High and Low: The Transformation of the Rape-Revenge Movie.' In *Women and Film: A Sight and Sound Reader,* Pam Cook and Philip Dodd, 76–84. London: Scarlet Press.

Comolli, Jean-Louis, and Narboni, Jean, 1969. 'Cinema/Ideology/Criticism.' *Cahiers du cinéma,* October, 38–42.

Corsi, Barbara. 2001. *Con qualche dollaro in meno: Storia economica del cinema italiano.* Rome: Editori Riuniti.

Cousins, Mark, and Althar Hussain. 1984. *Michel Foucault.* New York: St Martin's Press.

Couzens Hoy, David, ed. 1986. *Foucault: A Critical Reader.* Oxford: Blackwell.

De Lauretis, Teresa. 1989. *Technologies of Gender: Essays on Theory, Film, and Fiction.* Basingstoke and London: Macmillan.

Deleuze, Gilles. 1989. *Cinema 2: The Time Image.* Trans. Hugh Tomlinson and Robert Galeta. London: Athlone.

Della Porta, Donatella. 1995. *Social Movements, Political Violence, and the State: A Comparative Analysis of Italy and Germany.* Cambridge: Cambridge University Press.

– 1996. *Movimenti collettivi e sistema politico in Italia, 1960–1995.* Rome and Bari: Editori Laterza.

De Man, Paul. 1984. 'Autobiography as De-Facement.' In *The Rhetoric of Romanticism,* 67–81. New York: Columbia University Press.

De Martino, Giulio. 1998. *La prospettiva del '68: Una forma di vita e di coscienza politica.* Naples: Liguori.

Drake, Richard. 1996. *The Aldo Moro Murder Case.* Cambridge, MA: Harvard University Press.

– 2006. 'The Aldo Moro Murder Case in Retrospect.' *Journal of Cold War Studies* 8, no. 2 (Spring): 114–25.

Eco, Umberto. 2000. *Opera aperta.* Milan: Bompiani.

'È morto Franco Cristaldi.' 1992. *Cinema d'oggi,* no. 13: 1 and 3–4.

Ente Autonomo Gestione Cinema. 1984. *Italian Cinema of the Eighties.* Rome: EAGC.

Fagioli, Massimo. 1980. 'Una storia una ricerca un film.' In Bellocchio 1980b, 17–38.

– 1991. *La marionetta e il burattino.* Rome: Nuove Edizioni Romane.

– 1992. 'Il sogno della farfalla: Il soggetto.' *Il sogno della farfalla,* no. 1, 13–66.

– 1996. *Istinto di morte e conoscenza.* Rome: Nuove Edizioni Romane.

– 2007. *Bambino, donna, e trasformazione dell'uomo.* Rome: Nuove Edizioni Romane.

Femia, Joseph V. 1982. *Gramsci's Political Thought: Hegemony, Consciousness and the Revolutionary Process*. Oxford: Clarendon Press.

Finzi, Silvia Vegetti. 1986. *Storia della psicoanalisi: Autori opere teorie, 1895–1985*. Milan: Mondadori.

Flores, Marcello, and Alberto de Bernardi. 1998. *Il sessantotto*. Bologna: Il Mulino.

Fofi, Goffredo. 1967. 'Vento dell'Est.' *Ombre rosse* 2 (September): 65–76.

– 1971a. *Il cinema italiano: Servi e padroni*. Milan: Fetrinelli.

– 1971b. 'Il posto della politica.' in *Nel nome del padre di Marco Bellocchio,* ed. G. Fofi. Bologna: Cappelli.

– 1980. 'La place de la politique: Entretien avec Marco Bellocchio.' *Positif* 137 (April): 10–19.

Foucault, Michel. 1980. *Power/Knowledge: Selected Interviews & Other Writings, 1972–1977*. Ed. Colin Gordon. New York: Pantheon Books.

Francheschini, Alberto, Pier Vittorio Buffa, and Franco Giustolisi. 1988. *Mara Renato e io: Storia dei fondatori delle Br*. Milan: Mondadori.

Freedheim, Donald K. 1998. *Storia della psicoterapia: Un secolo di cambiamenti*. Trans. Antonella Bianchi di Castelbianco and Maria Luisa Ruffa. Rome: Edizioni Scientifiche.

Freud, Sigmund. 1953–1974. 'Group Psychology and the Analysis of the Ego.' In *The Standard Edition of the Complete Psychological Works*, 24 vols, ed. and trans. James Strachey et al. Vol. 18: 65–143. London: Hogarth Press.

Fuscagni, Carlo. 1984. 'Television as a Film Producer in Italian Cinema of the '80s.' In *Italian Cinema of the 1980s*, 41–6. Rome: Ente Autonomo Gestione Cinema.

Gatt-Rutter, John. 1978. *Writers and Politics in Modern Italy*. London: Hodder and Staughton.

Giachetti, Diego. 1998. *Oltre il Sessantotto: Prima durante e dopo il movimento*. Pisa: Biblioteca Franco Serantini.

Gili, Jean A. 1976. *Francesco Rosi: Cinéma et pouvoir*. Paris: Éditions du Cerf.

Ginsborg, Paul. 1990a. *A History of Contemporary Italy: Society and Politics, 1943–1988*. London: Penguin.

– 1990b. 'Family, Culture and Politics in Contemporary Italy.' In Barański and Lumley 1990, 21–49.

Giuliani, Gianna, 1980. *Le strisce interiori: Cinema italiano e psicoanalisi*. Rome: Bulzoni.

Glynn, Ruth. 2006. 'Trauma on the Line: Terrorism and Testimony in the Anni di Piombo.' In *The Value of Literature in and after the Seventies: The Case of Italy and Portugal*, ed. M. Jansen and P. Jordão. Utrecht: University of Utrecht Igitur Publishing and Archiving.

Günsberg, Maggie. 2005. *Italian Cinema: Gender and Genre*. Basingstoke and New York: Palgrave Macmillan.

Harvey, Sylvia. 1978. *May '68 and Film Culture*. London: BFI.

Hawkes, David. 2003. *Ideology*. London: Routledge.

Heise, Ursula K. 1997. *Chronoschisms: Time, Narrative, and Postmodernism*. Cambridge: Cambridge University Press.

Horton, John, and Andrea T. Baumeister, eds. 1996. *Literature and the Political Imagination*. London and New York: Routledge.

Iser, Wolfgang. 1987. 'The Play of the Text.' In *Languages of the Unsayable: The Play of Negativity in Literature and Literary Theory*, ed. Sanford Budick and Wolfgang Iser, 325–39. New York: Columbia University Press.

Kermode, Frank. 1979. *The Genesis of Secrecy: On the Interpretation of Narrative*. Cambridge, MA: Harvard University Press.

Kline, T. Jefferson. 1987. *Bertolucci's Dream Loom: A Psychoanalytic Study of Cinema*. Amherst, MA: University of Massachusetts Press.

Kölger, Hans Herbert. 1996. *The Power of Dialogue: Critical Hermeneutics after Gadamer and Foucault*. Trans. Paul Hendrickson. Cambridge, MA: MIT Press.

Kolker, Robert Phillip. 1985. *Bernardo Bertolucci*. London: BFI.

Landy, Marcia. 2000. *Italian Film* (*National Film Traditions*). Cambridge: Cambridge University Press.

Laqueur, Walter, ed. 1978. *The Terrorism Reader: A Historical Anthology*. London: Wildwood House.

Lumley, Robert. 1990. *States of Emergency: Cultures of Revolt in Italy from 1968 to 1978*. London: Verso.

Mangano, Attilio, and Antonio Schina. 1998. *Le culture del Sessantotto: Gli anni sessanta, le riviste, il movimento*. Pistoia: CDP/Massari Editore.

Marcus, Millicent. 1987. *Italian Film in the Light of Neorealism*. Princeton: Princeton University Press.

– 1993. *Filmmaking by the Book: Italian Cinema and Literary Adaptation*. Baltimore and London: John Hopkins University Press.

Marx, Karl, and Friedrich Engels. 2002. *The Communist Manifesto*. London: Penguin.

Marx, Karl, Friedrich Engels, and Serge L. Levitsky. 1996. *Das Kapital: A Critique of the Political Economy*. Washington, DC: Regnery.

Meade, Robert C. Jr. 1990. *Red Brigades: The Story of Italian Terrorism*. London: Macmillan.

Miccichè, Lino. 1995. *Cinema italiano: Gli anni '60 e oltre*. Venice: Marsilio.

– 1997. *Il cinema del riflusso: Film e cineasti italiani degli anni '70*. Venice: Marsilio.

Michalczyk, John J. 1986. *The Italian Political Filmmakers*. London and Toronto: Associated University Presses.

Minnella, Maurizio Fantoni. 2004. *Non riconciliati: Politica e società nel cinema italiano dal neorealismo a oggi*. Turin: Utet.

Moretti, Mario, Carla Mosca, and Rossana Rossanda. 2002. *Brigate rosse: Una storia italiana*. Milan: Baldini e Castoldi.

Moscati, Italo, ed. 1997. *1967: Tuoni prima del maggio; Cinema e documenti degli anni che preparono la contestazione*. Venice: Marsilio.

– 1998. *1969: Un anno bomba: Quando il cinema scese in piazza*. Venice: Marsilio.

Moss, David, 1989. *The Politics of Left-Wing Violence in Italy, 1969–85*. London: Macmillan.

Neale, Steve. 1981. 'Art Cinema as Institution.' *Screen*, no. 22: 1, 11–39.

O'Leary, Alan. 2005. 'Film and the "Anni di piombo": Representations of Politically Motivated Violence in Recent Italian Cinema.' In *Culture, Censorship and the State in Twentieth-Century Italy*, ed. Guido Bonsaver and Robert S.C. Gordon, 168–78. Oxford: Legenda.

– 2008. 'Dead Man Walking: The Aldo Moro Kidnap and Palimpsest History in *Buongiorno, notte*.' *New Cinemas: Journal of Contemporary Film* 6, no. 1: 33–45.

Olick, Jeffrey K. 1999. 'Collective Memory: The Two Cultures.' *Sociological Theory* 17, no. 3 (November): 333–48.

Pardo, Piergiorgio. 1998. *Il sessantotto*. Milan: Xenia Edizioni.

Pennebacker, James W, Dario Paez, and Bernard Rimé, eds. 1997. *Collective Memory of Political Events: Social Psychological Perspectives*. Mahwah, NJ: Lawrence Erlbaum Associates.

Pertile, Lino. 1993. 'The Italian Novel Today: Politics, Language, Literature.' In *The New Italian Novel*, ed. Zygmunt Barański and Lino Pertile, 1–19. Edinburgh: Edinburgh University Press.

Pieroni, Alfredo. 2006. *Il figlio segreto del Duce: La storia di Benito Albino Mussolini e di sua madre Ida Dalser*. Milan: Garzanti.

Pirani, Francesca. 1992. 'Il sogno della farfalla.' In Fagioli 1992, 9–11.

Porton, Richard. 1999. *Film and the Anarchist Imagination*. London and New York: Verso.

Schalk, David L. 1979. *The Spectrum of Political Engagement: Mounier, Benda, Nizan, Brasillach, Sartre*. Princeton: Princeton University Press.

Sturrock, John. 1993. *The Language of Autobiography: Studies in the First Person Singular*. Cambridge: Cambridge University Press.

Tassone, Aldo. 1980. *Parla il cinema italiano*, Vol 2. Milan: Il Formichiere.

– ed. 2002. *La nouvelle vague 45 anni dopo*. Milan: Il Castoro.

Testa, Carlo. 2002. *Italian Cinema and Modern European Literatures: 1945–2000*. Westport, CT: Praeger.

Todorov, Tzvetan. 1973. *The Fantastic: A Structural Approach to a Literary Genre.* Trans. Richard Howard. Cleveland and London: The Press of Case Western Reserve University.

– 2003. *Hope and Memory: Lessons from the Twentieth Century.* Trans. David Bellos. Princeton: Princeton University Press.

Tormey, Alan. 1971. *The Concept of Expression: A Study in the Philosophical Psychology and Aesthetics.* Princeton: Princeton University Press.

Turim, Maureen. 1989. *Flashbacks in Film: Memory and History.* New York and London: Routledge.

Viano, Maurizio. 1993. *A Certain Realism: Making Use of Pasolini's Film Theory and Practice.* California: University of California Press.

Villanueva, Enrique, ed. 1991. *Consciousness.* Atascadero, CA: Ridgeview Publications.

Wood, Mary P. 2005. *Italian Cinema.* Oxford: Berg.

Zeni, Marco. 2005. *La moglie di Mussolini.* Trento: Erre e Erre.

Žižek, Slavoj. 1989. *The Sublime Object of Ideology.* London: Verso.

– 2002. *Welcome to the Desert of the Real: Five Essays on September 11 and Related Dates.* New York: Verso.

Index